Workshop on Cognitive Modeling and Computational Linguistics (CMCL 2022)

Dublin, Ireland
26 May 2022

ISBN: 978-1-7138-6729-6

Printed from e-media with permission by:

Curran Associates, Inc.
57 Morehouse Lane
Red Hook, NY 12571

CURRAN ASSOCIATES INC.
proceedings
.com

Some format issues inherent in the e-media version may also appear in this print version.

Printed with permission by Curran Associates, Inc. (2023)

For permission requests, please contact the Association for Computational Linguistics at the address below.

Association for Computational Linguistics
209 N. Eighth Street
Stroudsburg, Pennsylvania 18360

Phone: 1-570-476-8006
Fax: 1-570-476-0860

acl@aclweb.org

Additional copies of this publication are available from:

Curran Associates, Inc.
57 Morehouse Lane
Red Hook, NY 12571 USA
Phone: 845-758-0400
Fax: 845-758-2633
Email: curran@proceedings.com
Web: www.proceedings.com

CMCL 2022

Workshop on Cognitive Modeling and Computational Linguistics

Proceedings of the Workshop

May 26, 2022

The CMCL organizers gratefully acknowledge the support from the following sponsors.

In cooperation with Laboratoire Parole et Langage (France) and Japan Society for the Promotion of Science (Japan)

Introduction

Welcome to the 12th edition of the Workshop on Cognitive Modeling and Computational Linguistics (CMCL)!!

CMCL is traditionally the workshop of reference for research at the intersection between Computational Linguistics and Cognitive Science. This year, for the first time CMCL will be held in hybrid mode: virtual attendance will still be allowed, given the persistence of the COVID-19 pandemic, while the in-person meeting will take place in the beautiful Dublin.

This year, we received 20 regular workshop submissions and we accepted 10 of them, for a global 50% acceptance rate. We also received two extended abstracts as non-archival submissions, and both of them will be presented during the poster session. As in previous years, submissions have been highly varied across the cognitive sciences, with topics ranging from the relationship between vision and human linguistic-semantic knowledge, the relationship between eye gaze and self-attention in Transformer language models, and an account of the game Codenames. Work ranges from deep neural network approaches to Bayesian cognitive models, learning of phonetic and phonological categories, analyses of neurolinguistic data, and much more. We are thrilled to continue a workshop with the breadth and depth that is emblematic of the fields of cognitive science and natural language processing.

Last year, we held a shared task on eye-tracking prediction in a variety of measures. This year, we led an additional shared task that built on the success of the previous edition. In the second edition of the shared task on eye-tracking data prediction, this time we included multilingual data from English, Russian, German, Hindi, Chinese, Dutch and Danish, enabling research teams to try a variety of methods and language models far beyond prior eye tracking tasks. A total of six teams participated, of which 5 submitted papers describing their systems.

As always, we are extremely grateful to the PC members, without whose efforts we would be unable to ensure high-quality reviews and high-quality work for presentation at the workshop. We are indebted to their generosity and are proud of the community that supports CMCL. We also thank our invited speakers, Andrea E Martin and Vera Demberg for kindly accepting our invitation.

Finally, we thank our sponsors: the Japanese Society for the Promotion of Sciences and the Laboratoire Parole et Langage. Through their generous support, we are able to offer fee waivers to PhD students who were first authors of accepted papers, and to offset the participation costs of the invited speakers.

The CMCL 2022 Organizing Committee

Organizing Committee

Workshop Organizers

Emmanuele Chersoni, The Hong Kong Polytechnic University, China
Nora Hollenstein, University of Copenhagen, Denmark
Cassandra L Jacobs, University of Buffalo, USA
Yohei Oseki, University of Tokyo, Japan
Laurent Prévot, Aix-Marseille University, France
Enrico Santus, Bayer, USA

Program Committee

Program Committee

Laura Aina, Pompeu Fabre University of Barcelona
Raquel Garrido Alhama, Google
Philippe Blache, Aix-Marseille University
Christos Christodoulopoulos, Amazon
Aniello De Santo, University of Utah
Vesna G Djokic, University of Amsterdam
Micha Elsner, Ohio State University
Raquel Fernández, University of Amsterdam
Abdellah Fourtassi, Aix-Marseille University
Michael Frank, Stanford University
Robert Frank, Yale University
Diego Frassinelli, University of Konstanz
John Hale, University of Georgia
Yu-Yin Hsu, The Hong Kong Polytechnic University
Tim Hunter, UCLA
Samar Husain, IIT Delhi
Anna A Ivanova, MIT
Carina Kauf, MIT
Jordan Kodner, Stony Brook University
Gianluca Lebani, University Ca' Foscari of Venice
Fred Mailhot, Dialpad
Karl David Neergaard, University of Macau
Stephen Politzer-Ahles, The Hong Kong Polytechnic University
Giulia Rambelli, University of Pisa
Roi Reichart, Technion – Israel Institute of Technology
Rachel A Ryskin, University of California Merced
Lavinia Salicchi, The Hong Kong Polytechnic University
William Schuler, Ohio State University
Cory Shain, MIT
Ece Takmaz, University of Amsterdam
Lonneke van der Plas, Idiap Research Institute
Yao Yao, The Hong Kong Polytechnic University

Shared Task Program Committee

Sunit Bhattacharya, Charles University of Prague
Stephanie Brandl, University of Copenaghen
Patrick Haller, University of Zurich
Joseph Marvin Imperial, National University of the Philippines
Mitja Nikolaus, Aix-Marseille University
Lavinia Salicchi, The Hong Kong Polytechnic University
Ece Takmaz, University of Amsterdam
Zining Zhu, University of Toronto

Invited Speakers

Vera Demberg, Saarland University, Germany
Andrea E Martin, Max Planck Institute for Psycholinguistics, Netherlands

Table of Contents

Program

Tuesday, July 26, 2022

09:30 - 09:45 *Opening Remarks*

09:45 - 10:45 *Keynote Talk by Andrea E. Martin*

10:45 - 11:00 *Coffee Break*

11:00 - 12:30 *Session 1 (Oral Presentations)*

Eye Gaze and Self-attention: How Humans and Transformers Attend Words in Sentences
Joshua Bensemann, Alex Yuxuan Peng, Diana Benavides Prado, Yang Chen, Neset Tan, Paul Michael Corballis, Patricia Riddle and Michael Witbrock

Seeing the advantage: visually grounding word embeddings to better capture human semantic knowledge
Danny Merkx, Stefan Frank and Mirjam Ernestus

Visually Grounded Interpretation of Noun-Noun Compounds in English
Inga Lang, Lonneke Van Der Plas, Malvina Nissim and Albert Gatt

12:30 - 13:30 *Lunch Break*

13:30 - 15:00 *Session 2 (Oral Presentations)*

A Neural Model for Compositional Word Embeddings and Sentence Processing
Shalom Lappin and Jean-Philippe Bernardy

Codenames as a Game of Co-occurrence Counting
Réka Cserháti, Istvan Kollath, András Kicsi and Gábor Berend

About Time: Do Transformers Learn Temporal Verbal Aspect?
Eleni Metheniti, Tim Van De Cruys and Nabil Hathout

15:00 - 15:15 *Coffee Break*

15:15 - 15:30 *Shared Task Presentation*

CMCL 2022 Shared Task on Multilingual and Crosslingual Prediction of Human Reading Behavior
Nora Hollenstein, Emmanuele Chersoni, Cassandra L Jacobs, Yohei Oseki, Laurent Prévot and Enrico Santus

Tuesday, July 26, 2022 (continued)

15:30 - 17:00 *Poster Session*

Estimating word co-occurrence probabilities from pretrained static embeddings using a log-bilinear model
Richard Futrell

Predicting scalar diversity with context-driven uncertainty over alternatives
Jennifer Hu, Roger P. Levy and Sebastian Schuster

Less Descriptive yet Discriminative: Quantifying the Properties of Multimodal Referring Utterances via CLIP
Ece Takmaz, Sandro Pezzelle and Raquel Fernández

Modeling the Relationship between Input Distributions and Learning Trajectories with the Tolerance Principle
Jordan Kodner

NU HLT at CMCL 2022 Shared Task: Multilingual and Crosslingual Prediction of Human Reading Behavior in Universal Language Space
Joseph Marvin Imperial

Team DMG at CMCL 2022 Shared Task: Transformer Adapters for the Multi- and Cross-Lingual Prediction of Human Reading Behavior
Ece Takmaz

Team ÚFAL at CMCL 2022 Shared Task: Figuring out the correct recipe for predicting Eye-Tracking features using Pretrained Language Models
Sunit Bhattacharya, Rishu Kumar and Ondrej Bojar

HkAmsters at CMCL 2022 Shared Task: Predicting Eye-Tracking Data from a Gradient Boosting Framework with Linguistic Features
Lavinia Salicchi, Rong Xiang and Yu-Yin Hsu

Poirot at CMCL 2022 Shared Task: Zero Shot Crosslingual Eye-Tracking Data Prediction using Multilingual Transformer Models
Harshvardhan Srivastava

17:00 - 18:00 *Keynote Talk by Vera Demberg*

18:00 - 18:15 *Closing Remarks*

Seeing the advantage: visually grounding word embeddings to better capture human semantic knowledge

Danny Merkx
Radboud University
Nijmegen, The Netherlands
danny.merkx@ru.nl

Stefan L. Frank
Radboud University
Nijmegen, The Netherlands
stefan.frank@ru.nl

Mirjam Ernestus
Radboud University
Nijmegen, The Netherlands
mirjam.ernestus@ru.nl

Abstract

Distributional semantic models capture word-level meaning that is useful in many natural language processing tasks and have even been shown to capture cognitive aspects of word meaning. The majority of these models are purely text based, even though the human sensory experience is much richer. In this paper we create visually grounded word embeddings by combining English text and images and compare them to popular text-based methods, to see if visual information allows our model to better capture cognitive aspects of word meaning. Our analysis shows that visually grounded embedding similarities are more predictive of the human reaction times in a large priming experiment than the purely text-based embeddings. The visually grounded embeddings also correlate well with human word similarity ratings. Importantly, in both experiments we show that the grounded embeddings account for a unique portion of explained variance, even when we include text-based embeddings trained on huge corpora. This shows that visual grounding allows our model to capture information that cannot be extracted using text as the only source of information.

1 Introduction

Distributional semantic models create word representations that quantify word meaning based on the idea that a word's meaning depends on the contexts in which the word appears. Such representations (also called embeddings) are widely used as the linguistic input for computational linguistic models, with research showing that they can account for response times in lexical decision tasks (Mandera et al., 2017; Rotaru et al., 2018; Petilli et al., 2021), decode brain data (Xu et al., 2016; Abnar et al., 2018), account for brain activity during text comprehension (Frank and Willems, 2017), and correlate with human judgements of word similarity (Kiela et al., 2018; Derby et al., 2018, 2020).

While such embeddings have proven useful, they are not cognitively plausible as creating high quality embeddings requires billions of word tokens. For instance, the GloVe embeddings developed by Pennington et al. (2014) are trained on 840 billion words. It would require a human 80 years of constant reading at about 330 words per second to digest that much information. Obviously, humans are able to understand language after much less exposure, and furthermore, their sensory experience is much richer than solely reading texts.

Embodied cognition theory poses that our conceptual knowledge is based on the entirety of our sensory experience (Barsalou, 2008; Foglia and Wilson, 2013). For instance, reading the word *dog* elicits sensory experiences we have with dogs, such as their sound and how they look. Embodied cognition theory thus assumes that all our sensory experiences contribute to our conceptual knowledge and processing, which should be reflected in human behaviour. Early priming studies have indeed found that visual similarities can elicit priming effects (D'Arcais et al., 1985; Schreuder et al., 1998).

If visual features are part of our conceptual knowledge, word embeddings incorporating visual features should be able to explain human behavioural data to a degree unattainable by purely text-based methods (that is, if we assume visual sensory experiences can never be fully captured by textual descriptions). That is why recent research has taken an interest in multimodal word embeddings, combining text with a second source of information, resulting in visually grounded embeddings (VGEs) in the case of visual information.

1.1 Related work

Using image tags as a source of visual context, Bruni et al. (2013) create visual distributional semantic embeddings and use dimensionality reduction to map visual and text-based embeddings to the common VGE space. Derby et al. (2018) combine

Proceedings of the Workshop on Cognitive Modeling and Computational Linguistics, pages 1 - 11
May 26, 2022 ©2022 Association for Computational Linguistics

text-based embeddings with the network activations of an object recognition model and show that these visual features improve the embeddings' performance in downstream tasks. Petilli et al. (2021) use visual embeddings created by an object recognition network, and show that the embedding similarities are predictive of priming effects over and above text-based similarities.

The studies described above involve separately trained word and visual embeddings. An end-to-end approach to combine visual and linguistic information is through a deep neural network based caption-to-image retrieval (C2I) models (e.g., Karpathy and Fei-Fei 2015; Kamper et al. 2017). While these models are trained to encode images and corresponding written or spoken captions in a common embedding space such that relevant captions can be retrieved given an image and vice versa, the resulting embeddings have been shown to capture sentence-level semantics (Chrupała et al., 2017; Merkx and Frank, 2019; Merkx et al., 2021). Kiela et al. (2018) showed that pretrained embeddings correlated better with human intuition about word meaning after being fine-tuned as learnable parameters in their C2I model.

1.2 Current study

In this study we investigate whether VGEs created by a C2I model explain human behavioural data. Our research question is: can VGEs capture aspects of word meaning that (current) text-based approaches cannot? To answer this question we investigate novel end-to-end trained VGEs and test them on two types of human behavioural data thought to rely on conceptual/semantic knowledge. Secondly, we take care to separate the contribution of the image modality from that of the linguistic information to see whether visual grounding captures word properties that cannot be learned by purely text-based methods. We do this by comparing our VGEs to three well-known text-based methods.

Throughout our experiments we will use two versions of the text-based methods: custom trained on the same data as our VGEs and pretrained on large corpora. From a cognitive modelling perspective, the former of these is more interesting. While the use of large corpora may not be problematic for natural language processing applications where performance comes first, we aim to create cognitively plausible embeddings, that is, from a realistic amount of linguistic exposure. However, the inclusion of pretrained embeddings serves to answer our main research question.

1.2.1 Semantic similarity judgements

In our first experiment we test whether the VGEs correlate better with a measure of human intuition about word meaning than text-based embeddings. A well-known method to capture human intuition about word meaning is simply by asking subjects how similar two words are in meaning. To evaluate word embeddings, one can then see if embedding similarities for those word pairs correlate with the human judgements (e.g., Bruni et al., 2013; Baroni et al., 2014; Speer and Chin, 2016; Kiela et al., 2018; Derby et al., 2020).

While the study by Kiela et al. (2018) performed a similar investigation on pretrained word embeddings fine-tuned through their C2I model, they did not take into account the fact that text might also contain visual knowledge. It is not unreasonable to assume that some visual knowledge can be gained from a large corpus of sentences solely describing visual scenes. We account for this visual knowledge from text by incorporating word embeddings trained on the image descriptions in order to investigate the contribution of the *image* modality included in the VGEs.

Collecting word similarity ratings typically involves showing participants two words and asking them to rate how similar or related their meanings are, or picking the most related out of several pairs. Semantic relatedness refers to the strength of the association between two word meanings. For instance, 'dog' and 'leash' have a strong relationship but are not similar in meaning. Semantic similarity refers to two words sharing semantic properties, for instance 'dogs' and 'cats' which are both animals that people keep as pets (Hill et al., 2015).

1.2.2 Semantic priming

In the second experiment, we test whether our VGEs are predictive of semantic priming effects from a large priming experiment (Hutchison et al., 2013). Semantic priming effects occur when activation of a semantically related prime word facilitates the processing of the target word, resulting in shorter reaction times. If all our sensory experiences contribute to word meaning, we would expect visual perceptual properties of the prime-target pair to influence the response times.

Petilli et al. (2021) performed a similar experiment using visual embeddings derived from activation features from an object recognition network and text-based word embeddings. Their results show that after accounting for the text-based similarity, the visual embedding similarities contribute to explaining the human reaction times only for lexical decision trails with a short stimulus onset asynchrony (SOA), and not for the naming task or long SOA trials. They attribute this to: 1) the lexical decision task being more sensitive to semantic effects than the naming task (Lucas, 2000), and 2) visual information being activated in early linguistic processing and rapidly decaying (Pecher et al., 1984; Schreuder et al., 1998). We will further test these interactions in our own experiment.

2 Methods

In our experiments, we compare the VGEs from our own model with three well known text-based distributional semantic models: FastText (Bojanowski et al., 2017), Word2Vec (Mikolov et al., 2013a) and GloVe (Pennington et al., 2014). For the purpose of this study, we take two approaches: 1) we train our own text-based distributional models to allow for a fair comparison to the VGEs, and 2) we use the pretrained models to investigate whether our VGEs capture semantic information that even models trained on large text corpora do not. The code used in this study can be found at `https://github.com/DannyMerkx/speech2image/tree/CMCL2022`

2.1 Training data

MSCOCO is a database intended for training image recognition, segmentation and captioning models (Chen et al., 2015). It has 123,287 images and 605,495 written English captions, that is, five captions paired to each image. Captions were collected by asking annotators to describe what they saw in the picture. Five thousand images (25,000 captions) are reserved as a development set.

The captions are provided in tokenised format. In order to use them in our models we only decapitalised all words and removed the punctuation at the end of each sentence. This results in a total of 6,184,656 word tokens and 28,415 unique word types, to which we add start- and end-of-sentence tokens for training our visually grounded model.

The images are pre-processed by resizing the images such that the shortest side is 256 pixels, while keeping the original aspect ratio. We take ten 224 by 224 crops of the image: one from each corner, one from the middle and the same five crops for the mirrored image. We use ResNet-152 (He et al., 2016) pretrained on ImageNet to extract visual features from these ten crops and then average the features of the ten crops into a single vector with 2,048 features. These features are extracted by removing ResNet's classification layer and taking the activations of the penultimate layer.

2.2 Models

2.2.1 Visually grounded model

Our visually grounded model is based on our implementation presented in Merkx and Frank (2019), and we refer to that paper for the details. Here we will provide a brief overview of the model, any differences with Merkx and Frank (2019) and the parameter settings tested in this study.

The VGE model maps images and their corresponding captions to a common embedding space. It is trained to make the embeddings for matching images and captions as similar as possible, and those for mismatched images and captions dissimilar. The model consists of two parts; an image embedder and a caption embedder. The image embedder is a single-layer linear projection on top of the image features extracted with ResNet-152. We train only the linear projection and do not further fine-tune ResNet.

The caption embedder consists of a word embedding layer followed by a two-layer bi-directional recurrent Long Short Term Memory (LSTM) layer and finally a self-attention layer. The embedding layer has 300 dimensions and is used to represent the input words as learnable embeddings. The purpose of the LSTM is to create a contextualised hidden state for each time-step (input word). Its first layer has 1028 hidden units, while its second layer acts as a bottleneck with 300 hidden units. Finally, the purpose of the attention layer is to weigh each time-step in order to create a single fixed-length embedding for the entire caption. The attention layer has 128 hidden units.

The image embedder has 2×300 dimensions so that the output matches the size of the caption embeddings. Both image and caption embedding are L2 normalised and we take their distance as the loss signal for the batch hinge loss function (see Merkx and Frank, 2019). The networks are trained for 32 epochs using Adam with a cyclic learning rate schedule based on Smith (2017), which varies the learning rate smoothly between 10^{-3} and 10^{-6}.

The obvious way to extract word embeddings from the trained model would be to use the trained weights of the embedding layer. Unlike for instance in GloVe, where each word's embedding is based on its full co-occurrence distribution, these embeddings are not trained specifically to capture word context or meaning and they are not necessarily the best word embeddings. However, our initial tests showed that they performed very poorly as semantic embeddings when trained from a random initialisation [1]. Rather than taking the input embeddings we create our own embeddings from the hidden representations of the model.

We create our VGEs from the hidden activations of the bottleneck LSTM layer. We use the trained caption encoder to encode all training sentences in MSCOCO. However, we remove the attention layer that creates the sentence embedding and we retain the individual activations of the LSTM at each time step. As the word representations in this layer can be used to create semantic sentence embeddings that capture human intuition about sentence meaning (as we showed for instance in Merkx and Frank, 2019 and Merkx et al., 2021), we expect these representations to better capture word meaning than the input embeddings.

The embedding for each word is then created by summing and normalising its LSTM layer activations from all its occurrences in the dataset. As opposed to Merkx and Frank (2019), where we used a single recurrent layer and found no further benefit of additional layers in terms of sentence embedding quality, we found that the quality of our VGEs improves when we use a two-layer LSTM, with the second layer acting as a bottleneck from which we derive the embeddings.

2.2.2 Text-based models

The text-based distributional models are trained on the MSCOCO captions. We train Word2Vec and FastText using the *Gensim* package (Řehůřek and Sojka, 2010). We train GloVe using the code that Pennington et al. (2014) made publicly available[2].

Word2Vec and FastText were trained as the Skip-gram variant with embedding size 300, a context window of 10 and 10 negative samples. GloVe was trained with embedding size 300 and a context window of 10. All resulting word embeddings are then L2 normalised.

[1] Kiela et al. (2018) were able to use the input embeddings because they were initialised using pretrained embeddings.

[2] `https://nlp.stanford.edu/projects/glove/`

Table 1: Description of the word similarity/relatedness evaluation datasets. #available is the number of word pairs included in the evaluation. Type indicates whether the dataset captures similarity or relatedness. NA indicates subjects were not specifically instructed on the difference.

Dataset	#word-pairs	#available	type
WordSim353	353	240	NA
WordSim-S	203	147	Similarity
WordSim-R	252	166	Relatedness
SimLex999	999	793	Similarity
-SimLex999 Q1	249	141	Similarity
-SimLex999 Q4	250	249	Similarity
MEN	3000	2889	Relatedness
RareWords	2034	204	NA

In addition, we use the following pretrained vectors (all 300 dimensional): Word2Vec trained on 100 billion tokens of the Google News corpus (Mikolov et al., 2013b), FastText trained on 600 billion tokens of Common Crawl (Mikolov et al., 2018) and GloVe trained on 840 billion tokens of Common Crawl (Pennington et al., 2014).

2.3 Evaluation data

2.3.1 Semantic similarity judgements

We include both semantic relatedness and similarity datasets in our analysis. It has been argued that subjects' intuitive understanding of similarity is not necessarily in line with the 'scientific' notions of similarity and relatedness explained in the introduction (Hill et al., 2015). Thus, if subject are not clearly instructed on these notions of similarity or relatedness, we consider the nature of the dataset undefined.

The WordSim353 dataset by Finkelstein et al. (2002) contains 353 word pairs annotated with similarity ratings. While the name suggests it is a similarity rating dataset, more recent studies consider it a hybrid dataset, as subjects were not specifically instructed to judge relatedness or similarity. In a later study by Agirre et al. (2009), the WordSim353 data was split into similar and related pairs by annotating the word pairs. WordSim-S (similar) contains word pairs annotated as being synonyms, antonyms, identical, or hyponym-hyperonym. WordSim-R (related) contains word pairs annotated as being meronym-holonym, and pairs with none of the above relationships but with a similarity score greater than 5 (out of 10). Both sets contain all unrelated words (words not annotated with any of the above relationships and a similarity lower than 5).

SimLex999 was created with the caveats of the original WordSim353 in mind in order to create a dataset of 999 word pairs annotated for similarity rather than relatedness (Hill et al., 2015). SimLex999 furthermore contains concreteness ratings for the word pairs. Hill et al. (2015) divided the the dataset into concreteness quartiles based on the sum of the concreteness ratings for each pair. Using these quartiles we also look at the 25% most concrete word pairs versus the 25% most abstract pairs in the dataset, of course expecting our grounded model to perform best on the concrete words.

MEN contains 3000 word pairs annotated for semantic relatedness (Bruni et al., 2013). Ratings were collected by showing subjects two word pairs and asking them to select the most related one. MEN was specifically collected to test multi-modal models, by selecting only words that have a visual referent that appeared in a large image database.

The RareWords dataset contains 2034 word pairs, where at least one word of each pair has a low frequency in Wikipedia (Luong et al., 2013). Modelling low-frequency words is a challenge for many models of distributional semantics.

Not all of the words in these databases are available in our training data and thus some will not have a word embedding. Table 1 contains an overview of the datasets described here and the number of word pairs that could be entered in our evaluations.

2.3.2 Semantic priming

The Semantic Priming Project (SPP) dataset (Hutchison et al., 2013) contains lexical decision times and naming times from a large priming experiment. The database is large for its kind, with 1,661 target words (and 1,661 non-words for the lexical decision task), each paired with a strong and weak prime and two unrelated primes. Furthermore, each prime-target pair was presented with a short (200ms) and a long (1200ms) SOA. Every combination of prime-target and SOA received responses from 32 subjects.

This gives us 26,576 (1661 target words $\times$ 4 priming conditions $\times$ 2 SOAs $\times$ 2 tasks) trials (disregarding the non-word word trials). We preprocessed the data by removing target words that mistakenly had more or fewer than the required four primes, trials with erroneous responses and missing data. We also lowered any capitals in the prime and target words, averaged the response times over the 32 subjects, and removed any prime-target pair that did not occur in our training data, resulting in 18,326 datapoints.

2.4 Analysis

2.4.1 Semantic similarity judgements

To test whether the word embedding models capture human intuitions on word similarity, we use the models to calculate embedding cosine similarities for each word pair and correlate them with the human annotations. From the correlations r we derive R^2 values, that is, the percentage of variance in the human similarity judgements that is explained by the model similarity scores. This allows us to evaluate our custom trained word embeddings to see which method best extracts word-level semantics from the MSCOCO dataset.

Next, we also compute semi-partial correlations between the human annotations and our VGE model using each of the text-based models as a control. Simply put, the semi-partial correlation between the VGE similarities and human annotations removes the effect of the control (i.e., text-based similarities) from the VGE similarities. Semi-partial R^2 gives us the percentage of variance that is uniquely explained by the VGE similarities. Given that all models are trained on the same textual data, with only the VGEs having access to the visual modality, this allows us to see whether visual grounding captures information that the text-based methods do not.

Finally we also test the semi-partial correlations using the pretrained embeddings as a control. For each pretrained model we also add in its custom MSCOCO-trained equivalent as a control, to take into account the information that text-based models can extract from the MSCOCO captions.

2.4.2 Semantic priming

Using linear regression models, we analyse how well embedding similarities predict human (log-transformed) reaction times in the SPP data using the Statsmodels package in Python (Seabold and Perktold, 2010). We code SOA and Task as factor variables. The reaction times are not on the same scale due to differences in the required response for the lexical decision and naming tasks so we standardise the log-transformed reaction time data separately for each combination of SOA and Task. This removes the main effects of SOA and Task but we include them in the regression as we are interested in their interactions with the similarity measures.

We fit a baseline regression including the target length (number of characters), Task and SOA as regressors. We furthermore include several regressors based on SUBTLEX-US (Brysbaert and New, 2009): log-transformed word-frequency counts, contextual diversity (the number of SUBTLEX-US documents a word appears in) and the orthographic neighbourhood density (the number of SUBTLEX-US words that are one character edit away) for the target words.

Next, for each of our embedding models, we include the prime-target embedding similarities as a regressor to the baseline model. We also add two two-way interactions to test the claims made in Petilli et al. (2021): 1) the interaction between the embedding similarities and Task to test the difference between lexical decision and naming in terms of sensitivity to semantic effects and 2) the interaction between the embedding similarities and SOA to test their claim about the time-frame in which visual information plays a role. These regression models allow us to compare the word embedding models to each other and to the baseline using the Akaike Information Criterion (AIC), where a lower AIC indicates a better model fit.

We also test if our VGEs can explain variance in the human reaction times that the text-based methods do not. We do this by refitting the regression models for each of the text-based similarity measures and adding the VGE similarity measures and their interactions with Task and SOA as extra regressors. For each of these regressions we then calculate the log-likelihood ratio (LLR) with the corresponding regression without the VGEs, indicating the decrease in model deviance due to adding the VGE similarity measures. Higher LLRs indicate a larger contribution of the VGEs to explaining variance in the human response times beyond what the text-based embedding similarities explain. Because the LLR follows a χ^2 distribution, we can test whether including the VGEs significantly improves the regression model.

We apply a similar approach to the pretrained text-based embeddings, but we also want to account for the information that text-based embedding models can extract from the MSCOCO captions. We do this by fitting a regression model as in the previous step except that we include both the pretrained and MSCOCO trained embeddings and their interactions with SOA and Task. We then follow the same procedure as described above by adding the VGE similarities and calculate LLRs to see if adding VGEs improves the regression fit.

3 Results

3.1 Semantic similarity judgements

Figure 1 shows the R^2 (explained variance) based on the Pearson correlation coefficients between the human similarity annotations and the embedding similarities. On top of the text-based R^2 values, we display the semi-partial R^2 of the VGEs using the text-based model as control. As total explained variance equals the semi-partial R^2 plus R^2 of the control(s), this clearly visualises both the total amount of explained variance and the amount of *extra* variance that is uniquely explained by the VGEs. All Pearson correlations were positive, as expected, except for two non-significant semi-partial correlations which are therefore not included in the figure.

For the MSCOCO models (left panel) we see that while GloVe has the worst performance on each dataset, there is no single best model. Furthermore, while the VGEs are outperformed by FastText and Word2Vec on SimLex999, we see that VGE performs best on the most concrete words (Q4) in SimLex999. A bit surprising then, is that VGE is outperformed by FastText and Word2Vec on MEN, which contains solely picturable nouns.

Looking at the semi-partial R^2, that is, the extra variance explained by the VGEs after controlling for one of the other embedding models, we see that for nearly every dataset and every model, the VGEs explain a significant portion of variance that is not explained by the text-based models. This is not very surprising on WordSim, where the VGEs were the best performing embeddings by quite a margin. However, we also see that even though the VGEs are outperformed by FastText and Word2Vec on MEN, they still explain a large extra portion of variance even though the R^2 for these models was already quite high.

Lastly, the pretrained models (right panel) outperform the MSCOCO models. This was expected, as the used training data is several orders of magnitude larger than MSCOCO. However, the semi-partial correlations still show that the VGEs explain a significant portion of extra variance on SimLex999 Q4 and MEN.

3.2 Semantic priming

The ΔAIC scores in Table 2 show that all word embedding models trained on MSCOCO improve

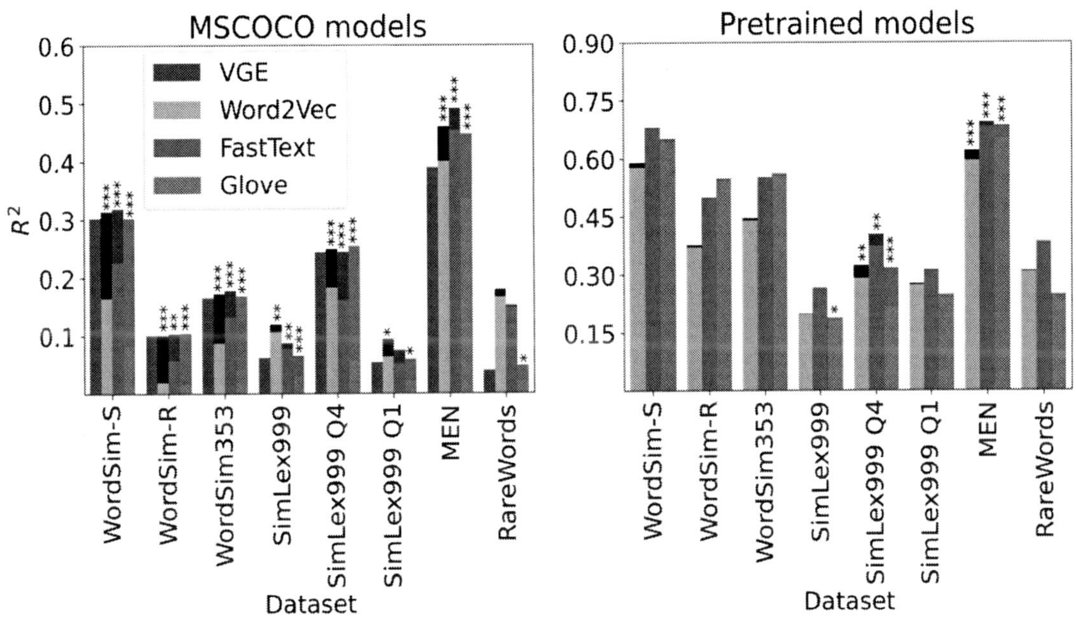

Figure 1: The coloured bars indicate the R^2 scores of the four word embedding models. The grey-scale bars on top of the R^2 scores of the text-based models indicate the semi-partial R^2 scores and their significance ($*p < .05, **p < .01, ***p < .001$, corrected using the Benjamini and Hochberg (1995) procedure with a false discovery rate of 0.05) of the VGEs after controlling for the variance explained by that text-based model. Left panel: models trained on MSCOCO. Right panel: pretrained text-based models.

Table 2: AIC comparison of regression models (lower is better). Δ indicates the difference in AIC compared to the VGE model or the Baseline model. β indicates the coefficient of the embedding similarity main effect (lower is better) and its significance.

Model	**AIC**	**ΔVGE**	**ΔBaseline**	β
VGE	46997.55	—	−211.04	−.67***
FastText	47101.90	104.35	−106.86	−.54***
GloVe	47163.70	166.15	−44.88	−.20**
Word2Vec	47184.45	186.90	−24.13	−.22**
Baseline	47208.58	211.03	—	—

Table 3: LLRs between regression models with the indicated text-based similarity measures and the same model with the VGE similarities as extra regressors. β VGE are the regression coefficients for the VGE similarities in each model. Higher LLRs indicate a larger improvement in model quality due to adding the VGEs.

	MSCOCO		**+ Pretrained**	
	LLR	β VGE	LLR	β VGE
Word2Vec	193.72***	−.77***	69.72***	−.49***
FastText	111.46***	−.63***	47.32***	−.42***
GloVe	168.34***	−.72***	49.80***	−.36***

the regression fit above the baseline. The embedding similarity effects were all negative, that is, a higher similarity correctly predicts a lower reaction time. We furthermore see that the VGE-derived similarity measures result in the best model fit by quite a margin, as evidenced by the AIC scores and effect size.

We also find significant interactions between Task and the embedding similarities for the VGE ($\beta = 0.201, P = 0.009$) and FastText regression models ($\beta = 0.197, P = 0.027$), meaning that the effect of embedding similarity is stronger for the lexical decision task. We find no significant interactions between the embedding similarities and SOA.

Table 3 shows the LLRs between regression models including the (pretrained) text-based and our VGE word similarity measures and the corresponding model including only the text-based measures. We see that our VGEs significantly improve the regression fit for every type of text-based method, even when we include both the pretrained and MSCOCO text-based measures. The coefficients of the VGE effects in these models are all positive, meaning a higher VGE similarity predicts a lower reaction time.

In the regression models including the VGEs and the MSCOCO text-based embeddings we found significant interactions between the VGE similarities and Task in the regression models that also include Word2Vec ($\beta = 0.239, P = 0.007$) or GloVe ($\beta = 0.234, P = 0.01$) and no other interactions with Task or SOA.

Lastly, in the regression models including the VGEs and both pretrained and MSCOCO text-based embeddings, we find significant interactions with Task for Word2Vec ($\beta = 0.312, P < 0.001$), FastText ($\beta = 0.297, P = 0.001$) and GloVe ($\beta = 0.443, P < 0.001$) vectors, and none for the VGEs.

4 Discussion

We created Visually Grounded Embeddings using a caption-image retrieval model in order to test if these embeddings can capture information about word meaning that text-based approaches cannot. Importantly, by testing our VGEs on human behavioural measures typically thought to rely on conceptual/semantic knowledge, we test a central idea of embodied cognition theory, namely that our visual experiences contribute to our conceptual knowledge.

4.1 Semantic similarity judgements

Our first experiment showed that, when trained on the same corpus, our VGEs are on par with text-based methods. While there is no clear overall best method, the VGEs perform well on WordSim and, as might be expected, on the datasets with concrete picturable nouns. Even though the text-based methods outperform the VGEs on one of these (MEN), the VGEs still explain a significant amount of extra variance over and above what is explained by the text-based methods. This indicates that the text-based embeddings and VGEs capture non-overlapping conceptual knowledge, which we attribute to the visual grounding of the VGEs, given that the training materials were otherwise equal.

The only database where the VGEs performed notably worse than the text-based methods was RareWords. This is perhaps because during training, the VGEs are grounded in the image corresponding to the text input, even if not all words in the sentence are visible in the picture. As the words in RareWords are generally not picturable nouns, any visual information incorporated into the word-embedding is unlikely to be helpful, or, as evidenced by the results, counterproductive.

We furthermore found that our VGEs explain additional variance in the human similarity ratings even after accounting for both the MSCOCO text-based models and pretrained models trained on massive text corpora. The fact that the VGEs explain a significant amount of extra variance even after the text-based models have seen billions of tokens of text, suggests that some aspects of word meaning cannot be captured solely from text and as well as that visual similarity plays a role in human intuition about word meaning.

4.2 Semantic priming

In our second experiment, the VGEs outperformed the text-based methods on explaining human reaction times from the Semantic Priming Project. Even after we account for both the MSCOCO text-based models and pretrained models in our regression, the VGEs still explain a significant amount of variance in the reaction times.

In previous work, Petilli et al. (2021) only found a significant contribution of visual information in the short SOA lexical decision task. We found no further proof for their hypothesis that visual information is activated in early linguistic processing and thereafter rapidly decays. Rather, we find that our VGEs improve the model quality for both short and long SOA trials.

We did find a significant positive interaction with Task, meaning that the word embeddings explain less variance in the naming task than in the lexical decision task. This interaction was not specific to the VGEs but also occurred in the models including FastText and for all the pretrained embeddings. As claimed in Petilli et al. (2021) and Lucas (2000) this suggests that naming tasks are in general less sensitive to semantic effects.

5 Conclusion

We set out to test an end-to-end approach to combining visual and textual input in a single embedding, trained on a cognitively plausible amount of data. The results from our two experiments suggest that VGEs capture aspects of word meaning that text-based approaches cannot. Even though we include word embeddings trained on corpora several orders of magnitude greater than any human's exposure to language, our VGEs still explain a unique portion of variance in both human behavioural measures.

While our results indicate that visual grounding can provide complementary information for certain words, it may not play a role in our conceptual knowledge of rare, abstract words, as shown by our results on the RareWords corpus. Similar to Petilli et al. (2021) this then does not support the strongest formulations of embodied cognition theory which suggest total equivalence between conceptual and sensorimotor processing (Glenberg, 2015).

Of course, one could always claim that it is just current word-embedding models that do not fully capture word meaning yet. However, given that VGEs trained on a relatively small amount of visual data can complement text-based embeddings, we do not think even larger text-corpora or more complex embedding models can ever fully capture human semantic knowledge. The human experience is rich and varied, and our computational models can never fully capture human word knowledge while ignoring visual aspects of this experience.

6 Acknowledgements

The research presented here was funded by the Netherlands Organisation for Scientific Research (NWO) Gravitation Grant 024.001.006 to the Language in Interaction Consortium.

References

Samira Abnar, Rasyan Ahmed, Max Mijnheer, and Willem Zuidema. 2018. Word Embeddings have Complementary Roles in Decoding Brain Activity. *Proceedings of the 8th Workshop on Cognitive Modeling and Computational Linguistics (CMCL 2018), Salt Lake City, Utah, USA, January 7, 2018*, pages 57–66.

Eneko Agirre, Enrique Alfonseca, Keith Hall, Jana Kravalova, Marius Pasca, and Aitor Soroa. 2009. A study on similarity and relatedness using distributional and wordnet-based approaches. In *Proceedings of the 2009 Annual Conference of the North American Chapter of the Association for Computational Linguistics (HLT-NAACL-2009)*, pages 19–27, Boulder, Colorado.

Marco Baroni, Georgiana Dinu, and Germán Kruszewski. 2014. Don't count, predict! a systematic comparison of context-counting vs. context-predicting semantic vectors. *Proceedings of the 52nd Annual Meeting of the Association for Computational Linguistics (Volume 1: Long Papers)*, pages 238–247.

Lawrence W. Barsalou. 2008. Grounded cognition. *Annual Review of Psychology*, 59(1):617–645.

Yoav Benjamini and Yosef Hochberg. 1995. Controlling the false discovery rate: a practical and powerful approach to multiple testing. *Journal of the Royal Statistical Society B*, 57:289–300.

Piotr Bojanowski, Edouard Grave, Armand Joulin, and Tomás Mikolov. 2017. Enriching word vectors with subword information. *Transactions of the Association for Computational Linguistics*, 5:135–146.

Elia Bruni, Namh Khanh Tran, and Marco Baroni. 2013. Multimodal distributional semantics. *Journal of Artificial Intelligence Research*, 49:1–47.

Marc Brysbaert and Boris New. 2009. Moving beyond Kučera and Francis: A critical evaluation of current word frequency norms and the introduction of a new and improved word frequency measure for American English. *Behavior Research Methods*, 41(4):977–990.

Xinlei Chen, Hao Fang, Tsung-Yi Lin, Ramakrishna Vedantam, Saurabh Gupta, Piotr Dollar, and C. Lawrence Zitnick. 2015. Microsoft COCO Captions: Data Collection and Evaluation Server. *arXiv preprint arXiv: 1504.00325*.

Grzegorz Chrupała, Lieke Gelderloos, and Afra Alishahi. 2017. Representations of language in a model of visually grounded speech signal. In *Proceedings of the 55th Annual Meeting of the Association for Computational Linguistics (ACL)*, pages 613–622.

Steven Derby, Paul Miller, and Barry Devereux. 2020. Analysing word representation from the input and output embeddings in neural network language models. In *Proceedings of the 24th Conference on Computational Natural Language Learning*, pages 442–454.

Steven Derby, Paul Miller, Brian Murphy, and Barry Devereux. 2018. Using sparse semantic embeddings learned from multimodal text and image data to model human conceptual knowledge. In *Proceedings of the 22nd Conference on Computational Natural Language Learning*, pages 260–270, Brussels, Belgium. Association for Computational Linguistics.

Giovanni B. Flores D'Arcais, Robert Schreuder, and Ge Glazenborg. 1985. Semantic activation during recognition of referential words. *Psychological Research*, 45(1):39–49.

Lev Finkelstein, Evgeniy Gabrilovich, Yossi Matias, Ehud Rivlin, Zach Solan, Gadi Wolfman, and Eytan Ruppin. 2002. Placing search in context: The concept revisited. *ACM Transactions on Information Systems*, 20(1):116–131.

Lucia Foglia and Robert A Wilson. 2013. Embodied cognition. *Wiley Interdisciplinary Reviews: Cognitive Science*, 4(3):319–325.

Stefan L. Frank and Roel M. Willems. 2017. Word predictability and semantic similarity show distinct patterns of brain activity during language comprehension. *Language, Cognition and Neuroscience*, 32(9):1192–1203.

Arthur M. Glenberg. 2015. Few believe the world is flat: How embodiment is changing the scientific understanding of cognition. *Journal of Experimental Psychology*, 69(2):165–171.

Kaiming He, Xiangyu Zhang, Shaoqing Ren, and Jian Sun. 2016. Deep residual learning for image recognition. In *The IEEE Conference on Computer Vision and Pattern Recognition (CVPR)*.

Felix Hill, Roi Reichart, and Anna Korhonen. 2015. Simlex-999: Evaluating semantic models with genuine similarity estimation. *Computational Linguistics*, 41(4):665–695.

Keith A. Hutchison, David A. Balota, James H. Neely, Michael J. Cortese, Emily R. Cohen-Shikora, Chi-Shing Tse, Melvin J. Yap, Jesse J. Bengson, Dale Niemeyer, and Erin Buchanan. 2013. The semantic priming project. *Behaviour Research Methods*, 45:1099–1114.

Herman Kamper, Shane Settle, Gregory Shakhnarovich, and Karen Livescu. 2017. Visually grounded learning of keyword prediction from untranscribed speech. *INTERSPEECH 2017 – 18th Annual Conference of the International Speech Communication Association*, pages 3677–3681.

Andrej Karpathy and Li Fei-Fei. 2015. Deep visual-semantic alignments for generating image descriptions. In *The IEEE Conference on Computer Vision and Pattern Recognition (CVPR)*, pages 3128–3137.

Douwe Kiela, Alexis Conneau, Allan Jabri, and Maximilian Nickel. 2018. Learning visually grounded sentence representations. In *Proceedings of NAACL-HLT 2018*, pages 408–418. Association for Computational Linguistics.

Margery Lucas. 2000. Semantic priming without association: A meta-analytic review. *Psychonomic Bulletin & Review*, 7(4):618–630.

Thang Luong, Richard Socher, and Christopher Manning. 2013. Better word representations with recursive neural networks for morphology. In *Proceedings of the Seventeenth Conference on Computational Natural Language Learning*, pages 104–113, Sofia, Bulgaria. Association for Computational Linguistics.

Paweł Mandera, Emmanuel Keuleers, and Marc Brysbaert. 2017. Explaining human performance in psycholinguistic tasks with models of semantic similarity based on prediction and counting: A review and empirical validation. *Journal of Memory and Language*, 92:57–78.

Danny Merkx and Stefan L. Frank. 2019. Learning semantic sentence representations from visually grounded language without lexical knowledge. *Natural Language Engineering*, 25(4):451–466.

Danny Merkx, Stefan L. Frank, and Mirjam Ernestus. 2021. Semantic Sentence Similarity: Size does not Always Matter. In *INTERSPEECH 2021 – 22nd Annual Conference of the International Speech Communication Association*, pages 4393–4397.

Tomas Mikolov, Kai Chen, Greg Corrado, and Jeffrey Dean. 2013a. Efficient Estimation of Word Representations in Vector Space. *arXiv preprint arXiv: 1301.3781*.

Tomas Mikolov, Edouard Grave, Piotr Bojanowski, Christian Puhrsch, and Armand Joulin. 2018. Advances in pre-training distributed word representations. In *Proceedings of the International Conference on Language Resources and Evaluation (LREC 2018)*.

Tomas Mikolov, Ilya Sutskever, Kai Chen, Greg Corrado, and Jeffrey Dean. 2013b. Distributed representations of words and phrases and their compositionality. In *NIPS*.

Diane Pecher, René Zeelenberg, and Jeroen G. W. Raaijmakers. 1984. Does pizza prime coin? perceptual priming in lexical decision and pronunciation. *Psychological Research*, 45(4):339–354.

Jeffrey Pennington, Richard Socher, and Christopher D. Manning. 2014. Glove: Global vectors for word representation. In *Empirical Methods in Natural Language Processing (EMNLP)*, pages 1532–1543.

Marco A. Petilli, Fritz Günther, Alessandra Vergallito, Marco Ciapparelli, and Marco Marelli. 2021. Data-driven computational models reveal perceptual simulation in word processing. *Journal of Memory and Language*, 117.

Radim Řehůřek and Petr Sojka. 2010. Software Framework for Topic Modelling with Large Corpora. In *Proceedings of the LREC 2010 Workshop on New Challenges for NLP Frameworks*, pages 45–50, Valletta, Malta. ELRA.

Armand S. Rotaru, Gabriella Vigliocco, and Stefan L. Frank. 2018. Modeling the structure and dynamics of semantic processing. *Cognitive Science*, pages 1–28.

Robert Schreuder, Giovanni B. Flores D'Arcais, and Ge Glazenborg. 1998. Effects of perceptual and conceptual similarity in semantic priming. *Journal of Memory and Language*, 38(4):401–418.

Skipper Seabold and Josef Perktold. 2010. statsmodels: Econometric and statistical modeling with python. In *9th Python in Science Conference*.

Leslie N. Smith. 2017. Cyclical learning rates for training neural networks. In *2017 IEEE Winter Conference on Applications of Computer Vision (WACV)*, pages 464–472.

Robert Speer and Joshua Chin. 2016. An Ensemble Method to Produce High-Quality Word Embeddings. *arXiv preprint arXiv: 1604.01692*.

Haoyan Xu, Brian Murphy, and Alona Fyshe. 2016. Brainbench: A brain-image test suite for distributional semantic models. In *Proceedings of the 2016 Conference on Empirical Methods in Natural Language Processing*, pages 2017–2021.

A Neural Model for Compositional Word Embeddings and Sentence Processing

Jean-Philippe Bernardy and **Shalom Lappin**
Centre for Linguistic Theory and Studies in Probability
Department of Philosophy, Linguistics and Theory of Science
University of Gothenburg
jean-philippe.bernardy@gu.se shalom.lappin@gu.se

Abstract

We propose a new neural model for word embeddings, which uses Unitary Matrices as the primary device for encoding lexical information. It uses simple matrix multiplication to derive matrices for large units, yielding a sentence processing model that is strictly compositional, does not lose information over time steps, and is transparent, in the sense that word embeddings can be analysed regardless of context. This model does not employ activation functions, and so the network is fully accessible to analysis by the methods of linear algebra at each point in its operation on an input sequence. We test it in two NLP agreement tasks and obtain rule like perfect accuracy, with greater stability than current state-of-the-art systems. Our proposed model goes some way towards offering a class of computationally powerful deep learning systems that can be fully understood and compared to human cognitive processes for natural language learning and representation.

1 Introduction

The word embeddings that deep neural networks (DNNs) learn are encoded as vectors. The various dimensions of the vectors correspond to distributional properties of words, as measured in corpora. Combining word embeddings into phrasal and sentence vectors can be achieved through various means, often through task-specific models with many parameters of their own, optimised by gradient descent.

In this paper we use unitary matrices in place of arbitrary vector embeddings. Arjovsky et al. (2016) propose *Unitary-Evolution Recurrent Neural Networks* (URNs), to eliminate exploding or vanishing gradients in gradient descent. By the definition of unitary-evolution, at each step, a unitary transformation is applied to the state of the RNN. This means that each input symbol is interpreted as a unitary transformation, or equivalently as a unitary matrix. No activation functions are applied between the time-steps. This design provides a lightweight DNN, with several attractive mathematical and computational properties. URNs are strictly compositional. The effect of embeddings can be analysed independently of context. Therefore the model is transparent, in the sense that it can be analysed by direct inspection, rather than through black box testing methods. So, for example, researchers are forced to resort to probe techniques (Hewitt and Manning, 2019) to ascertain the syntactic structure which transformers and other DNNs represent.

Because of the reversibility of unitary transformations, long distance dependency relations can, in principle, be reliably and efficiently recognised, without additional special-purpose machinery of the kind required in an LSTM. This has been demonstrated to hold for copying and adding tasks (Arjovsky et al., 2016; Jing et al., 2017; Vorontsov et al., 2017) (See also section 6.4).

Here we view the unitary matrices learned by a URN as *word embeddings*. Doing so gives a richer structure to embeddings, with computational and formal advantages that are absent from the traditional vector format that dominates current work in deep learning.

We demonstrate these advantages by applying the URN architecture to two tasks: (i) bracket matching in a generalised Dyck language, and (ii) the more challenging task of subject-verb number agreement in English. These experiments confirm the long-distance capabilities of URNs, even on a linguistically interesting and difficult task.

The richer structure of unitary embeddings permits us to measure the relative effects and distances of different words and phrases. We illustrate the application of such metrics for both experiments.

In section 2 we describe the design of the URN, and our implementation of it. Sections 4 and 5 present our experiments and their results, leverag-

Proceedings of the Workshop on Cognitive Modeling and Computational Linguistics, pages 12 - 22
May 26, 2022 ©2022 Association for Computational Linguistics

ing the theory presented in section 3.[1] We discuss related work in section 6, and we draw conclusions and sketch future work in section 7.

The computational perspicuity of URNs allows them to be compared to psychologically and neurologically attested models of human learning and representation. Most deep neural networks, particularly powerful transformers, use non-linear activation functions which render their operation opaque and difficult to understand. By contrast, the computations of an URN are explicitly given as simple matrix multiplications, and they are open to inspection at each point in the processing sequence.

2 Models

In its full generality, a recurrent network is a function from an input state vector s_0 and a sequence of input vectors x_i, such that the state at each time-step is a function of the state at the previous step and the input at that step: $s_{i+1} = f(x_i, s_i)$. The function f is constant across steps, and it is called a "cell" of the network.

Since the simple recurrent networks of Elman (1990), the dominant architectures of RNNs, including the influential LSTM (Hochreiter and Schmidhuber, 1997), use non-linear activation functions (*sigmoid*, *tanh*, ReLU) at each time-step. Transformer models, like BERT, are even more opaque in their operations, due the their reliance on a large number of attention heads that apply non-linear functions at each level. By contrast our URNs invoke only linear cells. In fact, the cell that we use is a linear transformation of the unitary space,[2] so that it takes unit state vectors to unit state vectors, hence the term "unitary-evolution". Expressed as an equation, we have $f(x, s) = Q(x)s$, where $Q(x)$ is unitary. Therefore, only state vectors s_i of norm 1 play a role in URNs.

In our implementation of the URN architecture we limit ourselves to real numbers, and so $Q(x)$ is properly described as an orthogonal matrix. We follow this terminology in what follows.

Let n be the dimension of the state vectors s_i, and N the length of the sequence of inputs. We will consider only the case of n even. In all our experiments, we take s_0 to be the vector $[1, 0, \dots]$ without loss of generality. For predictions, we extract a probability distribution from state vectors by applying a dense layer with softmax activation to each s_i.

We need to ensure that $Q(x)$ is (and remains) orthogonal when it is subjected to gradient descent. In general, subtracting a gradient to an orthogonal matrix does not preserve orthogonality of the matrix. So we cannot make $Q(x)$ a simple lookup table from symbol to orthogonal matrix without additional restrictions. While one could project the matrix onto an orthogonal space (Wisdom et al., 2016; Kiani et al., 2022), our solution is to use a lookup table mapping each word to a skew-hermitian matrix $S(x)$.[3] We follow Hyland and Rätsch (2017) in doing this. We then let $Q(x) = e^{S(x)}$, which ensures the orthogonality of $Q(x)$. It is not difficult to ensure that $S(x)$ is skew-symmetric. It suffices to store only the elements of $S(x)$ above the diagonal, and let those below it be their anti-symmetric image, while the diagonal is set at zero.

Another important issue is that the number of parameters in $S(x)$ grows with the square of n. This would entail that doubling a model's power requires quadrupling the number of its parameters. To remedy this problem we limit ourselves to matrices $S(x)$ which have non-zero entries only on the first k rows (and consequently k columns). In this way we limit the total size of the embedding to $(n-1) + (n-2) + \cdots + (n-k+1)$, due to the constraint of symmetry. Consequently, $S(x)$ has at most rank $2k$. Below, we refer to this setup as consisting of *truncated* embeddings.

As an example, the 3×3 skew-symmetric matrix $\begin{pmatrix} 0 & a & b \\ -a & 0 & c \\ -b & -c & 0 \end{pmatrix}$ is 1-truncated if $c = 0$. This truncation reduces its informational content to the single row (and column) $(a\ b)$.

We use the acronym URN to refer to the general class of unitary-evolution networks, k-TURN to refer to our specific model architecture with k-truncation of embeddings (fig. 1), and Full-URN for our model architecture with no truncation.

We employ a standard training regime for our experiments. We apply a dropout function on both inputs of f, so that some entries of s_i or $Q(x_i)$ will be zeroed out according to a Bernoulli distribution

[1] The code and relevant linear algebra proofs for our model is available at `https://github.com/GU-CLASP/unitary-recurrent-network`.

[2] The subspace of vectors of unit norm

[3] A matrix S is skew-symmetric iff $S^T = -S$. Here, we rely on the the property that the exponential of any skew-symmetric matrix is orthogonal . The mathematical tools that we employ are standard (Gantmacher, 1959). The key results and their proofs are available at `https://github.com/GU-CLASP/unitary-recurrent-network/blob/main/proofs.pdf`.

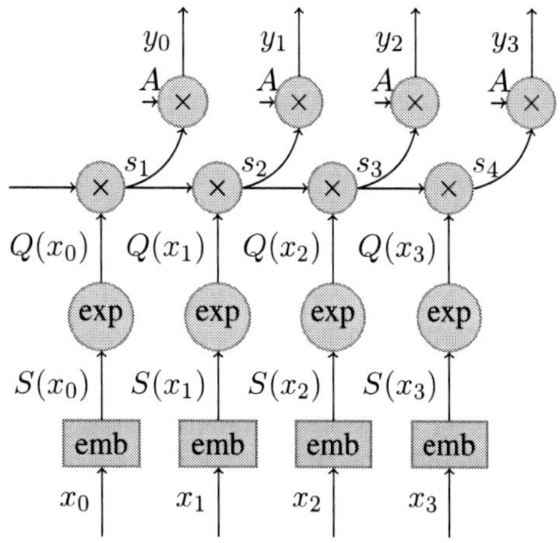

Figure 1: TURN architecture. Each input symbol x_i indexes an embedding layer, yielding a skew-symmetric matrix $S(x_i)$. Taking its exponential yields an orthogonal matrix $Q(x_i)$. Multiplying the state s_i by $Q(x_i)$ yields the next state, s_{i+1}.

of rate ρ.[4] The embeddings are optimised by means of the Adam gradient descent algorithm (Kingma and Ba, 2014), with no further adjustment. Our implementation uses the TensorFlow (Abadi et al., 2016) framework (version 2.2), including its implementation of matrix exponential.

3 Properties of Orthogonal Embeddings

The absence of activation functions in the URN make it more amenable to theoretical analysis than the general class of RNNs with activation functions, including LSTMs and GRUs. The key feature of this design is that the behaviour of the cell is entirely defined by the matrix $Q(x)$, the orthogonal embedding of x. The cell only multiplies by word embeddings, and we can focus solely on those embeddings to understand the model.

Since the work of Mikolov et al. (2013), vector embeddings have proven to be an extremely successful modelling tool. However, their structure is opaque. The only way of analysing their relations is through geometric distance metrics like cosine similarity. The unit vectors u and v are deemed similar if $\langle u, v\rangle$ is close to 1. Here we work with orthogonal matrix embeddings, which exhibit much richer structure. We use mathematical analysis to get a better sense of this structure, and relate it to vector embeddings.

[4]Even though we follow this regime to be standard, experiments indicate that dropout rates appear not critical when we restrict transformations to be unitary.

Composition of Embeddings A decisive benefit of unitary (and orthogonal) matrix embeddings is that they form a group. We can obtain the inverse of a word embedding simply by transposing it: $Q(x)^{-1} = Q(x)^T$. We can also compose two embeddings to obtain an embedding for the composition. Thanks to the associativity of multiplication, we have $f(x_1, f(x_0, s_0)) = Q(x_1)(Q(x_0)s_0) = (Q(x_1) \times Q(x_0))s_0$. So, we can define the embedding of any sequence as $Q(x_0 \ldots x_i) = Q(x_i) \times Q(x_{i-1}) \times \cdots \times Q(x_0)$. Using this notation, the final state of an URN is $Q(x_0 \ldots x_{N-1})s_0$. Hence, the URN is *compositional by design*.[5]

It is important to recognise that compositionality is strictly a consequence of the structure of a URN. It follows directly from the use of unitary matrix multiplication, through which the successive states in the RNN's processing sequence are computed, without activation functions, It is not necessary to demonstrate this result experimentally, since it is a formal consequence of the associativity of orthogonal matrix multiplication, as shown above. Because URNs do not incorporate additional nonlinear activation functions, a simple matrix is always sufficient to express any combination of word and phrasal embeddings.

Distance and Similarity For vector embeddings, one often uses cosine similarity as a metric of proximity. With unit vectors, this cosine similarity is equal to the inner product $\langle u, v\rangle = \sum_i u_i v_i$. In unitary space, it is equivalent to working with euclidean distance squared, because $\|u - v\|^2 = 2(1 - \langle u, v\rangle)$.

Notions of vector similarity and distance can be naturally extended to matrices. The Frobenius inner product $\langle P, Q\rangle = \Sigma_{ij} P_{ij} Q_{ij}$ extends cosine similarity, and the Frobenius norm $\|A\|^2 = \sum_{ij} A_{ij}^2$ extends euclidean norm. Furthermore, for orthogonal matrices they relate in an analogous way to unit vectors: $\|P - Q\|^2 = 2(n - \langle P, Q\rangle)$.

Why is the Frobenius norm a natural extension of cosine similarity for vectors? It is not merely due to the similarity of the respective formulas.

[5]One might expect that the composition of embeddings can be done at the level of skew-symmetric embeddings: $S(x_0 x_1) = S(x_0) + S(x_1)$. However, this will not work. The law $e^{S_0 + S_1} = e^{S_0} e^{S_1}$ holds only when S_0 and S_1 commute, which is, in general, not true in our setup. This non-commutativity makes it possible to obtain, by composition, embeddings of higher rank, by which way we make use of all the dimensions of the orthogonal group.

The connection is deeper. A crucial property of the Frobenius inner product (and associated norm) is that it measures the average behaviour of orthogonal matrices on state vectors. More precisely, the following holds: $\mathbb{E}_s[\langle Ps, Qs\rangle] = \frac{1}{n}\langle P, Q\rangle$, and $\mathbb{E}_s[\|Ps - Qs\|^2] = \frac{1}{n}\|P - Q\|^2$. In sum, as a fallback, one can analyse unitary embeddings using the methods developed for plain vector embeddings. Doing so is theoretically sound. Together with the fact that matrix embeddings can be composed, it means that one can analyse the distances between *phrases*.

Average Effect A useful metric for unitary embeddings is the squared distance to the identity matrix, $\|Q - I\|^2$. By the above result, it is the average squared distance between s and Qs — essentially, the average effect that Q has, relative to the task for which the URN is trained. Note that this sort of metric is unavailable when using opaque vector embeddings. In particular, the norm of a vector embedding is not directly interpretable as a measure of its effect. In the case of an LSTM, for example, vector embeddings first undergo linear transformations *followed by activation functions*, before effecting the state, in several separate stages.

Signature of Embeddings While the average effect is a useful measure, it is rather crude. Averaging over random state vectors considers all features as equivalent. But we might be interested in the effect of Q along specific dimensions, measured separately.

For this purpose, it is useful to note that any orthogonal matrix Q can be decomposed as the effect of $n/2$ independent rotations, in $n/2$ orthogonal planes. The angles of these rotations define how strongly Q effects the state vectors lying in this plane. We refer to such a list of angles as the *signature* of Q, and we denote it as $\text{sig}(Q)$. When displaying a signature, we omit any zero angle. This is useful because a k-truncated embedding has at most k non-zero angles in its signature. Non-zero angles will be represented graphically as a dial, with small angles pointing up ⦶, and large angles pointing down ⦶.

4 Natural Language Agreement Task

It may seem that the extreme simplicity of the TURN architecture renders it unsuitable for any non-trivial processing task. In fact, this is not at all the case.

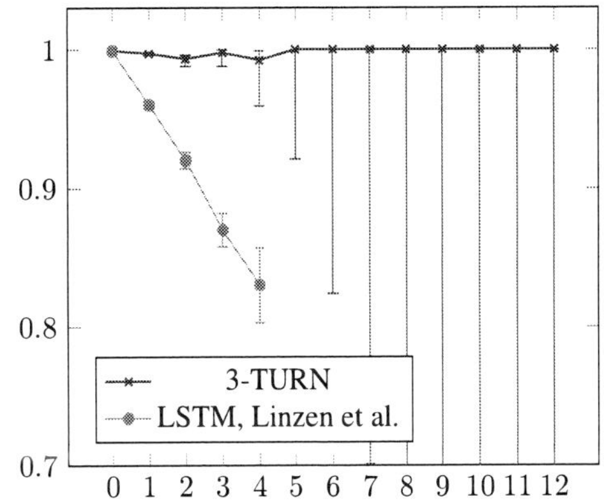

Figure 2: Accuracy per number of attractors for the verb number agreement task. Linzen et al. (2016) do not report performance of their LSTM past 4 attractors. Error bars represent binomial 95% confidence intervals.

Our first experiment applies a TURN to a natural language agreement task proposed by Linzen et al. (2016). This task is to predict the number of third person verbs in English text, with supervised training. In the phrase "The **keys** to the cabinet **are** on the table", the RNN is trained to predict the plural "**are**" rather than the singular "**is**".

The training data is composed of 1.7 million sentences with a selected subject-verb pair, extracted from Wikipedia. The vocabulary size is 50,000, and out-of-vocabulary tokens are replaced by their part-of-speech tag. Training is performed for ten epochs, with a learning rate of 0.01, and a dropout rate of $\rho = 0.05$. We use 90% of the data for training and 10% for validation and testing. A development subset is not necessary since no effort was made to tune hyperparameters. Our first experiment proved sufficient to illustrate our main claims. In any case, a TURN has few hyperparameters to optimise.

Linzen et al. (2016) point out that solving the agreement task requires knowledge of hierarchical syntactic structure. That is, if an RNN captures the long-distance dependencies involved in agreement relations, it cannot rely solely on the linear sequence of nouns (in particular their number inflections) preceding the predicted verb in a sentence. In particular, the accuracy must be sustained as the number *attractors* increases. An attractor is defined as a noun occurring between the subject and the verb which additionally exhibits the wrong number feature required to control the verb. In the above example sentence, "cabinet" is an attractor.

Figure 2 shows the results for a 50-unit TURN

word	effect	word	effect	word	effect
.	0.22	an	3.70	for	4.62
the	1.44	as	3.76	in	4.62
his	1.47	he	3.95	have	4.62
its	2.17	had	3.95	who	4.68
also	2.27	to	3.96	were	4.88
their	2.54	a	4.06	that	5.00
not	2.73	of	4.09	was	5.55
been	2.82	from	4.09	(	5.68
at	3.40	i	4.11	)	5.74
or	3.46	it	4.14	are	6.25
by	3.50	and	4.18	but	6.27
one	3.54	on	4.33	is	6.38
this	3.62	with	4.36	which	7.75
be	3.65	has	4.41	,	8.35

Table 1: Table of average effects for agreement experiment for the most frequent tokens in the corpus, ordered by average effect, from least to greatest

with 3-truncated embeddings for the agreement task, for up to 12 attractors. We see that the TURN "solves" this task, with error rates well under one percent. Crucially, there is no evidence of accuracy dropping as the number of attractors increases. Even though the statistical uncertainty increases with the number of attractors, due to decreasing numbers of examples, the TURN makes no mistakes for the higher number of attractor cases.

4.1 Average effect

In this section we illustrate the notion of average effect developed in 3, for this task.

We report the average effect for the embeddings of the most common words in the dataset (table 1), and other selected words and phrases obtained by composition. We stress that this is **not** done by measuring the average effect on the data set; but rather using the formula $||Q - I||^2$ for each unitary embedding Q. Looking at the table of effects for these words and phrases (ordered from smallest to largest effect) confirms the analysis of 3: tokens which are relevant to the task (e.g. verbs, relative pronouns) generally have a larger effect than those which are not (e.g. the dot, "not").

We also computed the distance between pairs of the most frequent nouns, with both singular and plural inflections (table 2). We observe, as our account predicts, that nouns with the same number inflection tend to be grouped (with a distance of 7.5 or less between them), while nouns with differing numbers are further apart (with a distance of 7.5 or more).

5 Dyck-language modelling task

To evaluate the *theoretical* long-distance modelling capabilities of an RNN in a way that abstracts away from the noise in natural language, one can construct synthetic data. Following Bernardy (2018) we use a (generalised) Dyck language. This language is composed solely of matching parenthesis pairs. So the strings "`{([])}<>`" and "`{()[<>]}`" are part of the language, while "`[}`" is not. This experiment is an idealised version of the agreement task, where opening parentheses correspond to subjects, and closing parentheses to verbs. An attractor is an opening parenthesis occurring between the pair, but of a different kind. Matching of parentheses corresponds to agreement. Because we use five distinct kinds of parentheses, the majority class baseline is at 20%. This makes it easier to evaluate the performance of a model on the matching task than for the third person agreement task, where the majority class baseline for the training corpus is above 70%.

We complicate the matching task with an additional difficulty. We vary the nesting depth between training and test phases. The *depth* of the string is the maximum nesting level reached within it. For instance "`[{}]`" has depth 2, while "`{([()]<>)}`" has depth 4. In this task, we use strings with a length of exactly 20 characters. We train on 102,400 randomly generated strings, with maximum depth 3, and test it on 5120 random strings of maximum depth 10. Training is performed with a learning rate of 0.01, and a dropout rate of $\rho = 0.05$, for 100 epochs.

The training phase treats the URN as a generative language model, applying a cross-entropy loss function at each position in the string. At test time, we evaluate the model's ability to predict the right kind of closing parenthesis at each point (this is the equivalent of predicting the number of a verb). We ignore predictions regarding opening parentheses, because they are always acceptable for the language.

We ran three versions of this experiment. One with truncated embeddings, one with full embeddings, and a third using a baseline RNN with full embeddings that are not constrained to be orthogonal. In all cases, the size of matrices is 50 by 50. We report accuracy on the task by number of attractors in fig. 3.

	article	year	area	world	family	articles	years	areas	worlds	families
article	0.00	7.04	6.51	6.89	5.82	9.26	9.84	10.01	10.87	9.39
year	7.04	0.00	7.62	6.30	5.38	8.22	9.06	9.75	10.14	8.64
area	6.51	7.62	0.00	6.42	6.34	9.57	9.70	10.39	11.63	10.39
world	6.89	6.30	6.42	0.00	5.17	7.32	8.82	9.17	9.13	7.83
family	5.82	5.38	6.34	5.17	0.00	7.71	7.72	8.78	9.49	8.82
articles	9.26	8.22	9.57	7.32	7.71	0.00	5.11	4.79	4.28	4.57
years	9.84	9.06	9.70	8.82	7.72	5.11	0.00	6.42	6.61	7.14
areas	10.01	9.75	10.39	9.17	8.78	4.79	6.42	0.00	5.93	6.09
worlds	10.87	10.14	11.63	9.13	9.49	4.28	6.61	5.93	0.00	7.79
families	9.39	8.64	10.39	7.83	8.82	4.57	7.14	6.09	7.79	0.00

Table 2: Distances between embeddings of most frequent nouns and their plural variants. Words which can be both nouns and verbs were excluded.

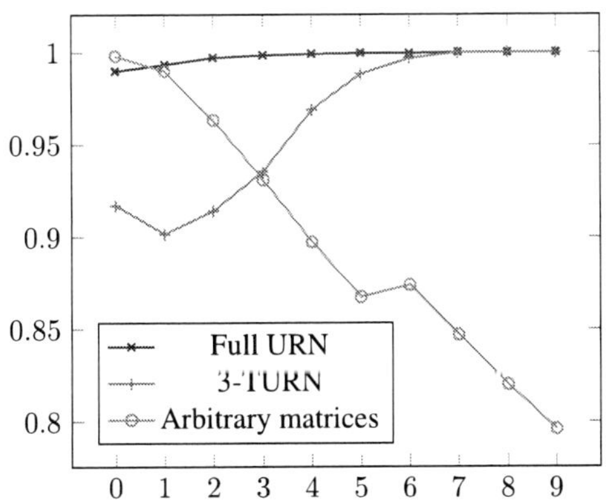

Figure 3: Accuracy of closing parenthesis prediction by number of attractors.

	⊘	⊖	⦸
⦸	0.33	0.35	1.35
⊖	0.46	1.73	0.2
⊘	1.09	0.2	0.34

Table 3: Similarity for each pair of rotation planes, for the embeddings of (and [. Headers show the rotation effected on the compared planes. A value of 2 indicates that the planes are equal (up to rotation of the basis vectors), and a value of 0 indicates that they are orthogonal.

We note that even the baseline model is capable of generalising to longer distances. Up to 9 attractors, it achieves performance that is well above a majority class baseline (20%). However, it shows steadily decreasing accuracy as the number of attractors increases.

By contrast, the URN models remain accurate as the number of attractors grows. Perhaps surprisingly, the URN improves in relation to the number of attractors. We will solve this apparent puzzle below, through analysis of the embeddings. The explanation will hinge on the fact that truncating embeddings affects performance only when the number of attractors is low.

Comparing the arbitrary embeddings model with with full URN highlights the importance of limiting the network to orthogonal matrices. The performance of the full URN is better over the long term and in general, with a validation loss of 1.47213 compared to 1.52914 for the arbitrary case. This happens despite the fact that the orthogonal system is a special case of the arbitrary network, and so orthogonal embeddings are, in principle, available to the baseline RNN. But it is not able to converge on the preferred solution (even for absolute loss). In sum, restricting to orthogonal matrices acts like a regularising constraint which offers a significant net benefit in generalisation and tracking power.

5.1 Analysis

As in the previous experiment, matrix embeddings can be analysed regardless of contexts, offering a direct view of how the model works. We consider the embeddings produced by training the 3-TURN model, and we start with the embeddings of individual characters and their signatures (table 4). The average effect, and even the signatures of all embeddings are strikingly similar. This does not imply that they are *equal*. Indeed, they rotate different planes.

We see in table 3 that the planes which undergo rotation by similar angles are far from orthogonal to each other— one pair even exhibits a similarity of 1.73. This corresponds to the fact that the transformations of (and [manipulate a common subset of coordinates. On the other hand, those planes that undergo rotation by different angles tend to be in a

character	average effect	signature
(	14.79	↖ ↙ ↓
<	14.34	↖ ↙ ↓
{	13.98	↖ ↙ ↓
[	14.25	↖ ↙ ↓
+	14.20	↖ ↙ ↓
)	14.85	↖ ↙ ↓
>	14.42	↖ ↙ ↓
}	14.07	↖ ↙ ↓
]	14.34	↖ ↙ ↓
−	14.26	↖ ↙ ↓
( )	0.06	↑ ↑ ↑ ↑
<>	0.06	↑ ↑ ↑ ↑
{ }	0.07	↑ ↑ ↑ ↑
[ ]	0.06	↑ ↑ ↑ ↑
+−	0.06	↑ ↑ ↑ ↑

Table 4: Average effect and signatures of parenthesis embeddings and matching pairs.

closer to orthogonal relationship.

Composition of Matching Parentheses To further clarify the formal properties of our model let's look at the embeddings of matching pairs, computed as the product of the respective embeddings of the pairs. Such compositions are close to identity (table 4). This observation explains the extraordinarily accurate long-distance performance of the URN on the matching task. Because a matching pair has essentially no effect on the state, by the time all parentheses have been closed, the state returns to its original condition. Accordingly, the model experiences the highest level of confusion when it is *inside* a deeply nested structure, and *not* when a deep structure is inserted between the governing opening parenthesis and the prediction conditioned on that parenthesis.

6 Related Work

6.1 Explainable NLP

It has frequently been observed that DNNs are complex and opaque in the way in which they operate. It is often unclear how they arrive at their results, or why they identify the patterns that they extract from training data. This has given rise to a concerted effort to render deep learning systems explainable (Linzen et al., 2018, 2019). This problem has become more acute with the rapid development of very large pre-trained transformer models (Vaswani et al., 2017), like BERT (Devlin et al., 2018), GPT2 (Solaiman et al., 2019), GPT3 (Brown et al., 2020), and XLNet (Yang et al., 2019).

URNs avoid this difficulty by being compositional by design. If they prove robust for a wide variety of NLP tasks, they will go some way to solving the problem of explainability in deep learning.

Learning Agreement The question of whether generative language models can learn long-distance agreement was proposed by Linzen et al. (2016). If accuracy is insensitive to the number of attractors, then we know that the model can work on long distances. The results of Linzen et al. (2016) are inconclusive on this question. Even though the model does better than the majority class baseline for up to four attractors, accuracy declines steadily as the number of attractor increases. This trend is confirmed by Bernardy and Lappin (2017), who ran the same experiment on a larger dataset and thoroughly explored the space of hyperparameters. It is also confirmed by Gulordava et al. (2018), who analysed languages other than English. Marvin and Linzen (2018) focused on other linguistic phenomena, reaching similar conclusions. Lakretz et al. (2021) recently showed that an LSTM may extract bounded nested tree structures, without learning a systematic recursive rule. These results do not hold directly for BERT-style models, because they are not generative, even though Goldberg (2019) provides a tentative approach. For a more detailed review of these results, see the recent account of Lappin (2021).

Our experiment shows that URNs can surpass state of the art results for this kind of task. This is not surprising. URNs are designed so that they *cannot forget information*, and so it is expected that they will perform well on tracking long distance relations. The conservation of information is explained by the fact that multiplying by an orthogonal matrix conserves cosine similarities: $\langle Qs_0, Qs_1 \rangle = \langle s_0, s_1 \rangle$. Therefore any embedding Q, be it of a single word or of a long phrase, maps a change in its input state to an equal change in its output state. Considering all possible states as a distribution, Q conserves the density of states. Hence, contrary to the claims of Sennhauser and Berwick (2018), URNs demonstrate that a class of RNNs can achieve rule-like accuracy in syntactic learning.

Dyck Languages Elman (1991) already observed that it is useful to experiment with artificial systems to filter out the noise of real world natural language data. However, to ensure that the model actually learns recursive patterns instead of bounded-level ones, it is necessary to test on more deeply nested structures than the ones that the model is trained on, as we did. Generalised Dyck languages are ideal for this purpose (Bernardy, 2018). While LSTMs (and GRUs) exhibit a certain capacity to generalise to deeper nesting their performance declines in proportion to the depth of the nesting, as is the case with their handling of natural language agreement data. Other experimental work has also illustrated this effect (Hewitt et al., 2020; Sennhauser and Berwick, 2018). Similar conclusions are observed for generative self-attention architectures (Yu et al., 2019), while BERT-like, non-generative self-attention architectures simply fail at this task (Bernardy et al., 2021).

By contrast URNs achieve excellent performance on this task, without declining in relation to either depth of nesting or the number of attractors. Careful analysis of the learned embeddings explains this level of accuracy in a principled way, as the direct consequence of their formal processing design.

6.2 Quantum-Inspired Systems

Unitary matrices are essential elements of quantum mechanics, and quantum computing. There, too, they insure that the relevant system does not lose information through time.

Coecke et al. (2010); Grefenstette et al. (2011) propose what they describe as a quantum inspired model of linguistic representation. It computes vector values for sentences in a category theoretic representation of the types of a pregroup grammar (Lambek, 2008). The category theoretic structure in which this grammar is formulated is isomorphic with the one for quantum logic.[6]

A difficulty of this approach is that it requires the input to be already annotated as parsed data. Another problem is that the size of the tensors associated with higher-types is very large, making them hard to learn. By contrast, URNs do not require a syntactic type system. In fact, our experiments indicate that, with the right processing network, it is possible to learn syntactic structure and semantic composition from unannotated input.

Compositionality of phrase and sentence matrices is intrinsic to the formal specification of the network.

6.3 Tensor Recurrent Neural Networks

Sutskever et al. (2011) describe what they call a "tensor recurrent neural network" in which the transition matrix is determined by each input symbol. This design appears to be similar to URNs. However, unlike URNs, they use non-linear activation functions, and so they inherit the complications that these functions bring.

6.4 Unitary-Evolution Recurrent Networks

Arjovsky et al. (2016) proposed Unitary-Evolution recurrent networks to solve the problem of exploding and vanishing gradients, caused by the presence of non-linear activation functions. Despite this, Arjovsky et al. (2016) suggest that they use ReLU activation between time-steps, unlike URNs. Moreover, we are primarily concerned with the structure of the underlying unitary embeddings. The connection between the two lines work is that, if an RNN suffers exploding/vanisihing gradients, it cannot track long-term dependencies.

Arjovsky et al. (2016)'s embeddings are computationally cheaper than ours, because they can be multiplied in linear time. Like us, they do not cover the whole space of unitary matrices. Jing et al. (2017) propose another representation which is computationally less expensive than ours, but which has asymptotically the same number of parameters. A third option is let back-propagation update the unitary matrices arbitrarily $n \times n$, and project them onto the unitary space periodically (Wisdom et al., 2016; Kiani et al., 2022).

Because we use a fully general matrix exponential implementation, our model is computationally more expensive than all the other options mentioned above. We can however report that when experimenting with the unitary matrix encodings Jing et al. (2017) and Arjovsky et al. (2016), we got much worse results for our experiments. This may be because we do not include a ReLU activation, while they do use one.

To the best of our knowledge, no previous study of URNs has addressed agreement or other language modelling tasks. Rather, they have been directed at data-copying tasks, which is of limited linguistic interest. This includes the work of Vorontsov et al. (2017), even though it is ostensibly concerned with long distance dependencies.

[6]See Lappin (2021) for additional discussion of this theory.

7 Conclusions and Future work

In conclusion, we have shown that the URN is a useful architecture for syntactic tasks, for which it can reach or surpass state-of-the art precision. We strongly suspect that it will also prove effective for NLP tasks requiring fine-grained semantic knowledge. Unlike other DNNs, a URN is transparent and mathematically grounded in straightforward operations of linear algebra. It is possible to trace and understand what is happening at each level of the network, and at each point in the sequence that makes up the processing flow of the network.

Additionally, URNs learn *unitary embeddings*. These offer two important advantages. First, they have a rich internal structure from which we can analyse the learned model. Second they handle compositionality without stipulated constraints, or additional mechanisms. Therefore we can obtain unitary embeddings for any phrase or sentence.

The refined distance, effect, and relatedness metrics that unitary embeddings facilitate, open up the possibility of more interesting procedures for identifying natural syntactic and semantic word classes. These can be textured and dynamic, rather than static. They can focus on specific dimensions of meaning and structure, and they can be driven by specific NLP tasks. If additional types of input data are encoded in a matrix, such as visual content, then these classes could also be grounded in extralinguistic contexts.

In order to render URNs efficient, it is necessary to reduce the number of parameters from which the matrix can be derived. We found that a simple k-truncation of underlying anti-symmetric matrices is a useful strategy to limit the size of word embeddings. It also makes the learned embeddings more accessible to formal analysis, because they can be decomposed as rotations along k planes. For the tasks that we considered, truncation does not seriously degrade the performance of the TURN model. Kiani et al. (2022) recently applied this strategy to another subset of tasks, suggesting general viability of this strategy.

In preliminary work we have applied URNs to the recognition of mildly context-sensitive languages containing cross serial dependencies of the sort found in Swiss German and in Dutch. The performance of the model is even more robust and stable than it is for the agreement tasks reported here. We will be extending this work to a variety of other linguistically and cognitively interesting NLP tasks.

Given the radical computational transparency of URN architecture, these models are natural candidates for comparison with human processing systems, both at the neurological level, and on more abstract psychological planes. Identifying and measuring the content of their acquired knowledge for particular tasks can be done through direct observation of their processing patterns, and the application of straightforward distance metrics. In this respect they are of particular interest in the study of the cognitive foundations of linguistic learning and representation.

8 Acknowledgements

The research reported in this paper was supported by grant 2014-39 from the Swedish Research Council, which funds the Centre for Linguistic Theory and Studies in Probability (CLASP) in the Department of Philosophy, Linguistics, and Theory of Science at the University of Gothenburg We thank three anonymous reviewers for their helpful comments on an earlier draft of this paper. We presented the main ideas of this paper to the CLASP Seminar, in December 2021, and to the Cognitive Science Seminar of the School of Electronic Engineering and Computer Science, Queen Mary University of London, in February 2022. We are grateful to the audiences of these two events for useful discussion and feedback.

References

Martín Abadi, Paul Barham, Jianmin Chen, Zhifeng Chen, Andy Davis, Jeffrey Dean, Matthieu Devin, Sanjay Ghemawat, Geoffrey Irving, Michael Isard, Manjunath Kudlur, Josh Levenberg, Rajat Monga, Sherry Moore, Derek G. Murray, Benoit Steiner, Paul Tucker, Vijay Vasudevan, Pete Warden, Martin Wicke, Yuan Yu, and Xiaoqiang Zheng. 2016. Tensorflow: A system for large-scale machine learning. In *OSDI*, volume 16, pages 265–283.

Martin Arjovsky, Amar Shah, and Yoshua Bengio. 2016. Unitary evolution recurrent neural networks. In *Proceedings of the 33rd International Conference on International Conference on Machine Learning - Volume 48*, ICML'16, pages 1120–1128. JMLR.org.

Jean-Philippe Bernardy. 2018. Can rnns learn nested recursion? *Linguistic Issues in Language Technology*, 16.

Jean-Philippe Bernardy, Adam Ek, and Vladislav Maraev. 2021. Can the transformer learn nested recursion with symbol masking? In *Findings of the ACL 2021*.

Jean-Philippe Bernardy and Shalom Lappin. 2017. Using deep neural networks to learn syntactic agreement. *Linguistic Issues In Language Technology*, 15(2):15.

T. Brown, B. Mann, Nick Ryder, Melanie Subbiah, J. Kaplan, P. Dhariwal, Arvind Neelakantan, Pranav Shyam, Girish Sastry, Amanda Askell, Sandhini Agarwal, Ariel Herbert-Voss, G. Krüger, Tom Henighan, R. Child, Aditya Ramesh, D. Ziegler, Jeffrey Wu, Clemens Winter, Christopher Hesse, Mark Chen, E. Sigler, Mateusz Litwin, Scott Gray, Benjamin Chess, J. Clark, Christopher Berner, Sam McCandlish, A. Radford, Ilya Sutskever, and Dario Amodei. 2020. Language models are few-shot learners. *ArXiv*, abs/2005.14165.

Bob Coecke, Mehrnoosh Sadrzadeh, and Stephen Clark. 2010. Mathematical foundations for a compositional distributional model of meaning. *Lambek Festschrift, Linguistic Analysis*, 36.

Jacob Devlin, Ming-Wei Chang, Kenton Lee, and Kristina Toutanova. 2018. Bert: Pre-training of deep bidirectional transformers for language understanding. *arXiv preprint arXiv:1810.04805*.

Jeffrey L. Elman. 1990. Finding structure in time. *Cognitive Science*, 14(2):179–211.

Jeffrey L Elman. 1991. Distributed representations, simple recurrent networks, and grammatical structure. *Machine learning*, 7(2-3):195–225.

Felix Ruvimovich Gantmacher. 1959. *The Theory of Matrices*. AMS Chelsea publishing.

Yoav Goldberg. 2019. Assessing bert's syntactic abilities. *ArXiv*, abs/1901.05287.

Edward Grefenstette, Mehrnoosh Sadrzadeh, Stephen Clark, Bob Coecke, and Stephen Pulman. 2011. Concrete sentence spaces for compositional distributional models of meaning. In *Proceedings of the Ninth International Conference on Computational Semantics (IWCS 2011)*.

Kristina Gulordava, Piotr Bojanowski, Edouard Grave, Tal Linzen, and Marco Baroni. 2018. Colorless green recurrent networks dream hierarchically. In *Proceedings of the 2018 Conference of the North American Chapter of the Association for Computational Linguistics: Human Language Technologies, Volume 1 (Long Papers)*, pages 1195–1205, New Orleans, Louisiana. Association for Computational Linguistics.

John Hewitt, Michael Hahn, Surya Ganguli, Percy Liang, and Christopher D Manning. 2020. Rnns can generate bounded hierarchical languages with optimal memory. *arXiv preprint arXiv:2010.07515*.

John Hewitt and Christopher D. Manning. 2019. A structural probe for finding syntax in word representations. In *Proceedings of the 2019 Conference of the North American Chapter of the Association for Computational Linguistics: Human Language Technologies, Volume 1 (Long and Short Papers)*, pages 4129–4138, Minneapolis, Minnesota. Association for Computational Linguistics.

Sepp Hochreiter and Jürgen Schmidhuber. 1997. Long short-term memory. *Neural Computation*, 9(8):1735–1780.

Stephanie L Hyland and Gunnar Rätsch. 2017. Learning unitary operators with help from u (n). In *Thirty-First AAAI Conference on Artificial Intelligence*.

Li Jing, Yichen Shen, Tena Dubček, John Peurifoi, Scott Skirlo, Yann LeCun, Max Tegmark, and Marin Soljačić. 2017. Tunable efficient unitary neural networks (EUNN) and their application to RNN. In *arXiv*.

Bobak Kiani, Randall Balestriero, Yann Lecun, and Seth Lloyd. 2022. projunn: efficient method for training deep networks with unitary matrices.

Diederik P. Kingma and Jimmy Ba. 2014. Adam: A method for stochastic optimization. *CoRR*, abs/1412.6980.

Yair Lakretz, Théo Desbordes, Jean-Rémi King, Benoît Crabbé, Maxime Oquab, and Stanislas Dehaene. 2021. Can rnns learn recursive nested subject-verb agreements? *arXiv preprint arXiv:2101.02258*.

Joachim Lambek. 2008. Pregroup grammars and Chomsky's earliest examples. *Journal of Logic, Language and Information*, 17:141–160.

Shalom Lappin. 2021. *Deep Learning and Linguistic Representation*. CRC Press, Taylor & Francis, Boca Raton, London, New York.

Tal Linzen, Grzegorz Chrupała, and Afra Alishahi, editors. 2018. *Proceedings of the 2018 EMNLP Workshop BlackboxNLP: Analyzing and Interpreting Neural Networks for NLP*. Association for Computational Linguistics, Brussels, Belgium.

Tal Linzen, Grzegorz Chrupała, Yonatan Belinkov, and Dieuwke Hupkes, editors. 2019. *Proceedings of the 2019 ACL Workshop BlackboxNLP: Analyzing and Interpreting Neural Networks for NLP*. Association for Computational Linguistics, Florence, Italy.

Tal Linzen, Emmanuel Dupoux, and Yoav Golberg. 2016. Assessing the ability of LSTMs to learn syntax-sensitive dependencies. *Transactions of the Association of Computational Linguistics*, 4:521–535.

Rebecca Marvin and Tal Linzen. 2018. Targeted syntactic evaluation of language models. In *Proceedings of the 2018 Conference on Empirical Methods in Natural Language Processing*, pages 1192–1202, Brussels, Belgium. Association for Computational Linguistics.

Tomas Mikolov, Ilya Sutskever, Kai Chen, Greg Corrado, and Jeffrey Dean. 2013. Distributed representations of words and phrases and their compositionality.

In *Proceedings of the 26th International Conference on Neural Information Processing Systems - Volume 2*, NIPS'13, pages 3111–3119.

Luzi Sennhauser and Robert Berwick. 2018. Evaluating the ability of LSTMs to learn context-free grammars. In *Proceedings of the 2018 EMNLP Workshop BlackboxNLP: Analyzing and Interpreting Neural Networks for NLP*, pages 115–124, Brussels, Belgium. Association for Computational Linguistics.

Irene Solaiman, Miles Brundage, J. Clark, Amanda Askell, Ariel Herbert-Voss, Jeff Wu, A. Radford, and J. Wang. 2019. Release strategies and the social impacts of language models. *ArXiv*, abs/1908.09203.

Ilya Sutskever, James Martens, and Geoffrey E. Hinton. 2011. Generating text with recurrent neural networks. In *Proceedings of the 28th International Conference on Machine Learning, ICML 2011, Bellevue, Washington, USA, June 28 - July 2, 2011*, pages 1017–1024. Omnipress.

Ashish Vaswani, Noam Shazeer, Niki Parmar, Jakob Uszkoreit, Llion Jones, Aidan N. Gomez, Lukasz Kaiser, and Illia Polosukhin. 2017. Attention Is All You Need. *arXiv:1706.03762 [cs]*.

Eugene Vorontsov, Chiheb Trabelsi, Samuel Kadoury, and Chris Pal. 2017. On orthogonality and learning recurrent networks with long term dependencies. In *arXiv*.

Scott Wisdom, Thomas Powers, John Hershey, Jonathan Le Roux, and Les Atlas. 2016. Full-capacity unitary recurrent neural networks. *Advances in neural information processing systems*, 29:4880–4888.

Zhilin Yang, Zihang Dai, Yiming Yang, Jaime G. Carbonell, Ruslan Salakhutdinov, and Quoc V. Le. 2019. XLNet: Generalized autoregressive pretraining for language understanding. *ArXiv*, abs/1906.08237.

Xiang Yu, Ngoc Thang Vu, and Jonas Kuhn. 2019. Learning the dyck language with attention-based seq2seq models. In *Proceedings of the 2019 ACL Workshop BlackboxNLP: Analyzing and Interpreting Neural Networks for NLP*, pages 138–146.

Visually Grounded Interpretation of Noun-Noun Compounds in English

Inga Lang[1], **Lonneke van der Plas**[1], **Malvina Nissim**[2] and **Albert Gatt**[3]

[1]Idiap Research Institute, `firstname.lastname@idiap.ch`
[2]University of Groningen, `m.nissim@rug.nl`
[3]Utrecht University, `a.gatt@uu.nl`

Abstract

Noun-noun compounds (NNCs) occur frequently in the English language. Accurate NNC interpretation, i.e. determining the implicit relationship between the constituents of a NNC, is crucial for the advancement of many natural language processing tasks. Until now, computational NNC interpretation has been limited to approaches involving linguistic representations only. However, research suggests that grounding linguistic representations in vision or other modalities can increase performance on this and other tasks. Our work is a novel comparison of linguistic and visuo-linguistic representations for the task of NNC interpretation. We frame NNC interpretation as a relation classification task, evaluating on a large, relationally-annotated NNC dataset. We combine distributional word vectors with image vectors to investigate how visual information can help improve NNC interpretation systems. We find that adding visual vectors yields modest increases in performance on several configurations of our dataset. We view this as a promising first exploration of the benefits of using visually grounded representations for NNC interpretation.

1 Introduction

Conceptual combination is the cognitive process that allows us to combine two mental concepts into one, for example by juxtaposing or otherwise merging two concepts. For instance, a house located on a beach might typically be called a 'beach house'. Noun-noun compounds (NNCs) are the linguistic phenomenon in which two nouns are joined to form one single, syntactically inseparable unit. The process of combining nouns into new nominal units is both highly prevalent and infinitely productive in a language like English (Libben, 2014), and also exists in various forms in many other languages, including but not limited to German, Norwegian, Hindi, Tamil, Japanese, Chinese, Bulgarian, and Turkish (Nakov, 2013). In English, the *head* of the NNC is usually the rightmost word, and determines the semantic category of the compound. The leftmost word in English NNCs is referred to as the *modifier*. Although NNCs are a common occurrence, the highly productive nature of compounding (Algeo and Algeo, 1993) means that individual NNCs tend to have relatively low frequency counts (Kim and Baldwin, 2006). Compositional models have therefore been of particular interest to researchers working on computational NNC representations (e.g. Shwartz, 2019; Dima, 2016).

Due to of the high prevalence and complex nature of English NNCs, the ability to interpret compounds would greatly improve several important natural language processing tasks, such as machine translation (Baldwin and Tanaka, 2004; Balyan and Chatterjee, 2015), text summarization (e.g. Silber and McCoy, 2000), question answering (e.g. Mann, 2002), and natural language inference (e.g. MacCartney and Manning, 2008).

In this paper, we frame compound interpretation as a classification problem. The goal is to identify the semantic relationship between the nominal elements of a compound. We explicitly compare the contribution of linguistic and multimodal (visuo-linguistic) representations to this task.[1] In part, the motivation for this is theoretical, as a computational account of linguistic meaning has to address the link between symbolic and non-symbolic information (Bender and Koller, 2020; Bisk et al., 2020). A further motivation is the empirical observation that grounding representations in vision gives rise to richer meaning representations (Bruni et al., 2012; Collell Talleda and Moens, 2016). Composition in the visual modality has also been shown to be possible for certain NNCs (Pezzelle et al., 2016). A final motivation comes from find-

[1]The code for our experiments, as well as our visual embeddings, can be found here: `https://github.com/ingalang/multimodal_NC_interpretation`

Proceedings of the Workshop on Cognitive Modeling and Computational Linguistics, pages 23 - 35
May 26, 2022 ©2022 Association for Computational Linguistics

ings in cognitive science suggesting that visually grounded word representations yield results closer to human performance on some NNC processing tasks (Günther et al., 2020). Our goal is to assess to what extent visual grounding helps to accurately identify the semantic relationship between NNC constituents. For example, Figure 1 displays images of the constituents of 'beach house' as well as the compound itself. Does the relationship between the constituents in the NNC become easy to predict once such visual information is incorporated, in addition to the textual representation of the constituents?

Figure 1: Picture of a beach, a house, and a beach house from ImageNet.

2 Background

Early approaches to the automatic interpretation of noun compounds included rule-based approaches (Finin, 1980; Vanderwende, 1994) or semi-automatic approaches requiring some user interaction (Barker and Szpakowicz, 1998). Other work utilized frequency statistics of NNC constituents to build probabilistic models for NNC interpretation (Lauer, 1995; Lapata and Keller, 2004). Kim and Baldwin (2005, 2006) leveraged WordNet (Miller, 1998) similarities in supervised training approaches.

Some approaches to NNC interpretation deal with identifying an appropriate paraphrase for a compound which explicitly states the relation between the compound's constituents. Several paraphrasing-based approaches have viewed the task of freely paraphrasing noun compounds as a goal in itself (Hendrickx et al., 2019; Ponkiya et al., 2020; Shwartz and Dagan, 2019; Van de Cruys et al., 2013), whereas others have used paraphrases as inputs to a model, representing NNCs in some way through their paraphrases.

Other approaches to NNC relation classification tend to be centered around classifying NNCs based on a pre-defined set of compound relations using various representations of the compounds themselves as input. Both compositional and distributional representations have been tested. Dima (2016) and Shwartz (2019) both tested various ways of representing noun compounds. Dima (2016) performed the first experiments on compositional representations of English NNCs, using compositional models such as the FullAdd model (Zanzotto et al., 2010) and the Matrix model (Socher et al., 2012). Dima's results, which were tested on datasets by Tratz and Hovy (2010) and Ó Séaghdha (2008), reached a similar performance to the results obtained by the creators of said datasets, respectively. Yet, Dima's work utilized simpler methods and did not include lexical and relational information, as opposed to Tratz and Hovy and Ó Séaghdha.

Visuo-linguistic representations for NNC interpretation have received far less attention. Günther et al. (2020) created the first computational model of visuo-linguistic conceptual combination, reporting positive results on several NNC processing tasks. Pezzelle et al. (2016) found that certain compounds can be composed in the visual domain by simple addition of image feature vectors. However, none of these studies have touched upon NNC *interpretation* using visuo-linguistic data, an area that remains unexplored, to our knowledge.

The present work focuses on the interpretation of NNCs that possess at least some degree of compositionality. This is justified on the grounds that novel compounds, which are very common (Algeo and Algeo, 1993), must be interpreted compositionally on first encounter. We employ one compositional model, called the Full Additive model (Zanzotto et al., 2010), as well as simple vector concatenation, in our experiments to construct compound vectors from individual constituent vectors. We do this for linguistic and visual vectors separately, and then combine the two modalities using vector concatenation. The following section will describe how we obtain our visual and linguistic vectors as well as introduce the noun compound dataset that we use.

3 Data

To perform our experiments, we use two main sources of data: a relationally-labeled NNC interpretation dataset for training and testing Tratz (2011), and ImageNet (Deng et al., 2009) to extract visual feature embeddings. The following subsections will describe these datasets in more detail.

	Split	Train	Val	Test
Coarse	random	13835	928	3701
	lexical (full)	4650	1593	766
	lexical (mod)	9555	5316	3593
	lexical (head)	9048	5516	3900
Fine	random	13968	934	3725
	lexical (full)	4614	1574	843
	lexical (mod)	9511	5270	3846
	lexical (head)	8938	5640	4049

Table 1: Number of samples in each configuration (split and grain) of the Tratz (2011) dataset after our filtering.

3.1 Compound Dataset

Our main compound dataset for this work is a revised version of the Tratz (2011) noun compound dataset, which contains 19,158 distinct NNCs labeled with 37 fine-grained and 12 coarse-grained relation labels. The dataset is based on a previous one first published by Tratz and Hovy (2010), which contained 17509 compounds categorized by 43 fine-grained constituent relation labels. The compounds were annotated using Amazon's Mechanical Turk service.[2] They used a weighted majority-vote scheme based on ten annotation votes per compound, where Turkers voted on the quality on the other Turkers' decisions in order to even out potential inter-annotator disagreement. On their 43-class annotation task, Tratz and Hovy (2010) report a Cohen's k (Cohen, 1960) of 0.57 as a measure of inter-annotator agreement.

To be able to test how compound interpretation models perform when dealing with unseen constituents, the Tratz (2011) dataset is split in various ways to ensure no previously seen constituents are available in the validation and testing phase. Different *lexical* splits ensure that the test and validation dataset contain no constituents previously seen in the training data – the *lexical mod* split ensures no previously seen modifiers (e.g. 'beach' in 'beach house'), the *lexical head* split ensures no previously seen heads (e.g. 'house'), and the *lexical full* split ensures no previously seen constituents at all. The *random* split does not take into account whether constituents are found in the training data or not.

Before performing our experiments, we do some filtering on the data in which we remove the fine-grained classes PERSONAL_NOUN, PERSONAL_TITLE, and LEXICALIZED. Our reason for removing the PERSONAL_NOUN and PERSONAL_TITLE classes is that there is some doubt as to whether proper names and titles possess the same semantic characteristics as common nouns (Cumming, 2007). Several works on NNC interpretation remove proper nouns from their data (e.g. Kim and Baldwin, 2006; Shwartz, 2019). Others, like (Dima and Hinrichs, 2015), choose to keep these categories but still acknowledge that their presence in the dataset is questionable. We remove the LEXICALIZED class because our work is mainly centered around how to interpret compounds that have a certain degree of compositionality, seeing as novel compounds, which likely make up the majority of compound types in most corpora, will need to be interpreted compositionally. Table 1 gives an overview of the number of samples in the train, validation, and test sets for each configuration of the Tratz (2011) dataset.

3.2 Image Data

ImageNet (Deng et al., 2009) is a large-scale image database which is structured using the WordNet (Miller, 1998) taxonomy, using synsets to represent sets of word meanings. Since many word classes are difficult to represent visually, ImageNet only contains nouns, and no other lexical categories, from the WordNet hierarchy. ImageNet contains 14,197,122 images, indexed by 21841 synsets[3], which represent different senses of the words.

Selecting Synsets and Images from ImageNet In order to collect the images needed for our task, we have to select all the synsets that were linked to each individual word in our dataset, and then retrieve the image URLs linked to those specific synsets. ImageNet is structured in such a way that one word can be linked to several synsets, and one synset can be linked to several words. Image URLs are associated with specific synsets, not specific words, so to retrieve an image URL from a word, one needs to first select which synset(s) one wants to use to represent that word.

Determining the appropriate sense to use for each constituent in a sample based on their context on the compound level is not trivial. We decide to go for a simple heuristic approach, namely finding the synset that most probably represents the most common or basic meaning for each word, given that the synset has images linked to it (where possible). Our heuristic method consists of the following steps:

[2] https://www.mturk.com/

[3] As per January of 2022

1. For a given word, let us call this our *target word*, retrieve all synsets that have images linked to them.

2. For each of the retrieved synsets, get the list of words that contain that synset among its synsets (representing the potential senses of the word). Let us call this list of words *comparison words*.

3. For each list of *comparison words*, compute the cosine similarity (by a pre-trained word2vec model) between each *comparison word* and the *target word*, and then take the average of all of these cosine similarities.

4. The synset whose *comparison words* list has the highest cosine similarity to the *target word* is selected as the most common, or basic, meaning.

Note that this method does not necessarily yield the *most common* sense, but the most common *imageable* sense, that is, the most common sense of a word, out of those which have related images. This choice was made on the basis of two assumptions: 1) it would give us the chance to collect more images, as opposed to selecting images only when the most common meaning is imageable,[4] and 2) an imageable synset that does not reflect the most common meaning of a word might still have certain visual properties in common with another less imageable, but more common, meaning of said word.

	ImageNet	ResNet10	ResNet100	Total in data
Unique mods	38.7%	36.4%	32.4%	3126
Unique heads	40.1%	37.6%	31.6%	3187

Table 2: Overview of the percentages of unique modifiers and heads in the coarse-grained random split of the (Tratz, 2011) data that have ImageNet images available, and that we could obtain ResNet_{10} and ResNet_{100} vectors for.

Table 2 gives an example of the ImageNet coverage of unique heads and modifiers in one dataset configuration (the random + coarse setting).

4 Methods

We frame the NNC interpretation task as a classification problem, experimenting with passing linguistic and visuo-linguistic vectors as inputs to an SVM classifier. Our experimental process can be described in three steps:

1. Obtain linguistic vectors (from a pre-trained *word2vec* model) and visual feature vectors (from a pre-trained ResNet model) for the constituents of a compound (head and modifier). We experiment with both unimodal (word) embeddings, and visuo-linguistic embeddings, formed by concatenating the word embedding of a compound to the visual representation of a compound.

2. Combine the vector representations of each constituent (either linguistic, or visuo-linguistic).[5] We use two methods of combination: (a) simple concatenation, and (b) the Full Additive (FullAdd) method proposed by Zanzotto et al. (2010).

3. Observe and evaluate the performance of a setup depending on (a) modality of vectors (purely linguistic, or visuo-linguistic) and (b) mode of constituent vector combination.

To obtain linguistic vectors and visual vectors, we utilize pre-trained word2vec (Mikolov et al., 2013a) and ResNet (He et al., 2016) models, respectively. Our models, as well as our experimental setups and baselines, will be described in this section.

4.1 Models of Word Representation

We utilize a word2vec model (Mikolov et al., 2013a) to represent words in the linguistic modality, and visual vectors obtained by using a ResNet model (He et al., 2016) on ImageNet (Deng et al., 2009) images. The following subsections will describe these approaches in more detail.

4.1.1 word2vec

To obtain word embeddings to use as our linguistic vectors, we use a pre-trained word2vec model (Mikolov et al., 2013a). We employ a popular set of pre-trained word2vec embeddings that were trained on about 100 billion words from the GoogleNews dataset. These 300-dimensional word embeddings[6] were trained using a skip-gram approach with negative sampling (SGNS for short), as described in Mikolov et al. (2013b). Unlike previous work on

[4]In this case, we use 'imageable' to mean that ImageNet has images for it.

[5]In case a constituent lacks a vector representation in either modality, we instead use a vector of zeros.

[6]`https://code.google.com/archive/p/word2vec/`

this dataset published by e.g. Shwartz (2019), we decide to not train our own word2vec embeddings. This decision was made because our goal is investigating the effect of combining linguistic representations with visual ones, rather than comparing different kinds of linguistic representations, like Shwartz (2019) did.

4.1.2 ResNet

ResNet (He et al., 2016) is a deep residual neural network architecture for image recognition. ResNet models learn residual functions instead of unreferenced functions, allowing for the creation of models that are deeper than previous CNN models such as the VGG models (Chatfield et al., 2014), while still being less complex and faster to train (He et al., 2016). To extract visual embeddings based on images from ImageNet, we use a ResNet152 model trained on ImageNet data, implemented in the Keras (Chollet et al., 2015) library for Python. ResNet is trained on an object classification task, using 1.28 million images in its training phase. The model learns to take an image vector as input and outputs one out of the 1000 ImageNet category labels included in its training data.

To extract visual features using ResNet152, we flatten the final layer before the final classification (softmax) layer of the model, which has the size 7 x 7 x 2048, resulting in vectors of size 100352. Since a single, randomly selected image would not reflect all the potential visual aspects of an object, and finding the image that is closest to a prototypical representation of a concept is not trivial, we take the average of several image vectors to get a general visual representation for each noun. We use two experimental settings for visual features, where we extract and average feature vectors for 10 or 100 ImageNet images. We will refer to these vectors as ResNet_{10} and ResNet_{100}, respectively. See Table 2 for a summary of the image availability in the Tratz (2011) dataset. These vectors can then be reduced to our desired vector dimensions, for example 300 in order for them to be compatible with pre-trained 300-dimensional *word2vec* embeddings. For our ResNet vectors to be more appropriate as inputs to our SVM classifiers, we scale our vectors so that the values range from -1 to 1.

4.2 Modes of Vector Combination

To combine modifier and constituent vectors into compound vectors, we test two different modes of combination: simple vector concatenation, and the FullAdd model (Zanzotto et al., 2010). In both cases, the combination of a modifier vector and a head vector only happens within one modality, i.e. we would not combine a linguistic modifier vector with a linguistic head vector. For our visuo-linguistic setups, compound vectors are composed in each modality and then the resulting vectors are concatenated to form a visuo-linguistic representation of the compound. The following subsection will describe the FullAdd model in more detail.

4.2.1 The Full Additive Model

The Full Additive model, also referred to as FullAdd or the Estimated Additive model (Zanzotto et al., 2010) is a model where the two vectors $\vec{x}$ and $\vec{y}$, representing the constituent words c_1 and c_2, are multiplied by square matrices A and B, respectively, and then added together to create a compositional meaning representation of a phrase. A and B are the same for each vector $\vec{x}$ and $\vec{y}$, respectively, and are obtained through training on a training set of compound nouns that contains distributional vector representations of each compound and each constituent word. We can think of these vectors as being ordered in triples, where any triple of words *(z, x, y)*, which corresponds to *(compound, modifier, head)* in English, is represented by a triple of vectors $(\vec{z}, \vec{x}, \vec{y})$. For example, the training set could contain the vector triple $(\overrightarrow{\textit{soap opera}}, \overrightarrow{\textit{soap}}, \overrightarrow{\textit{opera}})$. The goal will be to learn a composition function for any word vectors $\vec{x}$, $\vec{y}$ such that $\vec{p} = f(\vec{x}, \vec{y})$ approximates $\vec{z}$, where $\vec{p}$ is the composed vector for any given noun compound, and $\vec{z}$ is the observed distributional vector for this noun compound. In other words, the function is trained using compounds for which we have a distributional representation, and can then be used to create compositional representations of compounds where a distributional representation is not available.

Intuitively, one can think of the process of training the two matrices (one for modifiers and one for heads) as finding a way of transforming a meaning representation of a single word into its *as-constituent* meaning. For example, by multiplying the vector for *chocolate* with the modifier matrix (which we call matrix A), we approximate the *as-modifer* meaning of *chocolate*, as in *chocolate cake*. The general equation for composing a compound vector $\vec{z}$ given two constituent word vectors $\vec{x}$ and $\vec{y}$ is given below:

$$\vec{z} = \mathbf{A}\vec{x} + \mathbf{B}\vec{y} \quad (1)$$

To implement our FullAdd model, we use the Distributional Semantic Composition Toolkit, or DISSECT (Dinu et al., 2013), which allows for the implementation of FullAdd as well as other composition models. To prepare the necessary data for FullAdd, we filter our training data so that we only keep the compounds for which the whole compound as well as the modifier and head separately have vectors associated with them in our word embedding model. Then we construct a semantic space using those word embeddings. Due to the requirements of the DISSECT implementation, heads and modifiers cannot be repeated in the space (e.g., we can not include both 'cat food' and 'dog food'). The two FullAdd matrices, **A** and **B**, can then be trained in the way described above. The resulting vectors are then used to compose compositional meaning vectors for our training, test, and validation data. In our FullAdd experiments, we train a FullAdd model for each modality (linguistic and visual) and then create composed vectors for each compound in each modality before combining the two modalities using concatenation.

4.3 Experimental Setups

For our experiments, we create three majority-class baselines in addition to our SVM classifier.[7] In this section, we will describe our baselines and our main experimental setups.

4.3.1 Baselines

We implement the following majority-class baselines:

- Overall Majority: For a given data sample, this baseline selects the overall majority class as observed in the training data.
- Modifier Majority: For a given data sample, this baseline selects the majority class represented among compounds in the training data with the same modifier as the sample.
- Head Majority: For a given data sample, this baseline selects the majority class represented among compounds in the training data with the same head as the sample.

[7]We did also perform a few NNC interpretation experiments using a BERT model, which were not included in this paper because of poor performance on the lexical splits of the Tratz (2011) dataset. See Table 7 in the appendix for an overview.

The 'Modifier Majority' and 'Head Majority' rely on using the modifiers or heads, respectively, from the training data to determine the assigned label of each data sample. However, we have several dataset configurations in which the training and test datasets do not share any heads, modifiers, or any constituents at all – see Table 1 for a summary. Thus, in these configurations, the head or modifier majority mechanism will not work. This means that for the lexical + mod split of our data, the Modifier Majority baseline will give the exact same results as the Overall Majority baseline. The same is the case for the lexical + head split together with the Head Majority baseline, as well as the full lexical split with both the Modifier Majority and Head Majority baselines.

4.3.2 Classifier Setup

Our classifier is an SVM that takes as inputs either linguistic representations (in the form of *word2vec* vectors that have either been concatenated or composed using the FullAdd function) or visuo-linguistic representations (in the form of linguistic vectors concatenated with the visual vectors described in section 4.1.2). We use an SVM with a one-vs-rest scheme for multiclass classification. The SVM has a linear kernel, L2 penalty and a C value of 0.5. We train our classifier on the Tratz (2011) data, passing either our linguistic or visuo-linguistic vectors as inputs.

5 Results and Evaluation

We evaluate our setup on the Tratz (2011) dataset and report F1 scores for all dataset configurations.

	Split	MC-O	MC-M	MC-H
Coarse	random	7.5	40.0	59.3
	lexical (full)	6.7	–	–
	lexical (mod)	7.8	–	58.8
	lexical (head)	7.0	38.6	–
Fine	random	5.3	34.5	54.1
	lexical (full)	5.6	–	–
	lexical (mod)	6.3	–	52.6
	lexical (head)	5.2	34.8	–

Table 3: F1 scores from our baseline classifiers. MC stands for Majority Class; O stands for Overall, M for Modifier, and H for Head.

Table 3 shows the weighted F1 scores of our baseline classifiers. The modifier- and head-majority classifiers require the test datasets to include previously seen modifiers and heads (respectively), which is why the table has some cells that are marked with '–', indicating that the score for this cannot be computed with the given majority-class strategy and thus would get the same score as the overall majority baseline. For this reason, we only have comparable scores from the modifier- and head-majority classifiers in the case of the random split, in which both the fine-grained setting and the coarse-grained setting show that the head-majority classifier performs the best. In other words, it seems that having a common head is a greater indicator of same-class membership than having a common modifier in the Tratz (2011) dataset.

	Split	w2v	w2v + ResNet10		w2v + ResNet100	
Coarse	random	66.3	66.0	*- 0.3*	**66.4**	*+ 0.1*
	lexical (full)	**44.2**	44.1	*- 0.1*	43.7	*- 0.5*
	lexical (mod)	57.9	**58.3**	*+ 0.4*	57.7	*- 0.2*
	lexical (head)	50.8	51.0	*+ 0.2*	**51.3**	*+ 0.5*
Fine	random	**66.7**	66.6	*- 0.1*	**66.7**	*+/- 0*
	lexical (full)	39.2	**39.4**	*+ 0.2*	38.4	*- 0.8*
	lexical (mod)	56.4	56.4	*+/- 0*	**56.5**	*+ 0.1*
	lexical (head)	47.1	**47.5**	*+ 0.4*	46.9	*- 0.2*

(a) F1 scores using FullAdd-composed compound vectors

	Split	w2v	w2v + ResNet10		w2v + ResNet100	
Coarse	random	74.1	**75.3**	*+ 1.2**	75.2	*+ 1.1**
	lexical (full)	49.1	**50.8**	*+ 1.7**	50.0	*+ 0.9*
	lexical (mod)	63.5	**64.0**	*+ 0.5*	63.1	*- 0.4*
	lexical (head)	55.5	**56.7**	*+ 1.2*	56.0	*+ 0.5*
Fine	random	73.0	**75.0**	*+ 2.0*	**75.0**	*+ 2.0*
	lexical (full)	40.3	40.0	*- 0.3*	**40.7**	*+ 0.4*
	lexical (mod)	63.0	**63.5**	*+ 0.5*	63.4	*+ 0.4*
	lexical (head)	50.6	51.6	*+ 1.0**	**52.0**	*+ 1.4**

(b) Results using concatenated compound vectors

Table 4: Weighted F1 scores from classification experiments using linguistic and visuo-linguistic vectors. The tables show results of using FullAdd-composed vectors as well as concatenation-composed vectors, with the change in F1 obtained when ResNet vectors are included. An asterisk next to an increase in F1 score means the bimodal result is significantly different from its unimodal counterpart following a Bonferroni-corrected McNemar test.

Table 4 shows the results of our experiments on the Tratz (2011) data after our filtering. All of the scores given in the tables are F1 scores, and an asterisk next to an increase in score means that the increase was found to be significant following a McNemar test (McNemar, 1947) and a Bonferroni correction (Neyman and Pearson, 1928) of the p-values.[8] As is evident when comparing tables 4a and 4b, using concatenated vectors as opposed to FullAdd composed vectors yields much higher F1 scores. Additionally, the results in table 4b, with concatenated vectors, are less ambiguous: in this experiment, at least one of the visuo-linguistic settings beats the purely linguistic setting in each experimental setting.

As has been shown in previous research on this dataset, the most challenging dataset split is the full lexical split, where no constituents in the validation and test data are previously seen in the training data. As expected, the fine-grained setting is generally more challenging than the coarse-grained one. As we can see from comparing tables 4a and 4b, the results in the former table are more ambiguous, meaning that we cannot conclude that one input type (linguistic or visuo-linguistic vectors) is better than another. In table 4b, however, we find that our visuo-linguistic vectors help increase scores in some cases. In the case of the ResNet_{10} vectors, the increase in scores is significant for the random and full lexical splits in the coarse-grained setting as well as for the lexical (head) split in the fine-grained setting. For our ResNet_{100} vectors, only the coarse + random and the fine + lexical (head) settings show a significant increase in scores. We find small increases overall for most NNC relation classes, rather than big increases for certain relation classes (see Figure 3 in Appendix A for an example).

Table 5 shows results of experiments run on a subset of the data for which ResNet_{10} vectors were available for both the modifier and head of each compound. We compare results on our baselines as well as our FullAdd and concatenation models with textual or visual vectors alone, on the same subset. As with the results on the full dataset, the concatenation method performs better than the FullAdd model here. Additionally, it seems that the visual vectors do contribute at least some valuable information on their own. It is important to note that Table 5 is not directly comparable to the tables in 4, since the former shows results on just a small subset of the data.

One might be inclined to question why our FullAdd experiments on this dataset perform worse than very similar experiments done by e.g. Shwartz (2019) and Dima (2016). This is likely due to the fact that Shwartz (2019) and Dima (2016) trained their own word embeddings specifically for this task, meaning that they were able to obtain distributed embeddings for more of the compounds in the Tratz (2011) dataset than what we had available through our pre-trained model, and as a con-

[8]We set our α level to the conventional 0.05, which resulted in a p-value threshold of 0.00625 after a Bonferroni correction.

		baselines			*word2vec*		*ResNet10*	
grain	**split**	**MC-O**	**MC-M**	**MC-H**	**FullAdd**	**concatenate**	**FullAdd**	**concatenate**
Coarse	random	9.8	40.6	48.4	56.0	70.7	30.9	**62.7**
	lexical (full)	3.9	–	–	26.2	41.9	**6.9**	**28.5**
	lexical (mod)	6.3	–	47.1	45.7	59.7	20.4	47.0
	lexical (head)	5.7	32.0	–	30.8	47.1	19.8	**40.4**
Fine	random	3.3	32.5	38.9	53.7	66.6	16.9	**59.1**
	lexical (full)	4.6	–	–	23.6	31.2	**5.7**	**18.6**
	lexical (mod)	2.8	–	36.1	34.4	51.3	10.7	**41.1**
	lexical (head)	3.4	33.8	–	36.5	41.7	10.8	**34.4**

Table 5: Results (reported in F1) from experiments with unimodal vectors in either modality (word2vec vectors alone or ResNet_{10} vectors alone) on a subset of the data for which ResNet_{10} vectors were available. Baseline results on the same subset are included for comparison. Scores in bold are cases in which the ResNet_{10} vectors outperform the strongest baseline.

sequence had more training data for the FullAdd model. As our goal with this work is not to compare composition functions for linguistic vectors, we saw training our own embeddings as being superfluous for this study.

Overall, we see that, in our experiments with concatenated compound vectors, adding visual information helps increase the scores in all cases, and in some cases the increases are statistically significant.

5.1 Concreteness Ratings

Intuitively, one could assume that visual information (i.e. images) would be easier to obtain for more concrete words, thus making visual information a more appropriate and/or helpful addition for compounds that have relatively concrete constituents. If this is the case, then we should find a higher benefit of incorporating visual information, the more concrete a word is.

We quantify concreteness using a dataset of concreteness ratings of almost 40,000 English lemmas, by Brysbaert et al. (2014). The ratings are continuous values between 1 and 5, where 5 is the most concrete. The ratings were obtained by surveying more than 4,000 participants in a crowdsourcing study and taking the mean of the ratings obtained for each word.

As a first analysis of our results in light of these concreteness ratings, we performed several logistic regression analyses where we looked at the concreteness ratings of modifiers and heads as predictors of classification success. Table 6 in Appendix A gives a full overview of these results. What we find is that the dataset configuration seems to matter more than the modality, but that the concreteness ratings of both modifiers and heads are, in some cases, good predictors of classifier success. However, in the significant cases, we discover a negative

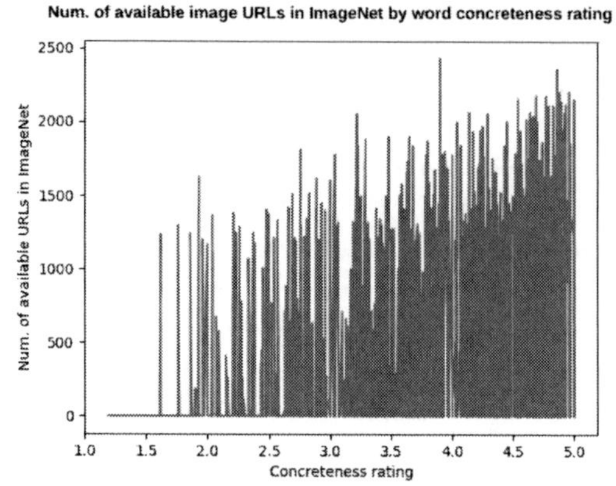

Figure 2: Word concreteness rating by number of available URLs in ImageNet

relationship between concreteness and classification success – i.e., the higher the concreteness of a modifier/head, the lower the chance of the classifier predicting the correct class. We performed an investigation into some of our results, filtering the samples by image availability (specifically, whether a constituent had fewer or more than 10 images available in ImageNet). The full results are found in Table 8 in Appendix A.

Figure 2 shows word concreteness ratings by number of URLs available in ImageNet, as determined by our image selection heuristic, for each of the words in the Tratz (2011) dataset that had concreteness ratings in the Brysbaert et al. (2014) dataset (regardless of whether they appeared as a modifier or head).

A correlation analysis revealed a low to moderate correlation between the concreteness ratings and the URL counts (Pearson's $r = 0.45$, $p < 0.001$). This indicates that, to some extent, the higher the concreteness rating of a constituent in a compound, the higher the chances of finding 10 or 100 images to represent said constituent as part of our image vectors. Yet, in experiments on the subset of compounds for which both constituents had ResNet_{10} vectors available, we find that our visual vectors alone are somewhat informative, as we saw in Table 5. Examples of words for which we were not able to obtain at least 10 images include *minute* (concreteness rating 3.04), *intelligence* (concreteness rating 2.24), and *state* (concreteness rating 3.52).

The negative relationship between constituent concreteness and classifier success seems counter-intuitive, but might be a result of a number of factors related to word frequency, polysemy, and the distribution of concrete vs. non-concrete words over the classes in the Tratz (2011) dataset. Although one might expect compounds containing concrete constituents to benefit more from visuolinguistic representations, we note that the negative correlation between concreteness and classification success is always found in the visuo-linguistic modality whenever it is found in the linguistic modality. In other words, this seems to be a general finding rather than a modality-specific one. As suggested by previous work, concrete and abstract words differ in the kinds of contexts they tend to appear in, where abstract words tend to occur near other abstract words, and concrete words occur in more varied contexts (Frassinelli et al., 2017). Additionally, it has been found that distributional semantic models like word2vec are worse at modeling word pair similarity for highly concrete words than for highly abstract words (Hill et al., 2015). Since our task is relation classification, our findings might also be partially influenced by the distribution of relation labels for concrete and non-concrete words. For example, abstract words may be more restricted in which relations they can partake in, and thus be easier to classify. We leave it up to future work to investigate these relationships, but we note that our visuo-linguistic representations do tend to outperform the purely linguistic ones, regardless of constituent concreteness ratings.

6 Conclusion and Future Work

In this paper, we have presented NNC interpretation experiments on the Tratz (2011) dataset, comparing linguistic and visuo-linguistic inputs to an SVM classifier. We have found that, in our best-performing case, concatenating visual feature vectors with linguistic vectors (word embeddings) helps increase F1 scores on the Tratz (2011) dataset in almost all experimental settings. Our findings indicate that utilizing visual information for this NNC relation classification task might indeed be a promising endeavor.

Future work should aim to further refine our approach by for example using more sophisticated methods for selecting images to represent words, exploring ways to represent abstract or nonimageable words, and finding better ways to visually ground polysemous words. In this regard, recent multimodal encoders pretrained on visual and linguistic data (e.g. Lu et al., 2019; Tan and Bansal, 2019), are a promising way forward. Another possible angle for future work could be to consider NNC interpretation in visual and linguistic contexts. In the future, we would also be eager to explore visual grounding in other aspects of computational NNC related tasks, such as NNC generation. Additionally, our approach should be tested on different datasets and in different circumstances, for example in a task that determines the probability of compound categories rather than fixed classes. One final potential angle for future work could be to look further into the task of visual composition. A first step could be to more closely examine the effects of using the FullAdd function with image vectors.

To conclude, our results are in line with previous work from both cognitive science and computational linguistics suggesting that more psychologically plausible models of NNC processing should incorporate grounding.

References

John Algeo and Adele S Algeo. 1993. *Fifty years among the new words: A dictionary of neologisms 1941-1991*. Cambridge University Press.

Timothy Baldwin and Takaaki Tanaka. 2004. Translation by machine of complex nominals: Getting it right. In *Proceedings of the Workshop on Multiword Expressions: Integrating Processing*, pages 24–31.

Renu Balyan and Niladri Chatterjee. 2015. Translating noun compounds using semantic relations. *Computer Speech & Language*, 32(1):91–108.

Ken Barker and Stan Szpakowicz. 1998. Semi-automatic recognition of noun modifier relationships. In *COLING 1998 Volume 1: The 17th International Conference on Computational Linguistics*.

Emily M. Bender and Alexander Koller. 2020. Climbing towards NLU: On meaning, form, and understanding in the age of data. In *Proceedings of the 58th Annual Meeting of the Association for Computational Linguistics*, pages 5185–5198, Online. Association for Computational Linguistics.

Yonatan Bisk, Ari Holtzman, Jesse Thomason, Jacob Andreas, Yoshua Bengio, Joyce Chai, Mirella Lapata, Angeliki Lazaridou, Jonathan May, Aleksandr Nisnevich, et al. 2020. Experience grounds language. *arXiv preprint arXiv:2004.10151*.

Elia Bruni, Gemma Boleda, Marco Baroni, and Nam-Khanh Tran. 2012. Distributional semantics in technicolor. In *Proceedings of the 50th Annual Meeting of the Association for Computational Linguistics (Volume 1: Long Papers)*, pages 136–145.

Marc Brysbaert, Amy Beth Warriner, and Victor Kuperman. 2014. Concreteness ratings for 40 thousand generally known english word lemmas. *Behavior research methods*, 46(3):904–911.

Ken Chatfield, Karen Simonyan, Andrea Vedaldi, and Andrew Zisserman. 2014. Return of the devil in the details: Delving deep into convolutional nets. *arXiv preprint arXiv:1405.3531*.

Francois Chollet et al. 2015. Keras.

Jacob Cohen. 1960. A coefficient of agreement for nominal scales. *Educational and psychological measurement*, 20(1):37–46.

Guillem Collell Talleda and Marie-Francine Moens. 2016. Is an image worth more than a thousand words? on the fine-grain semantic differences between visual and linguistic representations. In *Proceedings of the 26th International Conference on Computational Linguistics*, pages 2807–2817. ACL.

Tim Van de Cruys, Stergos Afantenos, and Philippe Muller. 2013. Melodi: A supervised distributional approach for free paraphrasing of noun compounds. In *7th International Workshop on Semantic Evaluation (SemEval 2013) in: 2nd Joint Conference on Lexical and Computational Semantics (SEM 2013)*, pages pp–144.

Samuel John Cumming. 2007. *Proper nouns*. Rutgers The State University of New Jersey-New Brunswick.

J. Deng, W. Dong, R. Socher, L. Li, Kai Li, and Li Fei-Fei. 2009. Imagenet: A large-scale hierarchical image database. In *2009 IEEE Conference on Computer Vision and Pattern Recognition*, pages 248–255.

J. Deng, W. Dong, R. Socher, L.-J. Li, K. Li, and L. Fei-Fei. 2009. ImageNet: A Large-Scale Hierarchical Image Database. In *CVPR09*.

Jacob Devlin, Ming-Wei Chang, Kenton Lee, and Kristina Toutanova. 2018. Bert: Pre-training of deep bidirectional transformers for language understanding. *arXiv preprint arXiv:1810.04805*.

Corina Dima. 2016. On the compositionality and semantic interpretation of english noun compounds. In *Proceedings of the 1st Workshop on Representation Learning for NLP*, pages 27–39.

Corina Dima and Erhard Hinrichs. 2015. Automatic noun compound interpretation using deep neural networks and word embeddings. In *Proceedings of the 11th International Conference on Computational Semantics*, pages 173–183.

Georgiana Dinu, Marco Baroni, et al. 2013. Dissect - distributional semantics composition toolkit. In *Proceedings of the 51st Annual Meeting of the Association for Computational Linguistics: System Demonstrations*, pages 31–36.

Rotem Dror, Segev Shlomov, and Roi Reichart. 2019. Deep dominance-how to properly compare deep neural models. In *Proceedings of the 57th Annual Meeting of the Association for Computational Linguistics*, pages 2773–2785.

Timothy Wilking Finin. 1980. *The semantic interpretation of compound nominals*. University of Illinois at Urbana-Champaign.

Diego Frassinelli, Daniela Naumann, Jason Utt, and Sabine Schulte m Walde. 2017. Contextual characteristics of concrete and abstract words. In *IWCS 2017—12th International Conference on Computational Semantics—Short papers*.

Fritz Günther, Marco Alessandro Petilli, and Marco Marelli. 2020. Semantic transparency is not invisibility: A computational model of perceptually-grounded conceptual combination in word processing. *Journal of Memory and Language*, 112:104104.

Kaiming He, Xiangyu Zhang, Shaoqing Ren, and Jian Sun. 2016. Deep residual learning for image recognition. In *Proceedings of the IEEE conference on computer vision and pattern recognition*, pages 770–778.

Iris Hendrickx, Preslav Nakov, Stan Szpakowicz, Zornitsa Kozareva, Diarmuid O Séaghdha, and Tony Veale. 2019. Semeval-2013 task 4: Free paraphrases of noun compounds. *arXiv preprint arXiv:1911.10421*.

Felix Hill, Roi Reichart, and Anna Korhonen. 2015. Simlex-999: Evaluating semantic models with (genuine) similarity estimation. *Computational Linguistics*, 41(4):665–695.

Su Nam Kim and Timothy Baldwin. 2005. Automatic interpretation of noun compounds using wordnet similarity. In *International Conference on Natural Language Processing*, pages 945–956. Springer.

Su Nam Kim and Timothy Baldwin. 2006. Interpreting semantic relations in noun compounds via verb semantics. In *Proceedings of the COLING/ACL 2006 Main Conference Poster Sessions*, pages 491–498.

Mirella Lapata and Frank Keller. 2004. The web as a baseline: Evaluating the performance of unsupervised web-based models for a range of nlp tasks. In *Proceedings of the Human Language Technology Conference of the North American Chapter of the Association for Computational Linguistics: HLT-NAACL 2004*, pages 121–128.

Mark Lauer. 1995. *Designing statistical language learners: Experiments on compound nouns*. Ph.D. thesis, Ph. D. thesis, Macquarie University.

Gary Libben. 2014. The nature of compounds: A psychocentric perspective. *Cognitive neuropsychology*, 31(1-2):8–25.

Jiasen Lu, Dhruv Batra, Devi Parikh, and Stefan Lee. 2019. Vilbert: Pretraining task-agnostic visiolinguistic representations for vision-and-language tasks. *arXiv preprint arXiv:1908.02265*.

Bill MacCartney and Christopher D Manning. 2008. Modeling semantic containment and exclusion in natural language inference. In *Proceedings of the 22nd International Conference on Computational Linguistics (Coling 2008)*, pages 521–528.

Gideon Mann. 2002. Fine-grained proper noun ontologies for question answering. In *COLING-02: SEMANET: Building and Using Semantic Networks*.

Quinn McNemar. 1947. Note on the sampling error of the difference between correlated proportions or percentages. *Psychometrika*, 12(2):153–157.

Tomas Mikolov, Kai Chen, Greg Corrado, and Jeffrey Dean. 2013a. Efficient estimation of word representations in vector space. *arXiv preprint arXiv:1301.3781*.

Tomas Mikolov, Ilya Sutskever, Kai Chen, Greg S Corrado, and Jeff Dean. 2013b. Distributed representations of words and phrases and their compositionality. In *Advances in neural information processing systems*, pages 3111–3119.

George A Miller. 1998. *WordNet: An electronic lexical database*. MIT press.

Preslav Nakov. 2013. On the interpretation of noun compounds: Syntax, semantics, and entailment. *Natural Language Engineering*, 19(3):291–330.

Jerzy Neyman and Egon S Pearson. 1928. On the use and interpretation of certain test criteria for purposes of statistical inference, part i. *Biometrika A*, 20:1–2.

Diarmuid Ó Séaghdha. 2008. Learning compound noun semantics. Technical report, University of Cambridge, Computer Laboratory.

Sandro Pezzelle, Ravi Shekhar, and Raffaella Bernardi. 2016. Building a bagpipe with a bag and a pipe: Exploring conceptual combination in vision. In *Proceedings of the 5th Workshop on Vision and Language*, pages 60–64.

Girishkumar Ponkiya, Rudra Murthy, Pushpak Bhattacharyya, and Girish Palshikar. 2020. Looking inside noun compounds: Unsupervised prepositional and free paraphrasing using language models. In *Proceedings of the 2020 Conference on Empirical Methods in Natural Language Processing: Findings*, pages 4313–4323.

Vered Shwartz. 2019. A systematic comparison of english noun compound representations. *arXiv preprint arXiv:1906.04772*.

Vered Shwartz and Ido Dagan. 2019. Still a pain in the neck: Evaluating text representations on lexical composition. *Transactions of the Association for Computational Linguistics*, 7:403–419.

H Gregory Silber and Kathleen F McCoy. 2000. Efficient text summarization using lexical chains. In *Proceedings of the 5th international conference on Intelligent user interfaces*, pages 252–255.

Richard Socher, Brody Huval, Christopher D Manning, and Andrew Y Ng. 2012. Semantic compositionality through recursive matrix-vector spaces. In *Proceedings of the 2012 joint conference on empirical methods in natural language processing and computational natural language learning*, pages 1201–1211.

Hao Tan and Mohit Bansal. 2019. LXMERT : Learning Cross-Modality Encoder Representations from Transformers. In *Proceedings of the 2019 Conference on Empirical Methods in Natural Language Processingand the 9th International Joint Conference on Natural Language Processing (EMNLP-IJCNLP'19)*, pages 5100–5111, Hong Kong, China. Association for Computational Linguistics.

Stephen Tratz. 2011. *Semantically-enriched parsing for natural language understanding*. University of Southern California.

Stephen Tratz and Eduard Hovy. 2010. A Taxonomy, Dataset, and Classifier for Automatic Noun Compound Interpretation. In *Proceedings of the 48th Annual Meeting of the Association for Computational Linguistics*, pages 678–687, Uppsala, Sweden. Association for Computational Linguistics.

Lucy Vanderwende. 1994. Algorithm for automatic interpretation of noun sequences. In *COLING 1994 Volume 2: The 15th International Conference on Computational Linguistics*.

Fabio Massimo Zanzotto, Ioannis Korkontzelos, Francesca Fallucchi, and Suresh Manandhar. 2010. Estimating linear models for compositional distributional semantics. In *Proceedings of the 23rd International Conference on Computational Linguistics (Coling 2010)*, pages 1263–1271.

Appendix

A Detailed Results Tables

This appendix contains supplementary tables that describe some of our findings in more detail.

Figure 3 shows the F1 scores for each relation in the random + coarse dataset configuration for word2vec vectors and word2vec + $ResNet_{10}$ vectors. As opposed to Table 5, Figure 3 shows results from our full dataset, rather than the subset of compounds with 'imageable' constituents.

		modifiers				*heads*			
		L		*VL*		*L*		*VL*	
split		**coef**	**p**	**coef**	**p**	**coef**	**p**	**coef**	**p**
Coarse	random	**-0.2049**	**<0.001**	**-0.1675**	**<0.001**	-0.18	0.008	-0.99	0.028
	lexical (full)	-0.1788	0.032	-0.1251	0.133	0.076	0.352	0.13	0.113
	lexical (mod)	**-0.2322**	**<0.001**	**-0.2740**	**<0.001**	**-0.1924**	**<0.001**	**-0.2093**	**<0.001**
	lexical (head)	**-0.1710**	**<0.001**	**-0.2118**	**<0.001**	0.0053	0.888	0.0432	0.252
Fine	random	**-0.2128**	**<0.001**	**-0.2073**	**<0.001**	**-0.268**	**<0.001**	**-0.27**	**<0.001**
	lexical (full)	0.1108	0.171	0.1665	0.041	0.0854	0.340	0.0296	0.741
	lexical (mod)	**-0.1340**	**0.001**	**-0.1581**	**<0.001**	**-0.3257**	**<0.001**	**-0.3306**	**<0.001**
	lexical (head)	0.0393	0.278	0.0423	0.243	0.0659	0.090	0.0569	0.144

Table 6: Results from a logistic regression analysis of modifier and head concreteness as a predictor of the successful classification of compounds. The scores in boldface are ones where the p-values are lower than a Bonferroni-corrected α level of 0.05.

Table 6 contains a summary of several logistic regression analyses performed on our classification results in both the linguistic and visuo-linguistic modalities. The results show coefficients and p-values of analyses using modifier and head concreteness (separately) as predictors of classification success.

split	**grain**	**BERT**	**BERT + $ResNet_{10\_RAW}$**			**BERT + $ResNet_{10\_NORM}$**		
			F1	diff	$\epsilon, (B<BM_{RAW})$	F1	diff	$\epsilon, (B<BM_{NORM})$
random	coarse	**78.7**	69.7	*- 9*	0.99	**78.7**	*+/- 0*	0.47*
random	fine	57.9	50.7	*- 7.2*	0.94	**65.1**	*+ 7.2*	0.024*
lexical (full)	coarse	**31.6**	28.6	*- 3*	0.92	25.8	*- 5.8*	0.95
lexical (full)	fine	**19.5**	14.5	*- 5*	1.00	15.0	*- 4.5*	0.79
lexical (mod)	coarse	17.0	**36.6**	*+ 19.6*	0.036*	6.7	*- 10.3*	0.98
lexical (mod)	fine	8.3	**27.0**	*+ 18.7*	0.005*	8.3	*+/- 0*	0.55
lexical (head)	coarse	11.1	**40.2**	*+ 29.1*	0.004*	5.0	*- 6.1*	0.84
lexical (head)	fine	4.4	**29.5**	*+ 25.1*	0.036*	2.8	*- 1.6*	0.78

Table 7: Results from fine-tuning BERT with and without adding $ResNet_{10}$ vectors after 50 epochs of training, averaged over 10 runs. Each column of bimodal results shows weighted F1, the change in F1 between the unimodal and the given bimodal setting, and the epsilon value from the ASD algorithm that reveals to what extent the bimodal is better than the unimodal setting.

Table 7 shows the results of some NNC interpretation experiments that we did with a pre-trained BERT model (Devlin et al., 2018) and our ResNet visual embeddings. In these experiments, we fed compounds to a BERT model fitted with a linear classifier on top in order to get the classifications of the compounds. In the visuo-linguistic modality, we concatenated BERT's linguistic embeddings with our visual embeddings before passing them to a linear classification layer. We experimented with using raw ResNet embeddings (straight out of the ResNet model, without applying anything but dimensionality reduction) and normalized ResNet embeddings. The table shows F1 scores as well as the ϵ value returned by the *Almost Stochastic Dominance* (ASD) algorithm proposed by Dror et al. (2019) for comparing the performance of two neural network architectures. The algorithm works in such a way that an ϵ value of less than 0.5 means that algorithm B (in our case, one of the visuo-linguistic settings) is *almost stochastically dominant* over algorithm A (in our case, the purely linguistic setting).

Table 8 gives an overview of the results of our classification algorithm when used on linguistic (L) and visuo-linguistic (VL) vectors. The table shows the F1 scores for subsets of our test data, where we select data samples where either one, both, or none of the constituents in each sample had a $ResNet_{10}$ vector available (i.e., had 10 or more images available in ImageNet). The 'no filtering' column contains the exact same results, for the full dataset, as reported in our main article, and is included for comparison.

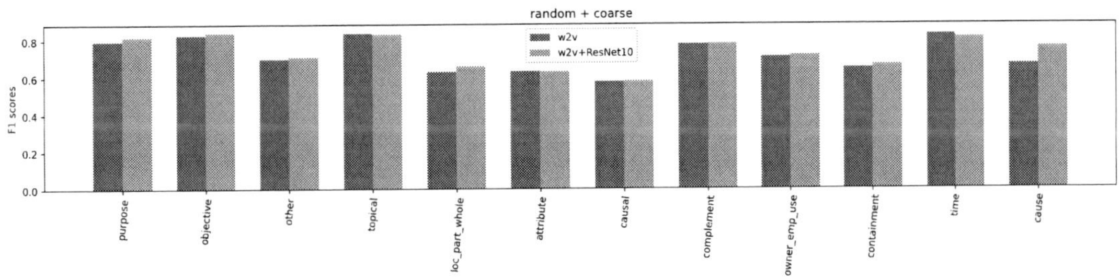

Figure 3: Per-relation F1 scores in the condition with the highest scores (the random + coarse configuration).

	constituents with 10+ images:	*no filtering*		*mods*		*heads*		*both*		*none*	
	split	**L**	**VL**	**L**	**VL**	**L**	**VL**	**L**	**VL**	**L**	**VL**
Coarse	random	74.1	**75.3***	70.46	71.43	72.78	74.65	70.76	72.59	76.84	77.9
	lexical (full)	49.1	**50.8***	41.29	46.04	48.4	51.24	41.3	43.22	56.84	53.77
	lexical (mod)	63.5	64.0	56.77	57.25	59.36	61.35	54.48	55.45	70.22	69.69
	lexical (head)	55.5	56.7	54.3	55.7	50.85	**54.64***	51.42	**55.96***	58.99	59.14
Fine	random	73.0	75.0	69.49	**71.72***	69.19	**72.06***	66.13	69.43	76.09	**77.78***
	lexical (full)	40.3	40.0	41.19	40.91	39.21	35.04	42.03	38.94	42.33	44.59
	lexical (mod)	63.0	63.5	60.13	60.2	54.32	55.77	51.88	53.38	68.71	69.35
	lexical (head)	50.6	**51.6***	52.06	53.35	51.18	51.6	52.88	53.91	50.17	51.53

Table 8: Results of our experiments using the concatenation method of composition and the ResNet_{10} vectors, filtered by the imageability (as modeled by whether or not 10 or more images were available) of the constituents. An asterisk next to a VL score means that the visuo-linguistic (VL) modality performed significantly better than the linguistic (L) modality following a McNemar test with a Bonferroni correction of the p-values.

Less Descriptive yet Discriminative: Quantifying the Properties of Multimodal Referring Utterances via CLIP

Ece Takmaz and **Sandro Pezzelle** and **Raquel Fernández**
Institute for Logic, Language and Computation
University of Amsterdam
{ece.takmaz|s.pezzelle|raquel.fernandez}@uva.nl

Abstract

In this work, we use a transformer-based pretrained multimodal model, CLIP, to shed light on the mechanisms employed by human speakers when referring to visual entities. In particular, we use CLIP to quantify the degree of descriptiveness (how well an utterance describes an image in isolation) and discriminativeness (to what extent an utterance is effective in picking out a single image among similar images) of human referring utterances within multimodal dialogues. Overall, our results show that utterances become less descriptive over time while their discriminativeness remains unchanged. Through analysis, we propose that this trend could be due to participants relying on the previous mentions in the dialogue history, as well as being able to distill the most discriminative information from the visual context. In general, our study opens up the possibility of using this and similar models to quantify patterns in human data and shed light on the underlying cognitive mechanisms.

1 Introduction

During a conversation, speakers can refer to an entity (e.g., the girl in Fig. 1) multiple times within different contexts. This has been shown to lead to subsequent referring expressions that are usually shorter and that show lexical entrainment with previous mentions (Krauss and Weinheimer, 1967; Brennan and Clark, 1996). This trend has been confirmed in recent vision-and-language (V&L) datasets (Shore and Skantze, 2018; Haber et al., 2019; Hawkins et al., 2020): referring utterances become more compact (i.e., less descriptive), and yet participants are able to identify the intended referent (i.e., they remain pragmatically informative).

Several approaches (Mao et al., 2016; Cohn-Gordon et al., 2018; Schüz et al., 2021; Luo et al., 2018, i.a.) have tackled the generation of image captions from the perspective of pragmatic informativity; Coppock et al. (2020) have compared the informativity of image captions and of referring expressions; and Haber et al. (2019); Hawkins et al. (2020) have explored how dialogue history contributes to discriminativeness. However, no work to date has investigated how these two dimensions, *descriptiveness* and *discriminativeness* or pragmatic informativity, interact in referring expressions uttered in dialogue.

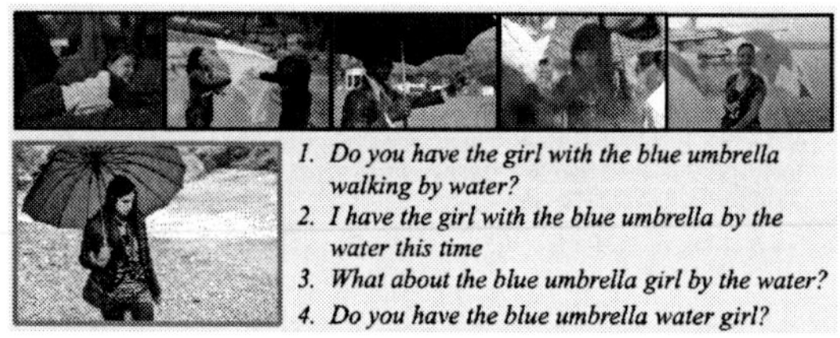

Figure 1: Referring utterance chain from PhotoBook (Haber et al., 2019). The chain has 4 ranks (4 references to the target image, in red outline). For simplicity, only the 5 distractor images from rank 1 are shown.

In this work, we use a transformer-based pretrained multimodal model to study the interplay between descriptiveness and discriminativeness in human referring utterances produced in dialogue. Due to their unprecedented success in numerous tasks, pretrained V&L models—such as LXMERT (Tan and Bansal, 2019), VisualBERT (Li et al., 2019), UNITER (Chen et al., 2020) and ALIGN (Jia et al., 2021)—have recently attracted a lot of interest aimed at understanding the properties and potential of their learned representations as well as the effect their architectures and training setups have (Bugliarello et al., 2021). These include probing such models in a zero-shot manner, i.e., without any specific fine-tuning (Hendricks and Nematzadeh, 2021; Parcalabescu et al., 2021); quantifying the roles of each modality (Frank et al., 2021); inspecting attention patterns (Cao et al., 2020); and evaluating their learned multimodal representations against human judgments (Pezzelle et al., 2021).

We focus on one model: Contrastive Language-

Proceedings of the Workshop on Cognitive Modeling and Computational Linguistics, pages 36 - 42
May 26, 2022 ©2022 Association for Computational Linguistics

Image Pre-training (CLIP, Radford et al., 2021), which learns via contrasting images and texts that can be aligned or unaligned with each other. This contrastive objective makes CLIP particularly suitable for modelling referential tasks that inherently include such comparisons. Here, we use CLIP to gain insight into the strategies used by humans in sequential reference settings, finding that although the descriptiveness of referring utterances decreases significantly, the utterances remain discriminative over the course of multimodal dialogue. The code to reproduce our results is available at `https://github.com/ecekt/clip-desc-disc`.

2 Data

We focus on PhotoBook (PB; Haber et al., 2019), a dataset of multimodal task-oriented dialogues where players aim to pick the images they have in common without seeing each other's visual contexts (which consist of 6 images coming from the same domain). The game is played over several rounds in which the previously seen images reappear in different visual contexts, giving the players an opportunity to refer to such images again. As a result, *chains* of utterances referring to a single image are formed over the rounds as the players build common ground. See Fig. 1 for a simplified representation of a chain.[1] In total, PB consists of 2,500 games, 165K utterances, and 360 unique images from COCO (Lin et al., 2014).

All our experiments are conducted on a subset of 50 PB games with manually annotated referring utterances, which contains 364 referential chains about 205 unique target images. We refer to this subset as PB-GOLD.[2] Although a dataset of automatically-extracted chains using all PB data is also available (Takmaz et al., 2020), as reported by the authors these chains may contain errors. We therefore opt for using the smaller but higher-quality PB-GOLD subset since we are interested in analysing human strategies. Given that we use a pretrained model without fine-tuning, experimenting with large amounts of data is not a requisite.

PB-GOLD's chains contain 1,078 utterances, i.e., 2.96 utterances per chain on average (min 1, max 4). We henceforth use the term 'rank' to refer to the position of an utterance in a chain. The average token length of utterances is 13.34, 11.03, 9.23, and 7.82, respectively, for ranks 1, 2, 3, and 4.[3] This decreasing trend, which is statistically significant at $p < 0.01$ with respect to independent samples t-tests between the ranks, is in line with the trend observed in the whole dataset (Haber et al., 2019). PB-GOLD's vocabulary consists of 926 tokens.

3 Model

We use CLIP (Radford et al., 2021), a model pretrained on a dataset of 400 million image-text pairs collected from the internet using a contrastive objective to learn strong transferable vision representations with natural language supervision.[4] In particular, we employ the ViT-B/32 version of CLIP, which utilizes separate transformers to encode vision and language (Vaswani et al., 2017; Dosovitskiy et al., 2021; Radford et al., 2019, 2021).

As the model learns to align images and texts, this enables zero-shot transfer to various V&L tasks such as image-text retrieval and image classification and even certain non-traditional tasks in a simple and efficient manner (Radford et al., 2019; Agarwal et al., 2021; Shen et al., 2021; Cafagna et al., 2021; Hessel et al., 2021). This makes it an intriguing tool to investigate the properties of visually grounded referring utterances. In this work, we freeze CLIP's weights and do not fine-tune the model or perform prompt engineering, since we aim to exploit the model's pretrained knowledge for the analysis of human referring strategies.

4 Descriptiveness

In our first experiment, we investigate the degree of descriptiveness exhibited by referring utterances in the PhotoBook game, i.e., the amount of information they provide about the image out of context. We consider each target image and corresponding referential utterance at a given rank *in isolation*, i.e., without taking into account the other competing images nor the dialogue history. We quantify descriptiveness as the alignment between an utterance and its image referent using `CLIPScore` (Hessel et al., 2021), assuming that a more descriptive utterance will attain a higher score. For all the target image-utterance pairs in the chains of PB-GOLD, we use CLIP to obtain a vector t representing the utterance and a

[1]Only 1 player's perspective for 1 context is represented.

[2]We use the gold set of the utterance-based chains v2 available at `https://dmg-photobook.github.io/`.

[3]We use TweetTokenizer: `https://www.nltk.org/api/nltk.tokenize.html`

[4]`https://github.com/openai/CLIP`

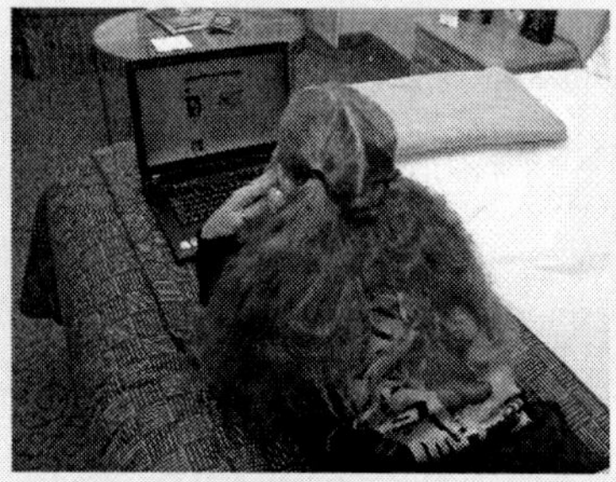

1. girl lying on a bed surfing the internet on a laptop computer
2. a girl sleeping on her belly on top of a bed looking at a laptop.
3. woman laying on her stomach on a bed in front of a laptop.
4. a girl with long brown hair with streaks of red lays on a bed and looks at an open laptop computer.
5. a young girl laying on a bed using her laptop.

Figure 2: Set of captions from COCO (Lin et al., 2014), the order of captions is arbitrary.

1. This is a kitchen with white cupboards and worktop.
2. There is a red wall painted behind the cooker section.
3. There is a wooden table to the right with pale floor tiles on the floor.
4. There is a sink to the left with a window near the sink.
5. There is a bunch of flowers beside the window.

Figure 3: Sequential description from Image Description Sequences (Ilinykh et al., 2019).

vector v representing the image. `CLIPScore` is then computed as the scaled cosine similarity between these two vectors, with range $[0, 2.5]$:[5] $\texttt{CLIPScore}(t, v) = 2.5 * max(cos(t, v), 0)$. We compute the average `CLIPScore` per rank over the whole PB-GOLD dataset.

Results. We find that earlier utterances are better aligned with the target image features and that there is a monotonically decreasing trend over the 4 ranks (Fig. 4, blue bars). The differences between all pairs of ranks are statistically significant (according to independent samples t-tests, $p < 0.01$), except for the comparison between the last 2 ranks ($p > 0.05$). Since earlier referring utterances tend to be longer (see Sec. 2), we check to what extent length may be a confounding factor. We find that there is only a weak correlation between token length and `CLIPScore` (Spearman's $\rho = 0.29, p < 0.001$).

We compare these results on PhotoBook with text-to-image alignment computed with the same method on two other datasets: (1) COCO (Lin et al., 2014),[6] which includes 5 captions per image provided independently by different annotators as shown in Fig. 2; here we do not expect to find significant differences in the level of descriptiveness across the captions, and (2) Image Description Sequences (IDS, Ilinykh et al., 2019)[7] where one participant describes an image incrementally as shown in Fig. 3, by progressively adding sentences with further details; here we do expect a similar pattern to PhotoBook, albeit for different reasons (because participants add less salient information; Ilinykh et al., 2019).

Fig. 4 shows that these expectations are confirmed. According to CLIP, COCO captions (green bars) are more descriptive than IDS descriptions and PB referring utterances, and are equally aligned with the image across 'ranks' (the order is arbitrary in this case). In contrast, IDS incremental descriptions (yellow bars) are intrinsically ordered and show a significant decreasing trend similar to PB.

5 Discriminativeness

In order for a listener to select the target image among distractor images, a referring utterance should be discriminative in its visual context. Our results in the previous section show that descriptiveness decreases over time—what is the trend regarding discriminativeness? To address this question, in our second experiment we use CLIP from the perspective of reference resolution.

We focus on local text-to-image alignment, initially ignoring the previous dialogue history. To this end, we feed CLIP a single referring utterance together with the visual context of the speaker who produced that utterance. CLIP yields softmax probabilities for each image contrasted with the single text. As a metric, we use accuracy: 1 if the target image gets the highest probability; 0 otherwise.

Results. The overall accuracy is 80.15%, which is well above the random baseline of 16.67%. In Fig. 5, we break down the results per rank (blue bars). A 4×2 chi-square test (4 ranks vs. correct/incorrect) did not yield significant differences

[5] The scaled factor was introduced by Hessel et al. (2021) to account for the relatively low observed cosine values.

[6] We use the set of COCO images in PB-GOLD (N=205).

[7] The images are from ADE20k corpus (Zhou et al., 2017)

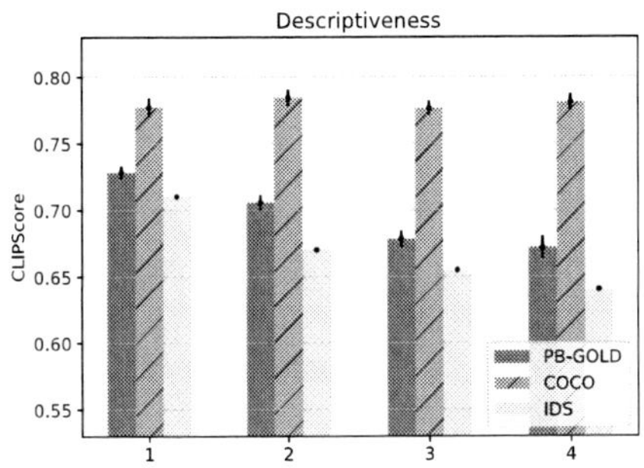

Figure 4: Descriptiveness (`CLIPScore`) for PB-GOLD, COCO and IDS. We only plot the first 4 'ranks' (x-axis) for COCO and IDS for comparability with PB-GOLD. The error bars illustrate the standard error.

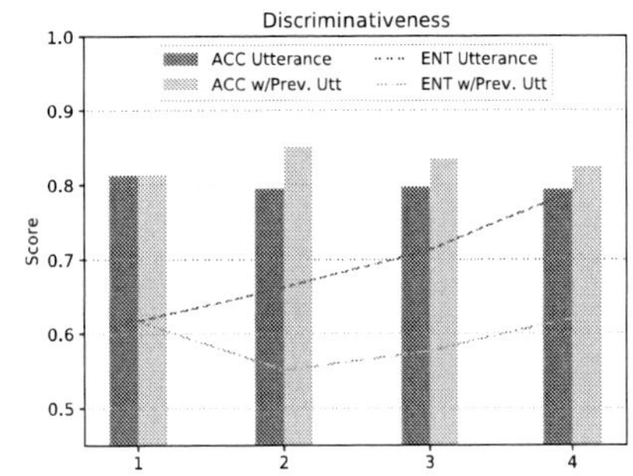

Figure 5: Discriminativeness (reference resolution accuracy, ACC) per rank with PB-GOLD utterances (Utterance) and utterances with history (w/Prev. Utt), along with their respective entropies (ENT).

in accuracy between the ranks, $p > 0.05$. Thus, although descriptiveness decreases over time, discriminativeness is not significantly affected. An analysis of the entropy of the softmax distributions reveals that entropy increases monotonically over the ranks (this difference is statistically significant according to an independent samples t-test between ranks 1 and 4; $H_1 = 0.62$, $H_4 = 0.79$, $p < 0.01$). That is, the model is more uncertain when trying to resolve less descriptive utterances. There is indeed a negative correlation between entropy and `CLIPScore` computed between the target image and the corresponding utterance (Spearman's $\rho = -0.5, p < 0.001$).

6 Analysis

How do participants manage to maintain discriminativeness while decreasing descriptiveness? Do they rely on the previous mentions present in the dialogue history? Do they refine their referring strategy by distilling the most discriminative information in a given context?

6.1 Dialogue history

The results of our experiment in the previous section show that the utterances in isolation are effective at referring; yet, uncertainty increases when the less descriptive utterances are considered out of context. To reduce such uncertainty, participants may rely on the dialogue history (Brennan and Clark, 1996; Shore and Skantze, 2018; Takmaz et al., 2020). We consider a scenario where participants keep in memory the previous mention when processing the current referring utterance. We model this scenario by prepending the previous referring utterance in the chain to the current utterance and feeding this into the reference resolution model described in Section 5. As shown in Fig. 5, the resulting discriminativeness is similar to the one obtained earlier (the differences are not significant; chi-square test, $p < 0.05$) and, as before, remains stable across ranks (chi-square test, $p > 0.05$). However, taking into account the previous mentions leads to a significant reduction of the entropy in general: e.g., at the last rank $H_4 = 0.79$ vs. $H'_4 = 0.62$ (t-test, $p < 0.05$). This suggests that relying on the dialogue history allows speakers to use less descriptive utterances by reducing discriminative uncertainty.

6.2 Most discriminative information

Besides exploiting the dialogue history, participants may refine their referring strategy by distilling the most discriminative information in a given context. To gain insight into this hypothesis, we explore what is discriminative in the images: we compute the discriminative features v_d of a target image by taking the average of the visual representations of distractor images to obtain the mean context vector and then subtracting this vector from the visual representation of the target image. We encode all 926 words in the vocabulary of PB-GOLD using CLIP, and retrieve the top-10 words whose representations are the closest to v_d in terms of cosine similarity (amounting to 1% of the vocabulary). We take these words to convey the most discriminative properties of an image in context. We analyse whether at least one of these retrieved words is mentioned exactly in the referring utterance, finding that this is indeed the case for a remarkable 60% of utterances.[8] As an illustration, for the example in Fig. 1, the words *walking* (mentioned at rank 1)

[8]Randomly sampling 10 words from the vocabulary for each utterance yields 11% (average of 5 random runs).

and *blue* (used at ranks 1, 2, 3, 4) are among the top-10 most discriminative words, while the word *water* (mentioned at ranks 1, 2, 3, 4) is close to the word *beach*, which is also retrieved as one of most discriminative words in this case.

The most discriminative words are likely to be reused in later utterances, even though the visual context changes from rank to rank. For instance, the most discriminative words mentioned at rank 1 constitute 60% of the discriminative words at rank 2, indicating that entrainment is likely for words that have high utility across contexts. We also find a significant increase in the proportion of discriminative content words to all the content words per utterance (only between ranks 1 and 4, 14% vs. 19%, $p < 0.01$).

7 Conclusion

We used a pre-trained multimodal model claimed to be a reference-free caption evaluator, CLIP (Radford et al., 2021), to quantify descriptiveness and discriminativeness of human referring utterances within multimodal dialogues. We showed that (i) later utterances in a dialogue become less descriptive in isolation while (ii) remaining similarly discriminative against a visual context.

We found that the addition of dialogue history helps decrease and control the entropy of resolution accuracy even when the speakers produce less descriptive referring utterances. In addition, we found that the proportion of discriminative words increases over the ranks. These suggest that participants playing the PhotoBook game (Haber et al., 2019) show a tendency towards distilling discriminative words and utilize the dialogue history to keep task performance stable over the dialogue. This outcome resonates with the findings by Giulianelli et al. (2021) who observe that PhotoBook dialogue participants tend to limit fluctuations in the amount of information transmitted within reference chains, in line with uniform information density principles (e.g., Genzel and Charniak, 2002; Jaeger and Levy, 2007).

Interestingly, future work could explore novel ways of incorporating the CLIP model or its representations into a reference resolution or generation model embedding dialogue history and visual context to obtain human-like outcomes.

Acknowledgments

We would like to thank Mario Giulianelli and Arabella Sinclair for their valuable comments on a draft of this paper. This project has received funding from the European Research Council (ERC) under the European Union's Horizon 2020 research and innovation program (grant agreement No. 819455).

References

Sandhini Agarwal, Gretchen Krueger, Jack Clark, Alec Radford, Jong Wook Kim, and Miles Brundage. 2021. Evaluating clip: Towards characterization of broader capabilities and downstream implications.

Susan E. Brennan and Herbert H. Clark. 1996. Conceptual pacts and lexical choice in conversation. *Journal of Experimental Psychology: Learning, Memory, and Cognition*, 22:1482–1493.

Emanuele Bugliarello, Ryan Cotterell, Naoaki Okazaki, and Desmond Elliott. 2021. Multimodal pretraining unmasked: A meta-analysis and a unified framework of vision-and-language BERTs. *Transactions of the Association for Computational Linguistics*.

Michele Cafagna, Kees van Deemter, and Albert Gatt. 2021. What vision-language models 'see' when they see scenes. *ArXiv*, abs/2109.07301.

Jize Cao, Zhe Gan, Yu Cheng, Licheng Yu, Yen-Chun Chen, and Jingjing Liu. 2020. Behind the scene: Revealing the secrets of pre-trained vision-and-language models. *ECCV Spotlight*.

Yen-Chun Chen, Linjie Li, Licheng Yu, Ahmed El Kholy, Faisal Ahmed, Zhe Gan, Yu Cheng, and Jingjing Liu. 2020. UNITER: Universal image-text representation learning. In *European Conference on Computer Vision*, pages 104–120. Springer.

Reuben Cohn-Gordon, Noah Goodman, and Christopher Potts. 2018. Pragmatically informative image captioning with character-level inference. In *Proceedings of the 2018 Conference of the North American Chapter of the Association for Computational Linguistics: Human Language Technologies, Volume 2 (Short Papers)*, pages 439–443, New Orleans, Louisiana. Association for Computational Linguistics.

Elizabeth Coppock, Danielle Dionne, Nathanial Graham, Elias Ganem, Shijie Zhao, Shawn Lin, Wenxing Liu, and Derry Wijaya. 2020. Informativity in image captions vs. referring expressions. In *Proceedings of the Probability and Meaning Conference (PaM 2020)*, pages 104–108, Gothenburg. Association for Computational Linguistics.

Alexey Dosovitskiy, Lucas Beyer, Alexander Kolesnikov, Dirk Weissenborn, Xiaohua Zhai,

Thomas Unterthiner, Mostafa Dehghani, Matthias Minderer, Georg Heigold, Sylvain Gelly, Jakob Uszkoreit, and Neil Houlsby. 2021. An image is worth 16x16 words: Transformers for image recognition at scale.

Stella Frank, Emanuele Bugliarello, and Desmond Elliott. 2021. Vision-and-language or vision-for-language? On cross-modal influence in multimodal transformers. In *Proceedings of the 2021 Conference on Empirical Methods in Natural Language Processing (EMNLP 2021)*. Association for Computational Linguistics.

Dmitriy Genzel and Eugene Charniak. 2002. Entropy rate constancy in text. In *Proceedings of the 40th annual meeting of the Association for Computational Linguistics*, pages 199–206.

Mario Giulianelli, Arabella Sinclair, and Raquel Fernández. 2021. Is information density uniform in task-oriented dialogues? In *Proceedings of the 2021 Conference on Empirical Methods in Natural Language Processing*, pages 8271–8283, Online and Punta Cana, Dominican Republic. Association for Computational Linguistics.

Janosch Haber, Tim Baumgärtner, Ece Takmaz, Lieke Gelderloos, Elia Bruni, and Raquel Fernández. 2019. The PhotoBook dataset: Building common ground through visually-grounded dialogue. In *Proceedings of the 57th Annual Meeting of the Association for Computational Linguistics*, pages 1895–1910, Florence, Italy. Association for Computational Linguistics.

Robert Hawkins, Minae Kwon, Dorsa Sadigh, and Noah Goodman. 2020. Continual adaptation for efficient machine communication. In *Proceedings of the 24th Conference on Computational Natural Language Learning*, pages 408–419, Online. Association for Computational Linguistics.

Lisa Anne Hendricks and Aida Nematzadeh. 2021. Probing image-language transformers for verb understanding. In *Findings of the Association for Computational Linguistics: ACL-IJCNLP 2021*, pages 3635–3644, Online. Association for Computational Linguistics.

Jack Hessel, Ari Holtzman, Maxwell Forbes, Ronan Le Bras, and Yejin Choi. 2021. CLIPScore: A reference-free evaluation metric for image captioning. In *Proceedings of the 2021 Conference on Empirical Methods in Natural Language Processing*, pages 7514–7528, Online and Punta Cana, Dominican Republic. Association for Computational Linguistics.

Nikolai Ilinykh, Sina Zarrieß, and David Schlangen. 2019. Tell me more: A dataset of visual scene description sequences. In *Proceedings of the 12th International Conference on Natural Language Generation*, pages 152–157, Tokyo, Japan. Association for Computational Linguistics.

T. Florian Jaeger and Roger P. Levy. 2007. Speakers optimize information density through syntactic reduction. In *Advances in neural information processing systems*, pages 849–856.

Chao Jia, Yinfei Yang, Ye Xia, Yi-Ting Chen, Zarana Parekh, Hieu Pham, Quoc V. Le, Yun-Hsuan Sung, Zhen Li, and Tom Duerig. 2021. Scaling up visual and vision-language representation learning with noisy text supervision. In *ICML*.

Robert M. Krauss and Sidney Weinheimer. 1967. Effect of referent similarity and communication mode on verbal encoding. *Journal of Verbal Learning & Verbal Behavior*, 6(3):359–363.

Liunian Harold Li, Mark Yatskar, Da Yin, Cho-Jui Hsieh, and Kai-Wei Chang. 2019. VisualBERT: A simple and performant baseline for vision and language. *arXiv preprint arXiv:1908.03557*.

Tsung-Yi Lin, Michael Maire, Serge Belongie, James Hays, Pietro Perona, Deva Ramanan, Piotr Dollár, and C. Lawrence Zitnick. 2014. Microsoft coco: Common objects in context. In *Computer Vision – ECCV 2014*, pages 740–755, Cham. Springer International Publishing.

Ruotian Luo, Brian L. Price, Scott D. Cohen, and Gregory Shakhnarovich. 2018. Discriminability objective for training descriptive captions. In *2018 IEEE/CVF Conference on Computer Vision and Pattern Recognition*, pages 6964–6974.

Junhua Mao, Jonathan Huang, Alexander Toshev, Oana Camburu, Alan L Yuille, and Kevin Murphy. 2016. Generation and comprehension of unambiguous object descriptions. In *Proceedings of the IEEE conference on computer vision and pattern recognition*, pages 11–20.

Letitia Parcalabescu, Albert Gatt, Anette Frank, and Iacer Calixto. 2021. Seeing Past Words: Testing the Cross-Modal Capabilities of Pretrained V&L Models. In *Proceedings of the First Workshop on Multimodal Semantic Representations (MMSR)*, Groningen. To appear.

Sandro Pezzelle, Ece Takmaz, and Raquel Fernández. 2021. Word representation learning in multimodal pre-trained transformers: An intrinsic evaluation. *Transactions of the Association for Computational Linguistics*, 9:1563–1579.

Alec Radford, Jong Wook Kim, Chris Hallacy, Aditya Ramesh, Gabriel Goh, Sandhini Agarwal, Girish Sastry, Amanda Askell, Pamela Mishkin, Jack Clark, Gretchen Krueger, and Ilya Sutskever. 2021. Learning transferable visual models from natural language supervision. In *ICML*.

Alec Radford, Jeff Wu, Rewon Child, David Luan, Dario Amodei, and Ilya Sutskever. 2019. Language models are unsupervised multitask learners. Technical report, OpenAI.

Simeon Schüz, Ting Han, and Sina Zarrieß. 2021. Diversity as a by-product: Goal-oriented language generation leads to linguistic variation. In *Proceedings of the 22nd Annual Meeting of the Special Interest Group on Discourse and Dialogue*, pages 411–422, Singapore and Online. Association for Computational Linguistics.

Sheng Shen, Liunian Harold Li, Hao Tan, Mohit Bansal, Anna Rohrbach, Kai-Wei Chang, Zhewei Yao, and Kurt Keutzer. 2021. How Much Can CLIP Benefit Vision-and-Language Tasks? *arXiv*, abs/2107.06383.

Todd Shore and Gabriel Skantze. 2018. Using lexical alignment and referring ability to address data sparsity in situated dialog reference resolution. In *Proceedings of the 2018 Conference on Empirical Methods in Natural Language Processing*, pages 2288–2297, Brussels, Belgium. Association for Computational Linguistics.

Ece Takmaz, Mario Giulianelli, Sandro Pezzelle, Arabella Sinclair, and Raquel Fernández. 2020. Refer, Reuse, Reduce: Generating Subsequent References in Visual and Conversational Contexts. In *Proceedings of the 2020 Conference on Empirical Methods in Natural Language Processing (EMNLP)*, pages 4350–4368, Online. Association for Computational Linguistics.

Hao Tan and Mohit Bansal. 2019. LXMERT: Learning cross-modality encoder representations from transformers. In *Proceedings of the 2019 Conference on Empirical Methods in Natural Language Processing and the 9th International Joint Conference on Natural Language Processing (EMNLP-IJCNLP)*, pages 5100–5111, Hong Kong, China. Association for Computational Linguistics.

Ashish Vaswani, Noam Shazeer, Niki Parmar, Jakob Uszkoreit, Llion Jones, Aidan N Gomez, Ł ukasz Kaiser, and Illia Polosukhin. 2017. Attention is all you need. In *Advances in Neural Information Processing Systems*, volume 30. Curran Associates, Inc.

Bolei Zhou, Hang Zhao, Xavier Puig, Sanja Fidler, Adela Barriuso, and Antonio Torralba. 2017. Scene parsing through ade20k dataset. In *2017 IEEE Conference on Computer Vision and Pattern Recognition (CVPR)*, pages 5122–5130.

Codenames as a Game of Co-occurrence Counting

Réka Cserháti and **István Kolláth** and **András Kicsi** and **Gábor Berend**
Institute of Informatics
University of Szeged
{cserhatir,kollathistvan}@gmail.com
{akicsi,berendg}@inf.u-szeged.hu

Abstract

Codenames is a popular board game, in which knowledge and cooperation between players play an important role. The task of a player playing as a spymaster is to find words (clues) that a teammate finds related to as many of some given words as possible, but not to other specified words. This is a hard challenge even with today's advanced language technology methods.

In our study, we create spymaster agents using four types of relatedness measures that require only a raw text corpus to produce. These include newly introduced ones based on co-occurrences, which outperform FastText cosine similarity on gold standard relatedness data. To generate clues in Codenames, we combine relatedness measures with four different scoring functions, for two languages, English and Hungarian. For testing, we collect decisions of human guesser players in an online game, and our configurations outperform previous agents among methods using raw corpora only.

1 Introduction

One of the central subjects of artificial intelligence research has long been the development of agents that play various games at the human level or better. Most studies in the field focus on combinatorial games, that can be easily formalized mathematically, such as chess and go (see, for example, Allis et al., 1994). The popular board game Codenames is different from these in many aspects and may provide an excellent experimental ground in areas such as predicting human behavior or implementing human-machine cooperation.

In the original game, two teams compete against each other. A board of 25 word cards contains cards belonging to the blue or red team, neutral cards, and an instant defeat card (black). A team wins if all cards of their team are revealed earlier than the cards of the other team, or if the opponent reveals the black card. However, only one person (the spymaster) from both teams knows which card is of what color. Therefore, the spymasters give the team a clue each turn, which consists of a clue word and a number. The other members of the team (guessers), in consultation with each other, reveal cards on the board they think are related to the clue word, until they bet on a wrong card, or reach the limit given by the spymaster as a number.

This means it is possible to create two types of agents for the game, spymasters and guessers. The main task of both agents is to be able to cooperate with human players. To create agents capable of such high-level cooperation, we need to be able to predict human behavior in the game. This task includes modeling the relatedness of words, with the aim of obtaining relatedness measures that represent human perception well.

This task is highly related to word association modeling, which has been studied extensively in psycholinguistics for a long time (Palermo and Jenkins, 1964; McNeill, 1966), but is by no means equivalent to it. In word association experiments, subjects should name any word associated with a given word as quickly as possible, but in this case, the spymaster's task is to find a word that is related to as many words from a given set as possible, but not or significantly less closely to a set of other words. The time allotted for the task is also limited at most very loosely (by the patience of the other players), and based on personal experiences, spymasters often use several minutes of thinking time to come up with the right clue. For this reason, connected words are often related in a complex way, even indirectly. The task of agents – to find words in the table related to the clue word – is more like simple associations, but time is not dominant here either, and more complex, indirect relations also matter. In a game between people, the relationship and common knowledge between the players can also count, but this is not an influencing factor in a game with an agent.

Proceedings of the Workshop on Cognitive Modeling and Computational Linguistics, pages 43 - 53
May 26, 2022

2 A Mathematical Model of the Game

Suppose that for a dictionary V, a similarity matrix $S \in \mathbb{R}^{|V|\times|V|}$ exists in which $S_{ij} = s(w_i, w_j)$ is the exact measure of the relationship between any two words w_i, w_j, that is, the relationships are just as strong according to every person. Then the implementation of the guesser agent is simple: from the words on the board, always choose the one that is most closely related to the clue word. This way, a greedy spy-agent is also simple: let v_i be the i-th word of the dictionary, and for every i, let $[w_{i1}, w_{i2}, ..., w_{in}]$ be the unrevealed words on the board, ordered by the relatedness to v_i, from the most closely related to the least related one. Then we look for i for which the largest number k exists, such that $w_{i1}, w_{i2}, ..., w_{ik}$ are all words belonging to the agent's team. Then v_i will be the clue word, and k the number of targeted words.

However, under such conditions, the behavior of the guessers is deterministic, which means the two spymasters are playing against each other. The dictionary, that is, the number of their possible decisions is finite, and spymasters know the outcome of each decision, which means they know each other's possible strategies. Thus, the game becomes a sequential game with perfect information, like e.g. chess, go, or tic-tac-toe. A greedy decision is not necessarily optimal, since a spymaster needs to consider what options they will have later, depending on their own and the other spymasters' decisions, and should optimize their move based on that. Within such a framework, the development of an optimal strategy may be the subject of further research, but is no more connected to computational and cognitive linguistics, so we will not discuss this further in this article.

The above conditions are, of course, far from reality, since such a distance function, which perfectly corresponds to the mental representations of all people, certainly does not exist. This is clear from the fact that in classical association tests, where the actual task is to find nearest neighbors, the subjects never give the same answer (Palermo and Jenkins, 1964; Postman and Keppel, 2014). However, it is a meaningful task to create a similarity function and construct a similarity matrix $S \in \mathbb{R}^{V\times V}$, in which $S_{ij} = s(w_i, w_j)$ approximates the average similarity perceived by people.

Furthermore, based on the similarity approximations, we can define a scoring function for possible clues, which realistically ranks them according to how many correct guesses a human guesser player is expected to give. Our distance matrix and our scoring function together determine a greedy spymaster agent. Since this task is challenging in itself, we disregard the possible non-greedy strategies and focus on optimizing similarity approximations and clue scoring functions for one round only.

3 Related Work

3.1 Associations

Word associations have been a subject of active research for a long time in cognitive science and psycholinguistics for various reasons. They were used to study mental functioning, memory, and certain diseases. Word associations were also applied for modeling the cognitive lexicon and some linguistic processes (summarized by Bel-Enguix et al., 2019).

One can create a graph (Bel-Enguix, 2014), and its transformation to a word embedding model (Bel-Enguix et al., 2019), specifically for modeling associations, but these require difficult-to-obtain association data. This would be a high resource requirement and would make it difficult to apply such methods in various languages.

Instead, we can use methods that require only raw corpora. For this, the results of Spence and Owens (1990) are the most important studies of associations. They have shown that the amount of co-occurrences of words in a corpus is a good indicator of the semantic relationship between them and is also suitable for measuring the strength of associations. Bel Enguix et al. (2014) also predict associations from co-occurrences, using a network of bigram counts. Similar to their methods, we use weighted co-occurrences explicitly to model the connection of words (for details, see 4.1.).

3.2 Language graphs

Although the canonical way to represent words is to assign them to vectors, if the goal is to model connections between words, a graph structure is at least as suitable. When each word is represented by a vector, the similarity between them is most often calculated as the cosine of the angle of the two vectors. In the case of graph representations, all words in the dictionary correspond to the vertices of a large graph, and the distance between them can be defined in many ways depending on the graph. One option is the length or weight of the shortest path between the two vertices. Knowledge graphs

(Miller, 1992; Speer and Havasi, 2012; Navigli and Ponzetto, 2010a) were already used to model word connections in previous Codenames agents, but other types of language graphs also exist, which could be utilized for this task as well.

Hope and Keller (2013), for example, use a graph of co-occurrences for word sense induction. Later Pelevina et al. (2016) use a similar method to disambiguate word embedding models.

Another graph, created as an alternative for word embeddings, is GraphGlove (Ryabinin et al., 2020), where the edges of the graph are optimized by the cost function of GloVe (Pennington et al., 2014b), so that the shortest path between two vertices gives the distance of the corresponding words.

3.3 Codenames agents

To the best of our knowledge, the first algorithms similar to Codenames agents have been created by Shen et al. (2018) specifically to model human associations. In their simplified game, the board always consists of three nouns, and the agent gives a clue that must be one of three adjectives, and refers to exactly two of the board words. Their clues were generated based on the following five similarity functions:

- probability of bigrams relative to word frequency,
- cosine similarity in Skip-gram (Mikolov et al., 2013),
- cosine similarity in GloVe (Pennington et al., 2014a),
- connection according to the knowledge graph ConceptNet5 (Speer and Havasi, 2012),
- similarity in topic modeling.

They found that the behavior of human players is best modeled on the probabilities of bigrams, which is in line with the results of (Spence and Owens, 1990) (although the latter calculated co-occurrences with much larger window size).

Kim et al. (2019) were the first to build agents designed explicitly to play the game. As a background to their relatedness measure, they used

- CBOW, Skip-gram and GloVe word embeddings (in multiple configurations),
- and the WordNet database (Miller, 1992) with a number of different distance functions.

However, in their study, they do not evaluate the performance of agents with human data, but by pairing spymaster and guesser agents, which reveals only the similarity of the two agents, regardless of their ability to interact with humans.

Jaramillo et al. (2020) calculated similarity functions from the following representations:

- TF-IDF similarity calculated from Wikipedia articles and dictionary definitions,
- a naive-Bayesian classification of words, and
- word embeddings extracted from the first layer of the GPT2 language model (Radford et al., 2019).

Of these methods, they find GPT2 vectors best suited to model word relatedness.

The latest article on the topic is (Koyyalagunta et al., 2021), in which, in addition to the previously used Skip-gram and GloVe word embeddings, to produce their similarity matrices they use

- FastText (Bojanowski et al., 2017),
- the BERT model (Devlin et al., 2018),
- and the BabelNet knowledge graph (Navigli and Ponzetto, 2010b), with a framework that associates words according to special rules, developed specifically for this purpose.

In addition to calculating the relatedness between words, the above works also differ in the scoring functions of the possible clues. Without limiting the generality, we assume that our agent plays in the blue team, that is, our clues refer to the blue words. Using the notations of Koyyalagunta et al. (2021), let $\tilde{c}$ be a possible clue word, I_n a set of targeted (intended) words, that is, the n closest blue words to $\tilde{c}$, R the set of all bad words that do not belong to the team (red words), and $s(\cdot,\cdot)$ a function that calculates the similarity or relatedness of two words. The scoring function of Kim et al. (2019) is then

$$g_{Kim}(\tilde{c}, n) = \begin{cases} \min_{b \in I_n} s(\tilde{c}, b), \\ \quad \text{if } \min_{b \in I_n} s(\tilde{c}, b) > \max_{r \in R} s(\tilde{c}, r) \\ 0, \quad \text{otherwise.} \end{cases} \tag{1}$$

Jaramillo et al. (2020) takes the same function, but adds penalties based on the color of the cards. Koyyalagunta et al. (2021), on the other hand, define another scoring function:

$$g_{Koyy}(\tilde{c}, n) = \left(\sum_{b \in I_n} s(\tilde{c}, b) \right) - \lambda\big(\max_{r \in R} s(\tilde{c}, r) \big), \tag{2}$$

where λ is configurable parameter.

In addition, they introduce another method to score clues not only on the basis of word similarities, but also on the basis of their frequency and the similarity of Dict2vec vectors (Tissier et al., 2017) – but this is actually a modification of the original distance matrix.

Their results show that relatedness calculated by GloVe performs best in combination with dictionary definitions and frequency, but without the latter, cosine similarity in FastText proves to be the best measure.

Furthermore, Kumar et al. (2021) studied if the decisions of human players can be predicted in an amended version of Codenames. For the predictions, they used word2vec and GloVe word embeddings, as well as several similarity measures on free association datasets, in particular SWOW (De Deyne et al., 2019) and USF (Nelson et al., 2004). They found that similarity based on random walks in SWOW performed the best, from which they concluded that not only direct associations, but indirect connections are also important in this game.

4 Our Codenames Agents

Building on the studies of Spence and Owens (1990), we introduce several word relatedness measures based on co-occurrences, which we expect to be more suitable for modeling the human perception of word connections than representation methods created for other NLP tasks. We create spymaster agents with several new clue scoring functions combined to our relatedness measures. This way, our methods only require a raw text corpus of appropriate size, so they can be used for any language. We evaluate them in two languages (English and Hungarian), in an online game with human players.[1]

4.1 Relatedness measures

Considering the previous results on the relationship between associations and co-occurrences (Spence and Owens, 1990; Shen et al., 2018), we create our distance matrices not from the latest neural methods of NLP, but from co-occurrences counted in raw text. As English corpora we use the concatenation of the English Wikipedia and the English OpenSubtitles corpus, consisting of 5.692 billion tokens in total. For Hungarian, we use the lemmatized version of the Hungarian Webcorpus (Nemeskey, 2020), also including the Hungarian Wikipedia (1.414 billion tokens). We work with vocabulary sizes 15K in English and 10K in Hungarian, and remove stopwords.

4.1.1 FastText

Among the similarity measures of Koyyalagunta et al. (2021), generally FastText seems to be the best model. So, following the cited work, we create a relatedness matrix based on the cosine similarity of FastText vectors. That is, if $\mathbf{v}_i, \mathbf{v}_j$ are vectors corresponding to words w_i, w_j, then

$$s_F(w_i, w_j) = \cos(\mathbf{v}_i, \mathbf{v}_j).$$

For comparability with the other methods, we train our FastText models on the above corpora for English and Hungarian in 300 dimensions, using window size 10.

4.1.2 Normalized PMI

A standard and probably the most common method to calculate word relatedness from co-occurrences is computing the pointwise mutual information (PMI) of two words. However, PMI has well-known shortcomings, such as overvaluing the relatedness of rare words, and lacking a fixed upper and lower bound. Bouma (2009) introduced normalized PMI as

$$\text{PMI}_{\text{norm}}(x, y) = \left(\ln \frac{p(x,y)}{p(x)p(y)}\right) \Big/ -\ln p(x,y), \quad (3)$$

which has 1 and -1 as upper and lower bounds, and works well empirically as an association measure. According to a known practice, we keep positive values only.

Comparing this relatedness measure to data obtained from humans (MEN, Bruni et al., 2012 and WS-353 relatedness, Agirre et al., 2009), we found that taking the square root of PMI_{norm} increases the Pearson correlation coefficient between human annotations and our calculated relatedness from 0.72 to 0.76 for MEN, and from 0.57 to 0.63 for WS-353. Additionally, in our following methods, it is beneficial if the values do not concentrate around zero, therefore we use the square root of normalized PMI hereinafter:

$$\text{NPMI}(x, y) = \sqrt{\text{PMI}_{\text{norm}}(x, y)}. \quad (4)$$

[1]The game:
http://spymasters.herokuapp.com/
Source code and data:
https://github.com/xerevity/CodeNamesAgent

4.1.3 Squared NPMI matrix

In Codenames, to get ahead in the game, spymasters have to give clues that are connected to many words that are probably unconnected to each other. As Kumar et al. (2021) showed, they might associate words that are not in a strong direct connection, but are only indirectly related (e.g. religion is not related to tree, but both are related to Christmas, therefore religion could be a clue for tree).

To model such indirect connections, we multiply the relatedness matrix by itself, and use the values of the squared matrix S' as the relatedness measure between two words. By the definition of matrix multiplication,

$$S'_{ij} = \sum_{k=1}^{n} s_{i,k} \cdot s_{k,j},$$

that is, if we define G_0 as a graph whose neighborhood matrix is the NPMI matrix then S'_{ij} is the sum of the product of the weights on all two-length paths $v_i - v_k - v_j$ in G_0. Since all edge weights are between 0 and 1, considering the weight of a path as the product of its edge weights gives a valid relatedness measure: longer paths and paths that contain smaller weights will yield to smaller relatedness values.

Artetxe et al. (2018) also showed on word embeddings, that different powers of embedding matrices are beneficial for word similarity and word relatedness tasks, and that the optimal power is higher for relatedness than for similarity.

Another advantage of this method is, that it reduces the number of zeros in the matrix. This is most important in the case of a guesser agent, because if the matrix consists of many zero values, some clues may not have any related words on the board according to our relatedness measure. However, if we have a nonzero value for all board words, we can take the relatedness between the clue word and the bad words into account, which might be beneficial for a spymaster agent as well.

4.1.4 NPMI graph

In the method described above, we already used a relatedness measure based on a graph constructed from NPMI values, where the weight of a path was the product of the weights of the edges on the path. This way, a greater value of edge or path weights corresponds to a stronger connection between the nodes. However, a more common way is that edge weights represent distance, and path weights are the sum of the edges, so that stronger connections belong to smaller path weights. Since our NPMI values are between 0 and 1, we can define graph G as follows: an edge $e(v_1, v_2)$ between vertices corresponding to words w_1 and w_2 exists if and only if NPMI$(w_1, w_2) > 0$, and its weight is $w(e(v_1, v_2)) = 1 - \text{NPMI}(w_1, w_2)$. Now the distance between w_1 and w_2 is given by the weight of the shortest path between v_1 and v_2:

$$d_G(w_i, w_j) = \min_{\pi \in \Pi_G(v_i, v_j)} \sum_{e_k \in \pi} w(e_k), \quad (5)$$

We can turn these distance values into relatedness measures by subtracting them from 1:

$$s_G(w_1, w_2) = 1 - d_G(w_i, w_j). \quad (6)$$

This way, for two strongly related words, for which the shortest path is the edge between them, we get the NPMI as relatedness value. This method therefore has some of the advantageous properties of both above relatedness measures.

	NPMI	NPMI^2	Graph	FastText
NPMI		0.495	0.820	0.393
NPMI^2	0.349		0.578	0.621
Graph	0.442	0.602		0.427
FastText	0.295	0.524	0.319	

Table 1: Pearson (upper tringle) and Spearman (lower triangle) correlation coefficients between our relatedness measures.

4.1.5 Comparison and evaluation of relatedness measures

To investigate the relationship of the above defined relatedness measures, we compute correlations between the score they assign to 100.000 random word pairs. As Table 1 shows, none of the measures are near equivalent, but they have nonzero correlations. They also show high positive correlations with MEN (Bruni et al., 2012) and WS-353 relatedness (Agirre et al., 2009), as can be seen in Table 2, which is hopeful for their usability as relatedness in Codenames agents.

4.2 Clue scoring functions

Say that the agent plays in the blue team, i.e. we want to generate clues associated to the blue words, based on the distance functions above. The functions of Kim et al. (2019) (see (1)) determined the score of a possible reference based on relatedness

	MEN		WS-353	
	Pearson	Spearman	Pearson	Spearman
NPMI	**0.761**	**0.749**	0.632	**0.649**
NPMI^2	0.627	0.670	0.502	0.545
Graph	0.754	0.735	**0.650**	0.647
FastText	0.732	0.737	0.562	0.564

Table 2: Correlation between our relatedness measures and gold standard annotations.

of the clue word to the least related blue word targeted. The shortcoming of this, however, is that in addition to blue (good) words that are similar to the clue word, there may be bad words of a different color that are only very slightly less similar to the clue. We can assume that in this case, agents are less likely to choose the targeted words; or in general, the smaller the difference between the distances of two words from the clue according to our distance function, the more likely the human player will perceive the order of the two words reversed.

To avoid such problems, Koyyalagunta et al. (2021) (see (2)) add a penalty on the relatedness of the closest bad word to their scoring functions. This scoring function generally improves the quality of the generated clues, thus we use this as one of our scoring functions. However, this function does not require all bad words to be less similar to the clue word than the targeted words, and in our experiments there have been such cases that this caused a problem. Therefore we define *KoyyRestrict*, a restricted modification of g_{Koyy}:

$$g_{KoyyR}(\tilde{c}, n) = \begin{cases} g_{Koyy}(\tilde{c}, n), \\ \quad \text{if } \min_{b \in I_n} s(\tilde{c}, b) > \max_{r \in R} s(\tilde{c}, r) \\ 0, \quad \text{otherwise.} \end{cases} \tag{7}$$

Another disadvantage of this scoring function is that the sum of the similarities might be high even if only one targeted word is very related to the clue word, and the scores of the other targets are close to the scores of the bad words. Regarding this, replacing the sum (which is, in optimization for a certain n, equivalent with the arithmetic mean) with the harmonic mean of the relatedness scores might also lead to an improvement, especially if there are outliers among the vocabulary words with very high relatedness to a blue word. Thus, we introduce *Harmonic* scoring function as:

$$g_H(\tilde{c}, n) = \begin{cases} H(b|b \in I_n) - \lambda \cdot \max_{r \in R} s(\tilde{c}, r), \\ \quad \text{if } \min_{b \in I_n} s(\tilde{c}, b) > \max_{r \in R} s(\tilde{c}, r) \\ 0, \quad \text{otherwise,} \end{cases} \tag{8}$$

where H is the harmonic mean function:

$$H(x_1, x_2, \ldots, x_n) = \frac{n}{x_1^{-1} + x_2^{-1} + \cdots + x_n^{-1}}.$$

Finally, we also use a different version (*HarmonicDivide*) of the above, where the penalty on the bad words is performed as division instead of subtraction:

$$g_{HD}(\tilde{c}, n) = \frac{H(b|b \in I_n)}{\max(n \cdot \max_{r \in R} s(\tilde{c}, r), 1)}. \tag{9}$$

We combine these four scoring functions with all of the above relatedness measures, and evaluate the agents thus obtained in the next section.

5 Evaluation and Analysis

Following Koyyalagunta et al. (2021), we use $\lambda = 0.5$ for *Koyyalagunta* and *KoyyRestrict* scoring functions, but also for the *Harmonic* function. We pair all relatedness measures to all scoring functions, creating 16 agents in total, and generate clues for $n = 2$ and 3 targeted blue words using all of them. Differently from Koyyalagunta et al. (2021), we consider all of our vocabulary words as possible clue words. For each possible clue word, the best target words in the set I_n are the n closest words to the clue word, so scoring a possible clue is computationally inexpensive.

We randomly create 100 boards, with each containing 10 good and 10 bad words. For each board, we generate clues with the 32 configurations detailed above. This results in 1304 distinct clues in English, and 1399 in Hungarian. For evaluation, we create an online game, where human players get a board with one of the corresponding clues randomly, and have to choose the given number of words from the board which they think the clue refers to. The players do not know how the agents work, and to avoid that through the game they learn it at the end of the round they only see the color of their chosen words. We collected 443 rounds played in English, and 1365 in Hungarian. This way, we have 31.5 rounds on average to evaluate English configurations, and 64 rounds for Hungarian. For one board, players on average spent 39 seconds on guessing in English, while 37 seconds in Hungarian. We note that the players of the Hungarian game were most likely Hungarian native speakers, while the same cannot be said about the English game, therefore we consider the Hungarian data more reliable.

Evaluation	Relatedness	Koyy	KoyyR	HM	HM-Div	Koyy	KoyyR	HM	HM-Div
		2 targets				3 targets			
P@all	FastText	0.764	0.757	0.740	**0.829**	0.710	0.712	0.756	**0.759**
	NPMI	0.747	0.747	0.776	0.715	0.707	0.708	0.733	0.695
	NPMI^2	0.722	0.742	0.725	0.744	0.666	0.696	0.746	0.729
	Graph	0.795	0.795	0.827	0.715	0.727	0.735	**0.759**	0.695
P@targets	FastText	0.558	0.567	0.581	**0.625**	0.531	0.518	**0.585**	0.582
	NPMI	0.504	0.504	0.519	0.546	0.515	0.513	0.503	0.495
	NPMI^2	0.529	0.547	0.554	0.479	0.503	0.513	0.556	0.550
	Graph	0.533	0.533	0.574	0.546	0.541	0.542	0.511	0.495

Table 3: Rate of correct guesses made by human players in the Hungarian game. Numbers falling into the bootstrapped confidence interval of the best score are underlined in each category.

Evaluation	Relatedness	Koyy	KoyyR	HM	HM-Div	Koyy	KoyyR	HM	HM-Div
		2 targets				3 targets			
P@all	FastText	0.707	0.726	**0.783**	0.722	0.711	0.742	0.755	0.760
	NPMI	0.727	0.727	0.670	0.682	**0.764**	**0.764**	0.725	0.716
	NPMI^2	0.611	0.583	0.604	0.729	0.645	0.583	0.638	0.649
	Graph	0.714	0.714	0.679	0.682	0.750	0.750	0.723	0.716
P@targets	FastText	0.487	0.535	**0.581**	0.555	0.549	0.495	**0.577**	0.520
	NPMI	0.420	0.420	0.397	0.426	0.549	0.549	0.541	0.508
	NPMI^2	0.377	0.361	0.372	0.445	0.354	0.369	0.370	0.470
	Graph	0.392	0.392	0.384	0.426	0.552	0.552	0.533	0.508

Table 4: Rate of correct guesses made by human players in the English game. Numbers falling into the bootstrapped confidence interval of the best score are underlined in each category.

Similar to Koyyalagunta et al. (2021), we compute the precision of the agents as

$$\text{P@targets} = \frac{|I_n \cap U|}{n},$$

where I_n is the set of the targeted words, and U is the set of words chosen by the players. However, the scoring functions optimize clue words to stay away from red words, but not from non-targeted blue words, which might be almost as related to the clue as the targeted ones. If the user chooses such an untargeted word, the agent still performs well. So we define P@all,

$$\text{P@all} = \frac{|A \cap U|}{n},$$

where A is the set of all good (blue) words. In Table 3 and Table 4, we show the mean precision of the players' guesses on the clues of each agent. In each category (defined by language, evaluation method, and the number of targets), we construct a 0.95 level confidence interval for the best mean precision using bootstrap, and mark the numbers falling into this interval underlined.

Among the configurations, FastText similarity combined with the *Koyyalagunta* scoring function was evaluated previously by Koyyalagunta et al. (2021), where it was the best agent without any language-specific resource, i.e. using raw corpora only. The results show that this is outperformed by many of our new configurations.

On FastText relatedness, our *Harmonic* and *HarmonicDivide* scoring functions result in a substantial improvement. Most of the best performing configurations use FastText as similarity measure combined with these functions, although the advantage of these methods is less significant when the guesses are evaluated on all blue words instead of the targets of the agent. Also, the only agent that performs within the confidence interval of the best agent in their category is FastText combined with *HarmonicDivide*, therefore we consider it as our highest performing agent. The second best agents in this regard, falling short in one category only, are the *Graph* similarity combined with *Koyyalagunta* and *KoyyalaguntaRestrict* functions.

As we can see, different relatedness measures fit different scoring functions. As mentioned in 4.2, we think that the *Harmonic* functions are more beneficial where outliers with high relatedness can be found; more generally, the optimal clue scoring function depends on the distribution of the relatedness measures. The exact connection between them seems to be an exciting direction for future work.

Interestingly, the correlations of the relatedness measures to human-annotated relatedness data (seen in 4.1.5) are not predictive of their performance in Codenames, as in those experiments FastText had been outperformed by both NPMI and Graph relatedness. The results in the two languages are not perfectly in line either. For example, in English $NPMI^2$ and graph relatedness perform worse than the two other relatedness measures, while the same does not appear in Hungarian. We suspect that this is because $NPMI^2$ and graph relatedness capture more indirect connections, which are more problematic to see for non-native speakers.

6 Summary and Future Work

In this work, we separated the Codenames spymaster agent's task into two parts. To cooperate with humans, we first need to specify a relatedness matrix that sufficiently approximates the relationships as judged by humans, and then define a scoring function on top of this that ranks the possible clues according to how many good guesses a human player is expected to give.

Based on previous research on associations, we generated some of our relatedness matrices based on co-occurrences between words in a corpus. We evaluated these relatedness measures with human-annotated relatedness data. However, we found that these scores were not predictive of the performance of the Codenames agents based on these measures.

We also introduced innovations in terms of scoring functions, firstly by refining the scoring function of Koyyalagunta et al. (2021), and secondly by using the harmonic mean of the relatedness to the clue word. This improved the performance of the best agents substantially.

Our best agents overall were FastText cosine similarity combined with a function using harmonic mean, and path weights in a graph of co-occurrences, combined with functions using arithmetic mean of similarities. This raises the question about what relationship is there between relatedness and scoring functions.

In future work, we would like to collect data on human spymaster-player decisions and evaluate guesser agents on them, which will directly allow the optimization of the relatedness measure.

Although many NLP methods have already been used to generate distance matrices, others are worth trying. Examples include graph embedding of associations (Bel-Enguix, 2014) and GraphGlove (Ryabinin et al., 2020).

As each relatedness measure can be defined by a matrix, it is also possible to aggregate several matrices generated in different ways. For example, creating distance matrices based on co-occurrences, neural word representations, and knowledge graphs at the same time seems to be a promising new direction. The comparison of such different relatedness matrices could also provide important lessons in cognitive modeling and the interpretability of neural word representations.

Acknowledgements

We thank the testers of our game for the data needed for the evaluation, and the reviewers for their helpful suggestions contributing to the final version of the article.

Réka Cserháti was supported by the ÚNKP-21-1 – New National Excellence Program of the Ministry for Innovation and Technology from the source of the National Research, Development and Innovation Fund. This study was partially supported by the Ministry of Innovation and the National Research, Development and Innovation Office within the framework of the Artificial Intelligence National Laboratory Programme. Project no. TKP2021-NVA-09 has been implemented with the support provided by the Ministry of Innovation and Technology of Hungary from the National Research, Development and Innovation Fund, financed under the TKP2021-NVA funding scheme.

References

Eneko Agirre, Enrique Alfonseca, Keith Hall, Jana Kravalova, Marius Paşca, and Aitor Soroa. 2009. A study on similarity and relatedness using distributional and WordNet-based approaches. In *Proceedings of Human Language Technologies: The 2009 Annual Conference of the North American Chapter of the Association for Computational Linguistics*, pages 19–27, Boulder, Colorado. Association for Computational Linguistics.

Louis Victor Allis et al. 1994. *Searching for solutions in games and artificial intelligence*.

Mikel Artetxe, Gorka Labaka, Iñigo Lopez-Gazpio, and Eneko Agirre. 2018. Uncovering divergent linguistic information in word embeddings with lessons for intrinsic and extrinsic evaluation. In *Proceedings of the 22nd Conference on Computational Natural Language Learning*, pages 282–291, Brussels, Belgium. Association for Computational Linguistics.

Abhilasha Ashok Kumar, Ketika Garg, and Robert Hawkins. 2021. Contextual flexibility guides communication in a cooperative language game. In *Proceedings of the Annual Meeting of the Cognitive Science Society*, volume 43.

Gemma Bel-Enguix. 2014. Retrieving word associations with a simple neighborhood algorithm in a graph-based resource. In *Proceedings of the 4th Workshop on Cognitive Aspects of the Lexicon (CogALex)*, pages 60–63, Dublin, Ireland. Association for Computational Linguistics and Dublin City University.

Gemma Bel-Enguix, Helena Gómez-Adorno, Jorge Reyes-Magaña, and Gerardo Sierra. 2019. Wan2vec: Embeddings learned on word association norms. *Semantic Web*, 10(6):991–1006.

Gemma Bel Enguix, Reinhard Rapp, and Michael Zock. 2014. How well can a corpus-derived co-occurrence network simulate human associative behavior? In *Proceedings of the 5th Workshop on Cognitive Aspects of Computational Language Learning (CogACLL)*, pages 43–48, Gothenburg, Sweden. Association for Computational Linguistics.

Piotr Bojanowski, Edouard Grave, Armand Joulin, and Tomas Mikolov. 2017. Enriching word vectors with subword information. *Transactions of the Association for Computational Linguistics*, 5:135–146.

Gerlof Bouma. 2009. Normalized (pointwise) mutual information in collocation extraction.

Elia Bruni, Gemma Boleda, Marco Baroni, and Nam-Khanh Tran. 2012. Distributional semantics in technicolor. In *Proceedings of the 50th Annual Meeting of the Association for Computational Linguistics (Volume 1: Long Papers)*, pages 136–145, Jeju Island, Korea. Association for Computational Linguistics.

Simon De Deyne, Danielle J Navarro, Amy Perfors, Marc Brysbaert, and Gert Storms. 2019. The "small world of words" english word association norms for over 12,000 cue words. *Behavior research methods*, 51(3):987–1006.

Jacob Devlin, Ming-Wei Chang, Kenton Lee, and Kristina Toutanova. 2018. Bert: Pre-training of deep bidirectional transformers for language understanding. pages 4171–4186.

David Hope and Bill Keller. 2013. Uos: A graph-based system for graded word sense induction. In *Second Joint Conference on Lexical and Computational Semantics (* SEM), Volume 2: Proceedings of the Seventh International Workshop on Semantic Evaluation (SemEval 2013)*, pages 689–694.

Catalina Jaramillo, Megan Charity, Rodrigo Canaan, and Julian Togelius. 2020. Word autobots: Using transformers for word association in the game codenames. In *Proceedings of the AAAI Conference on Artificial Intelligence and Interactive Digital Entertainment*, volume 16, pages 231–237.

Andrew Kim, Maxim Ruzmaykin, Aaron Truong, and Adam Summerville. 2019. Cooperation and codenames: Understanding natural language processing via codenames. In *Proceedings of the AAAI Conference on Artificial Intelligence and Interactive Digital Entertainment*, volume 15, pages 160–166.

Divya Koyyalagunta, Anna Sun, Rachel Lea Draelos, and Cynthia Rudin. 2021. Playing codenames with language graphs and word embeddings. *Journal of Artificial Intelligence Research*, 71:319–346.

Abhilasha A. Kumar, Mark Steyvers, and David A. Balota. 2021. Semantic memory search and retrieval in a novel cooperative word game: A comparison of associative and distributional semantic models. *Cognitive Science*, 45(10):e13053.

David McNeill. 1966. A study of word association. *Journal of Verbal Learning and Verbal Behavior*, 5(6):548–557.

Tomas Mikolov, Ilya Sutskever, Kai Chen, Greg S Corrado, and Jeff Dean. 2013. Distributed representations of words and phrases and their compositionality. In *Advances in neural information processing systems*, pages 3111–3119.

George A. Miller. 1992. WordNet: A lexical database for English. In *Speech and Natural Language: Proceedings of a Workshop Held at Harriman, New York, February 23-26, 1992*.

Roberto Navigli and Simone Paolo Ponzetto. 2010a. BabelNet: Building a very large multilingual semantic network. In *Proceedings of the 48th Annual Meeting of the Association for Computational Linguistics*, pages 216–225, Uppsala, Sweden. Association for Computational Linguistics.

Roberto Navigli and Simone Paolo Ponzetto. 2010b. Babelnet: Building a very large multilingual semantic network. In *Proceedings of the 48th annual meeting of the association for computational linguistics*, pages 216–225.

Douglas L Nelson, Cathy L McEvoy, and Thomas A Schreiber. 2004. The university of south florida free association, rhyme, and word fragment norms. *Behavior Research Methods, Instruments, & Computers*, 36(3):402–407.

Dávid Márk Nemeskey. 2020. *Natural Language Processing Methods for Language Modeling*. Ph.D. thesis, Eötvös Loránd University.

David S Palermo and James J Jenkins. 1964. Word association norms: Grade school through college.

Maria Pelevina, Nikolay Arefiev, Chris Biemann, and Alexander Panchenko. 2016. Making sense of word embeddings. In *Proceedings of the 1st Workshop on Representation Learning for NLP*, pages 174–183, Berlin, Germany. Association for Computational Linguistics.

Jeffrey Pennington, Richard Socher, and Christopher Manning. 2014a. GloVe: Global vectors for word representation. In *Proceedings of the 2014 Conference on Empirical Methods in Natural Language Processing (EMNLP)*, pages 1532–1543, Doha, Qatar. Association for Computational Linguistics.

Jeffrey Pennington, Richard Socher, and Christopher D Manning. 2014b. Glove: Global vectors for word representation. In *Proceedings of the 2014 conference on empirical methods in natural language processing (EMNLP)*, pages 1532–1543.

Leo Postman and Geoffrey Keppel. 2014. *Norms of word association*. Academic Press.

Alec Radford, Jeffrey Wu, Rewon Child, David Luan, Dario Amodei, Ilya Sutskever, et al. 2019. Language models are unsupervised multitask learners. *OpenAI blog*, 1(8):9.

Max Ryabinin, Sergei Popov, Liudmila Prokhorenkova, and Elena Voita. 2020. Embedding Words in Non-Vector Space with Unsupervised Graph Learning. In *Proceedings of the 2020 Conference on Empirical Methods in Natural Language Processing (EMNLP)*, pages 7317–7331, Online. Association for Computational Linguistics.

Judy Hanwen Shen, Matthias Hofer, Bjarke Felbo, and Roger Levy. 2018. Comparing models of associative meaning: An empirical investigation of reference in simple language games. In *Proceedings of the 22nd Conference on Computational Natural Language Learning*, pages 292–301, Brussels, Belgium. Association for Computational Linguistics.

Robyn Speer and Catherine Havasi. 2012. Representing general relational knowledge in ConceptNet 5. In *Proceedings of the Eighth International Conference on Language Resources and Evaluation (LREC'12)*, pages 3679–3686, Istanbul, Turkey. European Language Resources Association (ELRA).

Donald P Spence and Kimberly C Owens. 1990. Lexical co-occurrence and association strength. *Journal of Psycholinguistic Research*, 19(5):317–330.

Julien Tissier, Christophe Gravier, and Amaury Habrard. 2017. Dict2vec: Learning word embeddings using lexical dictionaries. In *Proceedings of the 2017 Conference on Empirical Methods in Natural Language Processing*, pages 254–263.

Yang Xu and Charles Kemp. 2010. Inference and communication in the game of password. *Advances in neural information processing systems*, 23.

A Appendix: Example clues

Figure 1 is a board we used for evaluation, and Table 5 contains the clues generated by all of our agents for this board.

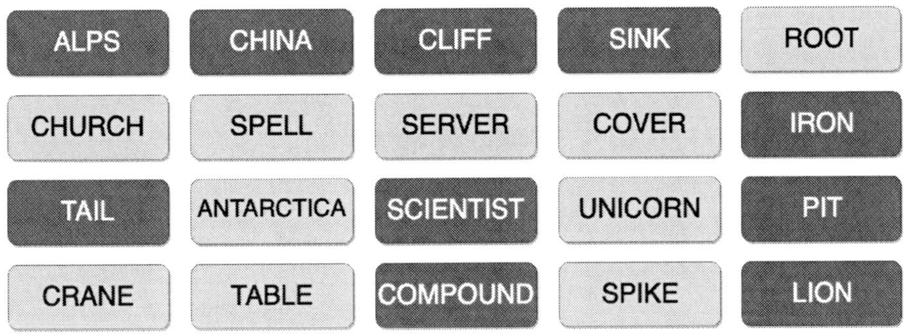

Figure 1: An example board used in evaluation

Relatedness	Scoring	Number	Clue word	Target words
FastText	Koyyalagunta	2	chapel	church, crane
FastText	Koyyalagunta	3	raven	unicorn, crane, spike
FastText	KoyyRestrict	2	chapel	church, crane
FastText	KoyyRestrict	3	shark	unicorn, crane, spike
FastText	Harmonic	2	menu	table, server
FastText	Harmonic	3	bean	root, crane, spike
FastText	HarmonicDivide	2	doll	unicorn, spike
FastText	HarmonicDivide	3	preview	cover, server, spike
NPMI	Koyyalagunta	2	directory	root, server
NPMI	Koyyalagunta	3	altar	church, table, server
NPMI	KoyyRestrict	2	directory	root, server
NPMI	KoyyRestrict	3	altar	church, table, server
NPMI	Harmonic	2	directory	root, server
NPMI	Harmonic	3	altar	church, table, server
NPMI	HarmonicDivide	2	directory	root, server
NPMI	HarmonicDivide	3	altar	church, table, server
$NPMI^2$	Koyyalagunta	2	user	server, root
$NPMI^2$	Koyyalagunta	3	voiced	crane, spike, unicorn
$NPMI^2$	KoyyRestrict	2	user	server, root
$NPMI^2$	KoyyRestrict	3	voiced	crane, spike, unicorn
$NPMI^2$	Harmonic	2	node	root, server
$NPMI^2$	Harmonic	3	voiced	crane, spike, unicorn
$NPMI^2$	HarmonicDivide	2	download	server, cover
$NPMI^2$	HarmonicDivide	3	itunes	server, cover, unicorn
Graph	Koyyalagunta	2	directory	root, server
Graph	Koyyalagunta	3	directory	root, server, table
Graph	KoyyRestrict	2	directory	root, server
Graph	KoyyRestrict	3	directory	root, server, table
Graph	Harmonic	2	directory	root, server
Graph	Harmonic	3	altar	church, table, server
Graph	HarmonicDivide	2	directory	root, server
Graph	HarmonicDivide	3	altar	church, table, server

Table 5: Clues generated for the board in Figure 1.

Estimating word co-occurrence probabilities from pretrained static embeddings using a log-bilinear model

Richard Futrell
Department of Language Science
University of California, Irvine
rfutrell@uci.edu

Abstract

I investigate how to use pretrained static word embeddings to deliver improved estimates of bilexical co-occurrence probabilities: conditional probabilities of one word given a single other word in a specific relationship. Such probabilities play important roles in psycholinguistics, corpus linguistics, and usage-based cognitive modeling of language more generally. I propose a log-bilinear model taking pretrained vector representations of the two words as input, enabling generalization based on the distributional information contained in both vectors. I show that this model outperforms baselines in estimating probabilities of adjectives given nouns that they attributively modify, and probabilities of nominal direct objects given their head verbs, given limited training data in Arabic, English, Korean, and Spanish.

1 Introduction

Word co-occurrence probabilities are a key ingredient in usage-based cognitive models of language. By word co-occurrence probabilities, I mean the probability of a word w given some other single word c, $p(w \mid c)$, where words w and c have some specific relationship, for example adjectives that attributively modify nouns or nouns serving as direct objects of verbs (Gries and Durrant, 2020).

These co-occurrence probabilities are psycholinguistically relevant because they feed into information-theoretic measures of 'thematic fit' and selectional restriction (Resnik, 1996; Lapata et al., 1999; Padó et al., 2007; Vecchi et al., 2017) which are relevant in predicting human online processing difficulty (e.g. McRae et al., 1998; Trueswell et al., 1994), and play a key role in language acquisition (Erickson and Thiessen, 2015). Most prominently, the widely-used pointwise mutual information (PMI) measure of association strength, $\text{PMI}(w, c) = \log \frac{p(w|c)}{p(w)}$ (Fano, 1961; Church and Hanks, 1990), relies on these conditional probabilities as an input. PMI makes appearances in models of grammar induction from text (Magerman and Marcus, 1990; Yuret, 1998; Clark and Fijalkow, 2020; Hoover et al., 2021), online sentence comprehension and production (Futrell et al., 2020b; Ranjan et al., 2022), and quantitative theories of word order variation (Futrell et al., 2020a; Sharma et al., 2020).

Word co-occurrence probabilities are hard to estimate accurately from text data because empirical counts of a particular pair of words in a particular relation are often sparse. This limitation makes it hard to evaluate cognitive theories that operate on co-occurrence probabilities. Although high-performance pretrained language models now exist (Radford et al., 2019; Devlin et al., 2019, etc.), the probabilities of interest often cannot be read off of these models directly, because w and c might be defined by relations that cannot be straightforwardly detected in terms of linear word order or templates. For example, suppose we are interested in the distribution of adjectives attributively modifying a noun in English. It would not do to ask a language model for the distribution of words immediately preceding a noun, because some of these words will not be attributive adjectives.

I propose to improve the estimation of word co-occurrence probabilities by leveraging pretrained static word embeddings to enhance generalization from potentially small training sets. My method enables generalization based on the semantic and syntactic information contained in word embeddings for both words w and c.

2 Model

Setting We are given a **vocabulary** of words V, a finite **target word set** $W \subseteq V$, a dataset of N pairs of words $\{\langle w_i, c_i \rangle\}_{i=1}^{N}$ where the **target word** w is an element of target word set W and the **context word** c is an element of the full vocabulary V, and a pretrained mapping from words to

Proceedings of the Workshop on Cognitive Modeling and Computational Linguistics, pages 54 - 60
May 26, 2022 ©2022 Association for Computational Linguistics

D-dimensional static embeddings $E : V \to \mathbb{R}^D$. Supposing the dataset consists of iid samples from some distribution $p(w, c) = p(c)p(w \mid c)$, our goal is to find a conditional distribution $q(w \mid c)$ with support W to approximate $p(w \mid c)$ in a way that leverages the static embeddings E.

Proposed model I propose a log-bilinear model (Mnih and Hinton, 2007, 2008) using word embeddings as input:[1]

$$q(w \mid c) = \frac{1}{Z(c)} \exp\left\{\phi(\mathbf{w})^\top \mathbf{A} \psi(\mathbf{c})\right\} \quad (1)$$

$$Z(c) = \sum_{w \in W} \exp\left\{\phi(\mathbf{w})^\top \mathbf{A} \psi(\mathbf{c})\right\}, \quad (2)$$

where $\mathbf{w} = E(w)$ and $\mathbf{c} = E(c)$ are the static embeddings of target word w and context word c respectively, the **target word encoder** $\phi(\cdot) : \mathbb{R}^D \to \mathbb{R}^K$ and **context word encoder** $\psi(\cdot) : \mathbb{R}^D \to \mathbb{R}^L$ are functions which may be parameterized as feed-forward neural networks with parameters denoted ϕ and ψ respectively, and $\mathbf{A}$ is a $K \times L$ interaction matrix. The model parameters ψ, ψ, and $\mathbf{A}$ are trained to minimize the cross-entropy loss

$$J(\phi, \psi, \mathbf{A}) = -\sum_{n=1}^{N} \log q(w_n \mid c_n). \quad (3)$$

Modeling decisions A modeler applying this approach needs to make a number of decisions, including the choice of static word embeddings and the structure of the word encoders $\phi(\cdot)$ and $\psi(\cdot)$. It is also possible to set $\psi = \phi$, using the same function to encode both the target word and the context word; this setup can reduce the number of parameters at the cost of less flexibility in fitting the training data.

Another major modeling decision involves the target word vocabulary W, which determines the support of $q(w \mid c)$ and is summed over during the calculation of the partition function (Eq. 2). In some cases, the modeler may not have access to a finite set W of possible target words. As long as the full vocabulary V is finite, it is possible to set $W = V$ and learn a probability distribution with support on all words in V.

Setting $W = V$ has the advantage that it allows the modeler not to commit to any particular target word set, thus avoiding the risk of prematurely excluding legitimate target words. It has the disadvantages that (1) calculation of the partition function (Eq. 2) is slower and/or more memory intensive, and (2) the learning problem is more difficult because probability mass is initially spread over the set V as opposed to a potentially much smaller set W.

Implementation In all experiments reported below, stochastic gradient descent is performed using the Adam algorithm with default initial learning rate (Kingma and Ba, 2015). All experiments are implemented in PyTorch with use of `opt_einsum` to compute the partition function (Smith and Gray, 2018; Paszke et al., 2019).

To handle out-of-vocabulary items, I include an unknown-word symbol UNK in the target word set W and full vocabulary V. If a target word w in a dataset is not present in the target word set W, or a context word c is not present in the full vocabulary V, then that word is mapped to UNK. In the embedding map, UNK is assigned to a normalized random vector drawn from a Gaussian distribution.

3 Related work

Distributional similarity information has been used to improve modeling of word co-occurrence probabilities in previous work. Dagan et al. (1994, 1999) defined a kernel-based interpolated language model where probability mass is explicitly spread over similar words, with variant models along these lines found in Wang et al. (2005) and Yarlett (2008). These models leverage similarity information about target words but not context words. In contrast, Bíró et al. (2007) proposed a method which uses similarity information about the context word but not the target word. Toutanova et al. (2004) developed a method that can exploit similarity information about both target and context, using a Markov Chain algorithm incorporating distributional and WordNet similarities. None of this previous work derived word similarity information from pretrained embeddings, because such embeddings did not exist at the time.

The log-bilinear model for conditional word probabilities was introduced in a language modeling context by Mnih and Hinton (2007, 2008). Mikolov et al. (2013a) influentially proposed to use the vector representations output by the word encoder in such a model as general word embeddings. The current work aims to return log-bilinear models to their language modeling roots, evaluating the capabilities of these models to estimate co-occurrence

[1] I have suppressed bias terms from the notation.

probabilities using pretrained embeddings as input, with a focus on word distributions where training data is limited. Here the target word vocabulary is typically small enough that the partition function (Eq. 2) can be computed directly on modern hardware, so that approximations such as noise-contrastive estimation (Mikolov et al., 2013b) are not necessary.

Recently Nikkarinen et al. (2021) introduced a neural-Bayesian nonparametric estimator for probability distributions on single words. Their setting has an unknown and generally infinite vocabulary V, and their model generalizes using a character-level LSTM. In contrast, the current model assumes a pre-existing known vocabulary V with embeddings, and generalizes based on those embeddings. A hybrid model may be possible in future work.

A related literature in corpus linguistics and NLP has explored the nature of restricted binary word co-occurrences, called collocations (for recent examples, see Savary et al., 2017; Kutuzov et al., 2017; Garcia et al., 2021; Espinosa Anke et al., 2021). This work focuses narrowly on the estimation of bilexical conditional probabilities, which are often inputs to models for collocation detection.

4 Experiments

I study the ability of the embedding-based log-bilinear model to estimate conditional distributions for (1) adjectives attributively modifying nouns and (2) nominal direct objects modifying verbs, in Arabic, English, Korean, and Spanish. I compare the model against baselines:

- Additive smoothing with $\alpha = 1$:

$$p_{\text{add}}(w \mid c; \alpha) \propto \text{count}(c, w) + \alpha,$$

  where $\text{count}(c, w)$ is the frequency of the pair of words c and w in the training data.

- An interpolated smoothed estimator:

$$p_{\text{interp}}(w \mid c) = p_{\text{add}}(w \mid c; \alpha) + \lambda p_{\text{MLE}}(w),$$

  where p_{MLE} is a maximum likelihood estimate, $\lambda = \frac{1}{4}$, and $\alpha = 1$.

- A softmax distribution on target words as a function of the context word embedding $\mathbf{c}$ (as proposed by Bíró et al., 2007):

$$p_{\text{softmax}}(w \mid c) \propto \exp\left\{\theta_w^\top \psi(\mathbf{c})\right\},$$

  where θ_w is an optimized weight vector for the target word w. This baseline uses the context word embedding $\mathbf{c}$ but not the target word embedding $\mathbf{w}$. It is equivalent to having the target word encoder return a one-hot vector representation of target word w.

- Models without word encoders, achieved by setting $\phi(\cdot)$ and $\psi(\cdot)$ to identity functions. Such models decode target words from the word embeddings directly.

All baselines are subject to the same vocabulary restrictions and out-of-vocabulary policy as the full log-bilinear models. As a standard test metric, I report the average negative log likelihood (NLL) of held-out data. I report NLLs for the full test set, as well as the challenging subset of the test set consisting of word pairs where the context word was never seen during training.

Below, I describe the experimental setting for the two tasks, and then I describe the results.

4.1 Distribution of attributive adjectives given nouns

I examine the distribution of attributive adjectives given the nouns that they modify, for example adjectives like *red* modifying nouns like *ball* in phrases like *the red ball.*

Data I use Universal Dependencies (UD) 2.8[2] (Nivre et al., 2020) and the automatically-parsed Wikipedia datasets released as part of the CoNLL 2017 Shared Task (Zeman et al., 2017) as a source of attributive adjective–noun pairs. I extract all pairs of words linked by a dependency of type *amod* where the head has universal part-of-speech (UPOS) `NOUN` and the dependent has UPOS `ADJ`. I represent the pair using the downcased wordforms of the adjective and noun.

For each language, I use the fastText aligned word vectors (Bojanowski et al., 2017; Joulin et al., 2018),[3] limiting the vocabulary set V to the top 200,000 vectors by frequency. For the target word vocabulary W, I take the 10,000 most frequent wordforms among all attributive adjectives extracted from the entire CoNLL Wikipedia dataset.

As training sets, I use 99,000 adjective–noun pairs drawn randomly from the Wikipedia datasets for each language, so training set size is fixed

[2] http://hdl.handle.net/11234/1-3687

[3] https://fasttext.cc/docs/en/aligned-vectors.html

	Attributive adjectives given nouns						Direct objects given verbs					
			Softmax		Log-Bilinear				Softmax		Log-Bilinear	
Data	Add.	Interp.	No Enc.	Enc.	No Enc.	Enc.	Add.	Interp.	No Enc.	Enc.	No Enc.	Enc.
Arabic	8.50	7.05	8.31	8.04	**5.79**	5.89	9.78	9.78	9.17	9.00	8.63	**8.47**
Unseen c	9.15	9.60	8.31	8.52	**6.93**	6.98	9.71	9.84	9.03	8.86	9.09	**8.76**
English	8.75	7.17	7.15	7.16	**6.40**	6.41	9.64	8.99	8.64	8.58	8.16	**8.04**
Unseen c	9.01	8.40	7.21	7.22	6.99	**6.96**	9.89	9.96	8.62	8.56	8.39	**8.35**
Spanish	8.70	7.49	8.13	8.10	**6.27**	**6.27**	9.70	9.10	8.64	8.52	7.96	**7.84**
Unseen c	9.17	9.50	8.15	8.21	7.16	**7.09**	9.80	9.62	8.48	8.48	8.35	**8.18**
Korean	7.96	5.39	5.51	5.61	**4.81**	4.82	9.71	9.76	9.20	9.18	8.34	**7.99**
Unseen c	7.16	5.92	5.45	5.48	5.44	**5.40**	9.67	9.91	9.16	9.14	9.58	**8.76**

Table 1: Average NLLs of adjectives given nouns and direct objects given verbs in UD corpora for models and baselines. 'Add.' is the additive smoothing baseline. 'Enc.' and 'No Enc.' refer to models with and without word encoders, respectively. *Unseen c* indicates performance on pairs where the context (the head noun for adjectives given nouns, and the head verb for direct objects given verbs) was never observed at train time.

across languages. I use an additional 1,000 pairs from the Wikipedia datasets as development sets for hyperparameter tuning and early stopping, and for test sets I extract all pairs from the relevant UD corpora.[4] Pairs where the target word w is not in the target word vocabulary W are removed from the development and test sets.

Training and hyperparameters Each model is trained for the number of iterations that gives minimum loss on the Wikipedia dev set. The word encoders are feed-forward neural networks with one hidden layer of 300 units and an output layer of 300 units, with ReLU activation. In training, I use batch size 32; I also experimented with batch size 512 but this resulted in rapid overfitting.

4.2 Distribution of nominal direct objects given verbs

I examine the distribution of nominal direct objects given verbs; for example, from a sentence such as *I kicked the red ball*, one would be interested in the probability of the direct object *ball* given its head noun *kicked*. All procedures here are the same as for the distribution of attributive adjectives given nouns except as described below.

Data I extracted direct objects as all pairs of words linked in a dependency of type *obj* where the head has UPOS `VERB` and the dependent has UPOS `NOUN`. Because nouns are more open-class than adjectives, I used a target word vocabulary of size 20,000.

[4]For English, I concatenate EWT and GUM. For Arabic, I concatenate NYUAD and PADT. For Spanish, I concatenate AnCora and GSD. For Korean, I concatenate Kaist and GSD.

4.3 Results

Results are shown in Table 1. The log-bilinear models outperform all others. In several cases (see for example Spanish and Korean adjectives), only the log-bilinear model is capable of outperforming the interpolated baseline.

When predicting adjectives from nouns, the log-bilinear models without word encoders sometimes outperform those with word encoders. These is perhaps not surprising: the input word embeddings were trained to be used in a log-bilinear skip-gram probability model, so they already form useful representations for word prediction.

Overall performance on predicting objects from verbs is worse than when predicting adjectives from nouns. This reflects the harder nature of the task and the larger support size required to model nouns rather than adjectives.

4.4 Additional experiments

I also trained full log-bilinear models with a number of other settings. I found that tying the word and context encoders does not substantially change performance, but that fine-tuning the input word embeddings leads to severe overfitting. Removing the target word vocabulary restriction (setting $W = V$) also substantially negatively impacts performance: for adjectives, the best test set NLL is 6.57 for Arabic, 6.75 for English, 6.95 for Spanish, and 4.89 for Korean.

5 Conclusion

I evaluated log-bilinear modeling as means to leverage pretrained word embeddings for the estimation of co-occurrence probabilities in different syntactic configurations. I found that this method delivers accurate probability estimates across languages, outperforming baselines. This method will be useful in all applications requiring such probabilities. Code implementing the method can be found at `https://github.com/langprocgroup/vectorprob`.

Acknowledgments

This work was supported by NSF Grant #1947307 and an NVIDIA GPU Grant to the author. I thank Charles Torres, Gregory Scontras, and William Dyer for helpful discussion.

References

István Bíró, Zoltán Szamonek, and Csaba Szepesvári. 2007. Sequence prediction exploiting similarity information. In *Proceedings of the 20th International Joint Conference on Artifical Intelligence*, pages 1576–1581.

Piotr Bojanowski, Edouard Grave, Armand Joulin, and Tomas Mikolov. 2017. Enriching word vectors with subword information. *Transactions of the Association for Computational Linguistics*, 5:135–146.

Kenneth Ward Church and Patrick Hanks. 1990. Word association norms, mutual information, and lexicography. *Computational Linguistics*, 16(1):22–29.

Alexander Clark and Nathanaël Fijalkow. 2020. Consistent Unsupervised Estimators for Anchored PCFGs. *Transactions of the Association for Computational Linguistics*, 8:409–422.

Ido Dagan, Lillian Lee, and Fernando CN Pereira. 1999. Similarity-based models of word cooccurrence probabilities. *Machine Learning*, 34(1):43–69.

Ido Dagan, Fernando CN Pereira, and Lillian Lee. 1994. Similarity-based estimation of word cooccurrence probabilities. In *32nd Annual Meeting of the Association for Computational Linguistics*, Las Cruces, New Mexico, USA. Association for Computational Linguistics.

Jacob Devlin, Ming-Wei Chang, Kenton Lee, and Kristina Toutanova. 2019. BERT: Pre-training of deep bidirectional transformers for language understanding. In *Proceedings of the 2019 Conference of the North American Chapter of the Association for Computational Linguistics: Human Language Technologies, Volume 1 (Long and Short Papers)*, pages 4171–4186, Minneapolis, Minnesota. Association for Computational Linguistics.

Lucy C Erickson and Erik D Thiessen. 2015. Statistical learning of language: Theory, validity, and predictions of a statistical learning account of language acquisition. *Developmental Review*, 37:66–108.

Luis Espinosa Anke, Joan Codina-Filba, and Leo Wanner. 2021. Evaluating language models for the retrieval and categorization of lexical collocations. In *Proceedings of the 16th Conference of the European Chapter of the Association for Computational Linguistics: Main Volume*, pages 1406–1417, Online. Association for Computational Linguistics.

Robert M Fano. 1961. *Transmission of Information: A Statistical Theory of Communication*. MIT Press, Cambridge, MA.

Richard Futrell, William Dyer, and Greg Scontras. 2020a. What determines the order of adjectives in English? Comparing efficiency-based theories using dependency treebanks. In *Proceedings of the 58th Annual Meeting of the Association for Computational Linguistics*, pages 2003–2012, Online. Association for Computational Linguistics.

Richard Futrell, Edward Gibson, and Roger P Levy. 2020b. Lossy-context surprisal: An information-theoretic model of memory effects in sentence processing. *Cognitive Science*, 44(3):e12814.

Marcos Garcia, Tiago Kramer Vieira, Carolina Scarton, Marco Idiart, and Aline Villavicencio. 2021. Assessing the representations of idiomaticity in vector models with a noun compound dataset labeled at type and token levels. In *Proceedings of the 59th Annual Meeting of the Association for Computational Linguistics and the 11th International Joint Conference on Natural Language Processing (Volume 1: Long Papers)*, pages 2730–2741, Online. Association for Computational Linguistics.

Stefan Th Gries and Philip Durrant. 2020. Analyzing co-occurrence data. In *A Practical Handbook of Corpus Linguistics*, pages 141–159. Springer.

Jacob Louis Hoover, Wenyu Du, Alessandro Sordoni, and Timothy J. O'Donnell. 2021. Linguistic dependencies and statistical dependence. In *Proceedings of the 2021 Conference on Empirical Methods in Natural Language Processing*, pages 2941–2963, Online and Punta Cana, Dominican Republic. Association for Computational Linguistics.

Armand Joulin, Piotr Bojanowski, Tomas Mikolov, Hervé Jégou, and Edouard Grave. 2018. Loss in translation: Learning bilingual word mapping with a retrieval criterion. In *Proceedings of the 2018 Conference on Empirical Methods in Natural Language Processing*, pages 2979–2984, Brussels, Belgium. Association for Computational Linguistics.

Diederik P Kingma and Jimmy Ba. 2015. Adam: A method for stochastic optimization. In *3rd International Conference on Learning Representations, ICLR 2015, San Diego, CA, USA, May 7-9, 2015, Conference Track Proceedings*.

Andrey Kutuzov, Elizaveta Kuzmenko, and Lidia Pivovarova. 2017. Clustering of Russian adjective-noun constructions using word embeddings. In *Proceedings of the 6th Workshop on Balto-Slavic Natural Language Processing*, pages 3–13, Valencia, Spain. Association for Computational Linguistics.

Maria Lapata, Scott McDonald, and Frank Keller. 1999. Determinants of adjective-noun plausibility. In *Ninth Conference of the European Chapter of the Association for Computational Linguistics*, pages 30–36, Bergen, Norway. Association for Computational Linguistics.

David M Magerman and Mitchell P Marcus. 1990. Parsing a natural language using mutual information statistics. In *AAAI*, volume 90, pages 984–989.

Ken McRae, Michael J Spivey-Knowlton, and Michael K Tanenhaus. 1998. Modeling the influence of thematic fit (and other constraints) in on-line sentence comprehension. *Journal of Memory and Language*, 38(3):283–312.

Tomás Mikolov, Kai Chen, Greg Corrado, and Jeffrey Dean. 2013a. Efficient estimation of word representations in vector space. In *1st International Conference on Learning Representations, ICLR 2013, Scottsdale, Arizona, USA, May 2-4, 2013, Workshop Track Proceedings*.

Tomás Mikolov, Ilya Sutskever, Kai Chen, Greg S Corrado, and Jeff Dean. 2013b. Distributed representations of words and phrases and their compositionality. In *Advances in Neural Information Processing Systems*, pages 3111–3119.

Andriy Mnih and Geoffrey E Hinton. 2007. Three new graphical models for statistical language modelling. In *ICML '07: Proceedings of the 24th International Conference on Machine Learning*, pages 641–648.

Andriy Mnih and Geoffrey E Hinton. 2008. A scalable hierarchical distributed language model. *Advances in Neural Information Processing Systems*, 21:1081–1088.

Irene Nikkarinen, Tiago Pimentel, Damián Blasi, and Ryan Cotterell. 2021. Modeling the unigram distribution. In *Findings of the Association for Computational Linguistics: ACL-IJCNLP 2021*, pages 3721–3729, Online. Association for Computational Linguistics.

Joakim Nivre, Marie-Catherine de Marneffe, Filip Ginter, Jan Hajič, Christopher D. Manning, Sampo Pyysalo, Sebastian Schuster, Francis Tyers, and Daniel Zeman. 2020. Universal Dependencies v2: An evergrowing multilingual treebank collection. In *Proceedings of the 12th Language Resources and Evaluation Conference*, pages 4034–4043, Marseille, France. European Language Resources Association.

Sebastian Padó, Ulrike Padó, and Katrin Erk. 2007. Flexible, corpus-based modelling of human plausibility judgements. In *Proceedings of the 2007 Joint Conference on Empirical Methods in Natural Language Processing and Computational Natural Language Learning (EMNLP-CoNLL)*, pages 400–409, Prague, Czech Republic. Association for Computational Linguistics.

Adam Paszke, Sam Gross, Francisco Massa, Adam Lerer, James Bradbury, Gregory Chanan, Trevor Killeen, Zeming Lin, Natalia Gimelshein, Luca Antiga, Alban Desmaison, Andreas Kopf, Edward Yang, Zachary DeVito, Martin Raison, Alykhan Tejani, Sasank Chilamkurthy, Benoit Steiner, Lu Fang, Junjie Bai, and Soumith Chintala. 2019. Pytorch: An imperative style, high-performance deep learning library. In H. Wallach, H. Larochelle, A. Beygelzimer, F. d'Alché-Buc, E. Fox, and R. Garnett, editors, *Advances in Neural Information Processing Systems 32*, pages 8024–8035. Curran Associates, Inc.

Alec Radford, Jeffrey Wu, Rewon Child, David Luan, Dario Amodei, Ilya Sutskever, et al. 2019. Language models are unsupervised multitask learners. *OpenAI blog*, 1(8):9.

Sidharth Ranjan, Rajakrishnan Rajkumar, and Sumeet Agarwal. 2022. Locality and expectation effects in Hindi preverbal constituent ordering. *Cognition*, 223:104959.

Philip Resnik. 1996. Selectional constraints: An information-theoretic model and its computational realization. *Cognition*, 61(1-2):127–159.

Agata Savary, Carlos Ramisch, Silvio Cordeiro, Federico Sangati, Veronika Vincze, Behrang QasemiZadeh, Marie Candito, Fabienne Cap, Voula Giouli, Ivelina Stoyanova, and Antoine Doucet. 2017. The PARSEME shared task on automatic identification of verbal multiword expressions. In *Proceedings of the 13th Workshop on Multiword Expressions (MWE 2017)*, pages 31–47, Valencia, Spain. Association for Computational Linguistics.

Kartik Sharma, Richard Futrell, and Samar Husain. 2020. What determines the order of verbal dependents in Hindi? Effects of efficiency in comprehension and production. In *Proceedings of the Workshop on Cognitive Modeling and Computational Linguistics*, pages 1–10, Online. Association for Computational Linguistics.

Daniel GA Smith and Johnnie Gray. 2018. Opt_einsum – A Python package for optimizing contraction order for einsum-like expressions. *Journal of Open Source Software*, 3(26):753.

Kristina Toutanova, Christopher D Manning, and Andrew Y Ng. 2004. Learning random walk models for inducing word dependency distributions. In *Proceedings of the Twenty-First International Conference on Machine Learning*, page 103.

John C Trueswell, Michael K Tanenhaus, and Susan M Garnsey. 1994. Semantic influences on parsing: Use of thematic role information in syntactic ambiguity resolution. *Journal of Memory and Language*, 33(3):285–318.

Eva M Vecchi, Marco Marelli, Roberto Zamparelli, and Marco Baroni. 2017. Spicy adjectives and nominal donkeys: Capturing semantic deviance using compositionality in distributional spaces. *Cognitive Science*, 41(1):102–136.

Qin Iris Wang, Dale Schuurmans, and Dekang Lin. 2005. Strictly lexical dependency parsing. In *Proceedings of the Ninth International Workshop on Parsing Technology*, pages 152–159, Vancouver, British Columbia. Association for Computational Linguistics.

Daniel G Yarlett. 2008. *Similarity-based generalization in language*. Ph.D. thesis, Stanford University.

Deniz Yuret. 1998. *Discovery of linguistic relations using lexical attraction*. Ph.D. thesis, Massachusetts Institute of Technology, Cambridge, MA.

Daniel Zeman, Martin Popel, Milan Straka, Jan Hajič, Joakim Nivre, Filip Ginter, Juhani Luotolahti, Sampo Pyysalo, Slav Petrov, Martin Potthast, Francis Tyers, Elena Badmaeva, Memduh Gokirmak, Anna Nedoluzhko, Silvie Cinková, Jan Hajič jr., Jaroslava Hlaváčová, Václava Kettnerová, Zdeňka Urešová, Jenna Kanerva, Stina Ojala, Anna Missilä, Christopher D. Manning, Sebastian Schuster, Siva Reddy, Dima Taji, Nizar Habash, Herman Leung, Marie-Catherine de Marneffe, Manuela Sanguinetti, Maria Simi, Hiroshi Kanayama, Valeria de Paiva, Kira Droganova, Héctor Martínez Alonso, Çağrı Çöltekin, Umut Sulubacak, Hans Uszkoreit, Vivien Macketanz, Aljoscha Burchardt, Kim Harris, Katrin Marheinecke, Georg Rehm, Tolga Kayadelen, Mohammed Attia, Ali Elkahky, Zhuoran Yu, Emily Pitler, Saran Lertpradit, Michael Mandl, Jesse Kirchner, Hector Fernandez Alcalde, Jana Strnadová, Esha Banerjee, Ruli Manurung, Antonio Stella, Atsuko Shimada, Sookyoung Kwak, Gustavo Mendonça, Tatiana Lando, Rattima Nitisaroj, and Josie Li. 2017. CoNLL 2017 shared task: Multilingual parsing from raw text to Universal Dependencies. In *Proceedings of the CoNLL 2017 Shared Task: Multilingual Parsing from Raw Text to Universal Dependencies*, pages 1–19, Vancouver, Canada. Association for Computational Linguistics.

Modeling the Relationship between Input Distributions and Learning Trajectories with the Tolerance Principle

Jordan Kodner
Stony Brook University
Department of Linguistics
Institute for Advanced Computational Science
Stony Brook, NY, USA
Jordan.Kodner@stonybrook.edu

Abstract

Child language learners develop with remarkable uniformity, both in their learning trajectories and ultimate outcomes, despite major differences in their learning environments. In this paper, we explore the role that the frequencies and distributions of irregular lexical items in the input plays in driving learning trajectories. I conclude that while the Tolerance Principle, a type-based model of productivity learning, accounts for *inter-learner uniformity*, it also interacts with input distributions to drive *cross-pattern variation* in learning trajectories.

1 Introduction

One of the most striking characteristics of child language acquisition is its uniformity (Labov, 1972). Children in the same speech community acquire the same grammars despite the lexical variation in each child's individual input: a recent quantitative study of child-directed speech (CDS) finds Jaccard similarities of only 0.25-0.37 between individual portions of the Providence Corpus (Richter, 2021), not much higher than the lexical similarity between CDS and adult genres (Kodner, 2019). Thus, to explain uniformity of outcomes, grammar learning must not depend primarily on lexical identity but on more general patterns in the learner's input.

Learners not only acquire the essentially same grammars but acquire them following similar trajectories. For example, English learners consistently acquire the verbal *-s* and *-ing* before the past *-ed* (Brown, 1973), the last of which shows a *u*-shaped developmental regression (Ervin and Miller, 1963; Pinker and Prince, 1988). Individuals may show relative delays correlating to estimated working vocabulary size (Fenson et al., 1994, ch. 5-6), but variability is otherwise limited. However, while individuals learning the same pattern show uniformity, expected learning paths vary across patterns. Among English learners, for example, *-ing* does not show *u-shaped* learning, unlike *-ed*. Children

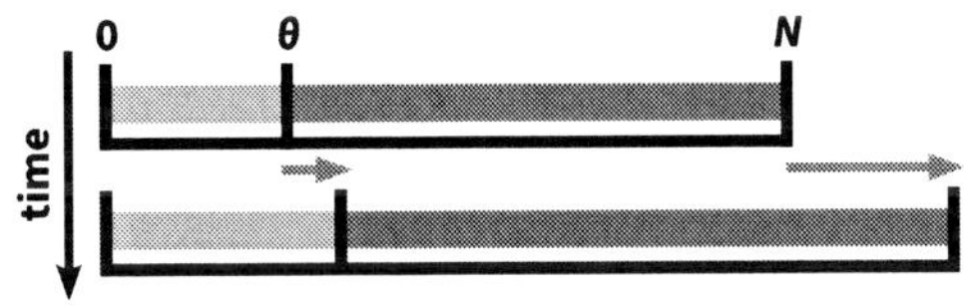

Figure 1: Visualizing the Tolerance Principle on a number line. e falls in the range $[0, N]$. If it lies below θ (gold), then the learner should acquire the pattern and memorize the exceptions. If e lies above θ (blue), the learner should resort to memorization instead. The number line extends as the learner's vocabulary grows.

learning Spanish verb stem alternations also show *u*-shaped learning, but they begin to over-regularize a year earlier than English past tense learners (Clahsen et al., 2002). One potential reason for this, differences in patterns' distributions in the input, is investigated here.

This paper introduces a quantitative means of assessing the role that the distribution of linguistic patterns in learner input plays in shaping learning trajectories and variation even prior to the grammar and individual cognitive factors. Adopting the Tolerance Principle (TP; Yang, 2016) as a type-based model of productivity learning, we find that the type-frequency and (indirectly) token frequency of exceptions to linguistic patterns have a dramatic effect on the expected learning trajectories across patterns while also quantifying expected uniformity across individuals within a given pattern.

2 The Learning Model

The *Tolerance Principle* (TP; Yang, 2016) is a cognitively motivated type-based learning model which casts generalization in terms of productivity in the face of exceptions. The model has gained support in recent years through its successful application to problems in syntax and semantics (e.g., Yang, 2016; Irani, 2019; Lee and Kodner, 2020), morphology (e.g., Yang, 2016; Kodner, 2020; Björnsdóttir, 2021; Belth et al., 2021),

Proceedings of the Workshop on Cognitive Modeling and Computational Linguistics, pages 61 - 67
May 26, 2022 ©2022 Association for Computational Linguistics

and phonology (e.g., Yang, 2016; Sneller et al., 2019; Kodner and Richter, 2020; Richter, 2021). It has increasingly received backing from a range of psycholinguistic experiments (Schuler, 2017; Koulaguina and Shi, 2019; Emond and Shi, 2020). It is adopted here because it makes categorical and auditable predictions about productivity and thus provides a clear means for investigating and the relationship between distributions in the input and the dynamics of learning.

The TP serves as a decision procedure for the learner. Once the learner hypothesizes a generalization in the grammar, it establishes the threshold θ_N at which it becomes more economical in terms of lexical access time to accept the hypothesis and exceptions rather than to just memorize items individually. (1) formalizes the TP. The *tolerance threshold* θ_N is defined as the number of known types that a generalization should apply to divided by its natural logarithm.[1]

(1) **Tolerance Principle** (Yang, 2016, p. 8): If R is a productive rule applicable to N candidates, then the following relation holds between N and e, the number of exceptions that could but do not follow R:

$$e \leq \theta_N \text{ where } \theta_N := \frac{N}{\ln N}$$

The derivation of the TP acknowledges that items in the input follow long-tailed Zipfian frequency distributions (Zipf, 1949) in which few items are well-attested and others are rarely attested in the input. Zipfian and other long-tailed distributions are quite common throughout language and are very prominent in lexical and inflectional frequencies (e.g., Miller, 1957; Jelinek, 1997; Baroni, 2005; Chan, 2008; Yang, 2013; Lignos and Yang, 2018)

Figure 1 provides a visualization of the Tolerance Principle over individual development. Crucially, N depends on a learner's current working vocabulary and is not a comment on the language's vocabulary in general. An individual learner's N and e increase as they learn more vocabulary, and a pattern may fall in and out of productivity.

3 Input Distributions driving Trajectories

This section uses the Tolerance Principle to calculate likely learning trajectories and variability in learning trajectories given distributions of regular and irregular forms in the input, and it discusses the impact that input distributions have on learning paths. It presents two illustrative examples and a case study from English past tense learning. For clarity, N_{tgt} and e_{tgt} are used here to represent the expected mature learner state, since N and e properly represent speaker-internal quantities and are not a description of the target language.

3.1 Calculating Trajectories with the TP

In the first illustrative example, $N_{tgt} = 82$ and $e_{tgt} = 32$. This pattern should not be productive for a mature speaker ($e_{tgt} > \theta_{Ntgt} = 18.6$), but learners may pass through a period of overgeneralization if their N and e support it at some point during development. To help with conceptualizing these developments, I introduce a visualization called a Tolerance Principle state space for this system in Figure 2. The x-axis indicates the number of regular forms that an individual has learned so far ($N - e$), and the y-axis indicates the number of irregular forms learned so far. Color indicates whether or not a learner at $(N - e, e)$ should learn a productive generalization. These are the two "zones" in the state space. The bottom left corner, $N = 0$, indicates the initial state for all learners, and the top right corner ($N = N_{tgt}$), indicates the mature state. In this example, the final state is in the non-productive zone.[2]

As learners mature, they "move" through the state space along some path from the bottom left to top right. The paths that individuals take are a function of the order in which they personally acquired regular and irregular items. Learners may pass in and out of the productive zone as they develop. In this example, a learner who passes temporarily through the productive zone may produce over-generalization errors, one source of u-shaped learning.

Not all paths through the state space are equally likely. It would be strange, for example, if a learner acquired all the irregular items before any of the regular items, or vice-versa. One could ask, for a learner who knows a given N, what is the likelihood that e of those are irregulars? Or equivalently in the state space, what is the likelihood that a learner should pass through a given point $(N - e, e)$? This can be modeled probabilistically

[1]See Yang (2016, pp. 10, 144) for the full mathematical derivation. θ_N approximates the Nth harmonic number

[2]The TP breaks down for very small N. This area is placed in the non-productive zone by convention.

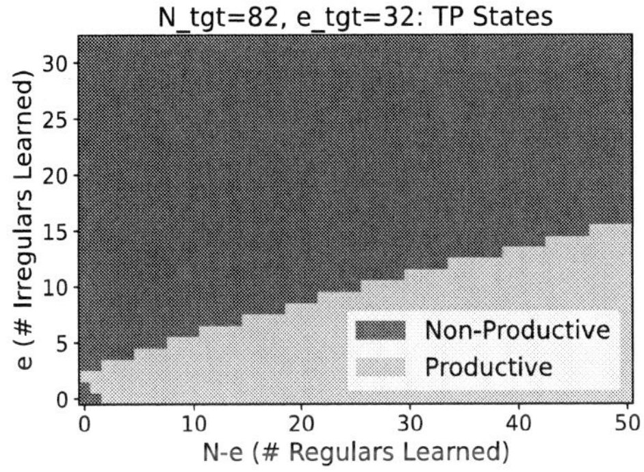

Figure 2: Tolerance Principle state space indicating productivity for every $(N - e, e)$ pair that a learner may pass through during vocabulary learning. N_{tgt}=82, e_{tgt}=32.

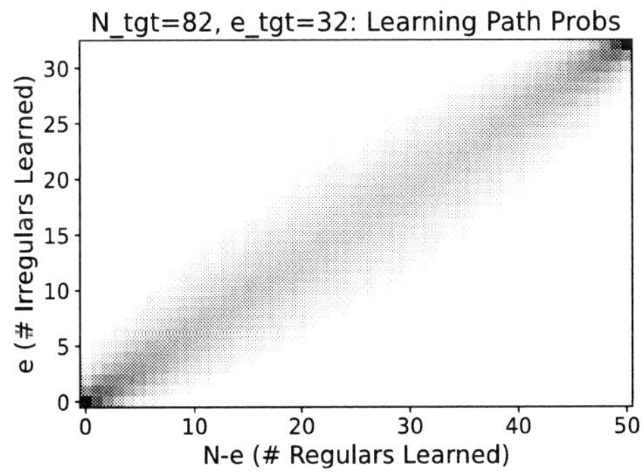

Figure 3: Likelihood of $(N - e, e)$ for each N. Darker indicates more likely path through the Fig. 2 TP space.

as a function of the relative token frequencies of the items. If irregulars are distributed uniformly throughout the distribution of types, path likelihood is well-approximated by a central hypergeometric distribution calculated for each N. Diagonals from top left to bottom right are "lines of constant N." Figure 3 visualizes this, with darker colors indicating more likely ratios of regulars and irregulars for a given N.

It is now possible to calculate the probability of falling in the productive and non-productive zones for each vocabulary size by summing over lines of constant N. The results, visualized in Figure 4 can be interpreted as the probability that a learner will generalize at each vocabulary size. Correlated with vocabulary size estimates by age, this can predict developmental trajectories. In this example, learners are will pass through a phase of early overgeneralization. This falls rapidly such that only about half should overgeneralize at $N = 15$. There is still a non-zero chance of over-generalizing be-

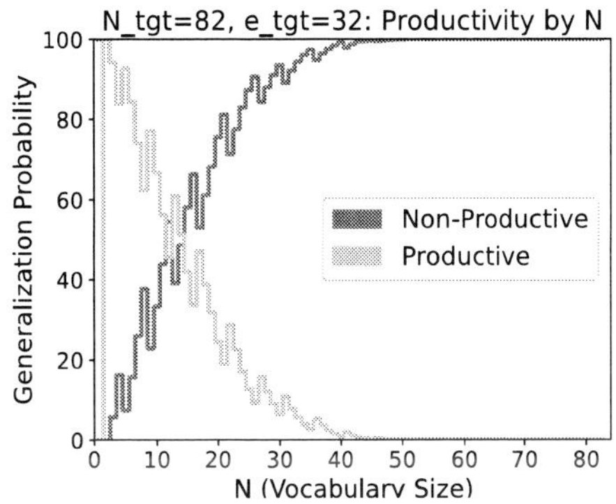

Figure 4: Likelihood of generalization and non-generalization by vocabulary size for Figs. 2-3.

fore $N = 45$, but after that point, all learners converge on adult-like non-productivity.

Note that productivity is driven entirely by the relative number of lexical items that follow or disobey the learner's hypothesized generalization and not the presence or absence of any individual lexical items. Learner outcomes are instead driven directly by the type frequency of patterns and the TP. Token frequencies play an indirect but crucial role as well. They determine the likely relative order that regular and irregular items are learned. The second illustration demonstrates this.

3.2 Effect of Irregular Token Frequency

This illustrative example examines the effect of irregular token frequency on learning trajectories by adopting a more realistic Zipfian input distribution.[3] The pattern $N_{tgt} = 90$, $e_{tgt} = 18$ should be acquired productively (N_{tgt} is in the productive zone of the state space visualized in Figure 5).

The 90 items are assumed to be distributed according to a Zipfian distribution. This should bow the most likely path through the state space, potentially pushing it into our out of the productive zone.[4] For example, if irregulars tend to fall on the frequent end of the distributions, these will tend to be heard, and therefore acquired earlier. This should bow the likely path upward and deeper into the non-productive zone. Three irregular distribu-

[3]Irregulars are often clustered in the high-frequency range (e.g., English past tense), but this is not universal. Other irregulars are more uniformly distributed in CDS (e.g., English plurals, Spanish verbs (Fratini et al., 2014)).

[4]Directly calculating each $(N - e, e)$ probability is intractable if every item has its own frequency. Wallenius' noncentral hypergeometric distr. allows class but not item weighting and was found to be a poor approximation. Thus, probabilities were calculated by simulating 100,000 trials.

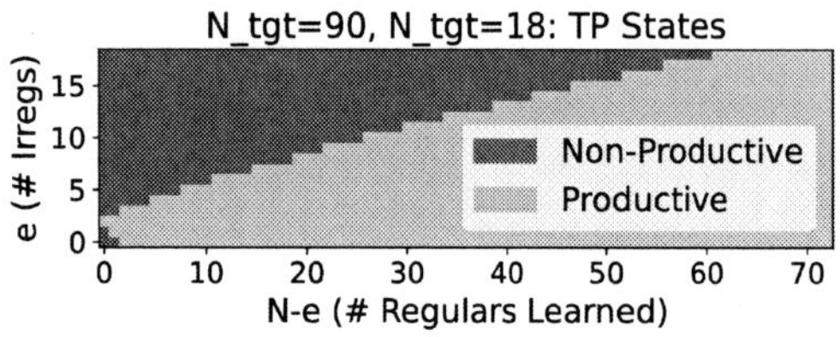

Figure 5: TP state space for $N_{tgt} = 90$, $e_{tgt} = 18$. This pattern should be acquired productively.

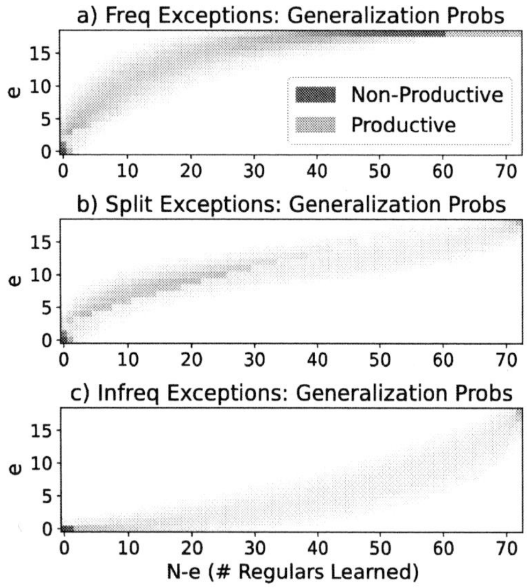

Figure 6: Likelihood of $(N-e, e)$ for each N and a) top-heavy, b) split, c) bottom-heavy e distributions.

tions are tested: They are **a)** the 18 most frequent items (the head of the Zipfian curve), **b)** the 9 most frequent and 9 least frequent items, and **c)** the 18 least frequent items. They are visualized in Figure 6 for three distributions of irregulars:

Even though the type distribution is the same in each case, the expected learning trajectories differ dramatically (Fig. 7). In the top-heavy case, nearly no learners are expected to be productive between $N = 20$ and $N = 80$, then everyone rapidly achieves productivity. In the bottom-heavy all learners achieve productivity as soon as they hypothesize the generalization. The split case predicts transient variation where all early learners are essentially adult-like, but many temporarily abandon productivity before relearning it later. This is because the likely path through the TP state space skirts the tolerance threshold, so slight variation in each individual's e predicts a large categorical difference in the grammar.

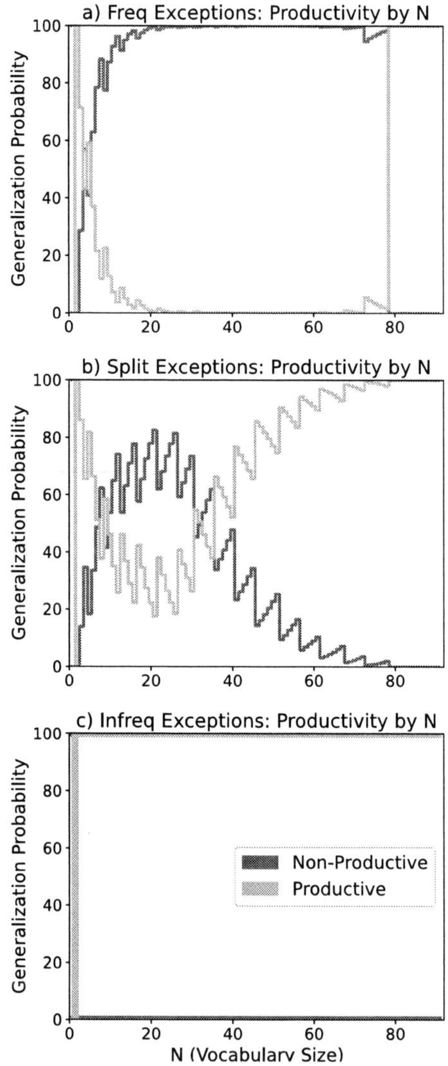

Figure 7: Likelihood of generalization and non-generalization by vocabulary size given Fig. 6.

3.3 Application to English Past Tense

This section applies the methods described thus far to real data: English past tense items extracted with frequencies from the CHILDES database (MacWhinney, 2000). Two expected learning paths were calculated: the default past *-ed* ($N = 1328$, $e = 98$ in this data) and the relatively common *sing-sang, ring-rung* sub-pattern (N=26, e=8). English learning children consistently acquire productive *-ed* around age three (Berko, 1958; Marcus et al., 1992). In contrast, the *sing-sang* pattern is not productive, though there is some transient variation (Berko, 1958; Xu and Pinker, 1995; Yang, 2016). This is because it has many exceptions (e.g., *sting-stung, bring-brought*).

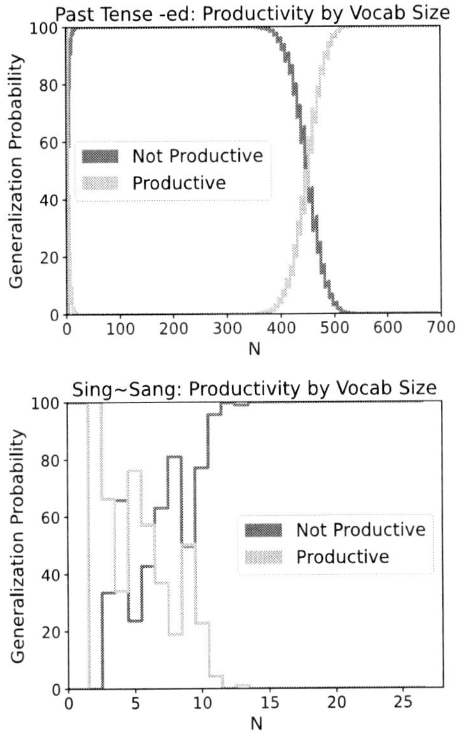

Figure 8: Generalization probability by vocabulary size for English past tense *-ed* and *sing~sang*. *-ed* was calculated on all data but trimmed to N=700 for visualization.

Figure 8 visualizes the results. Learners are predicted to show great uniformity in the acquisition of *-ed*. They consistently acquire the rule when they know 400-500 verbs. This qualitative uniformity is consistent with known developmental facts, but it is not immediately clear whether these particular numbers line up with the empirical evidence. Estimates of vocabulary size by age vary by method, but Marcus et al. (1992, ch. 5) report that Sarah and Adam from the Brown Corpus have produced 300-350 unique verbs by age three, but productive vocabulary underestimates working knowledge (Fenson et al., 1994, ch. 5-6), which is what is being modeled here.

The predictions for *sing-sang* is quite a bit different. There is significant variability when vocabulary size is small, but learners uniformly decide on non-productivity by around N=12. This appears to be consistent with wug-test results for children. In the original Berko (1958) study, only three of 86 pre-schoolers produce an *-ang(ed)* past form for stimuli *gling*+PAST or *bing*+PAST, suggesting low variability and low-productivity in that age group.[5]

[5]Adults and children seem to approach the wug test differently (Schütze, 2005), with many adults treating it as an analogy game (Derwing and Baker, 1977). Adults can be prompted to analogize the *sing-sang* pattern Berko (1958)

4 Discussion

This paper presents a means of modeling expected learning trajectories for productivity using the Tolerance Principle. As a type-based model of productivity learning, the TP only relies directly on the type attestation of regular and irregular items in the input. Since the grammar which is learned only depends on which side of the tolerance threshold the number of irregulars falls and not the lexical identity of the items or their exact number, it explains the general uniformity of outcomes observed across individual learners.

The TP was derived assuming that learners expect long-tailed frequency distributions in their input, and it provides an indirect role for token-frequency in learning. Higher frequency items are more likely to be attested early and learned early. Thus *while the type distribution of irregulars governs the ultimate learning outcome, their token distribution drives the learning trajectory*: the vocabulary size at which the adult-like grammar is settled on, the likelihood of over-regularization, and the degree of variability among individual learners.

One advantage of the TP for the purposes of this type of modeling is that it makes clear binary predictions about productivity. This study provides a novel means for making concrete predictions about the learning paths predicted by the TP. It remains to be seen how well these predictions fit the empirical data in a wider range of case studies. Another open question is whether other generalization models would make similar or different predictions, and if so, which best fit the empirical data.

The distribution of irregulars in the input can be measured empirically from corpora of child-directed speech since it is a property of the lexicon and of discourse concerns. The input has a clear effect on the path of learning even prior to adopting specific assumptions about the underlying grammar that children acquire. This suggests quantitatively re-evaluating the input as a way forward for explaining cross-linguistic differences in child language development as a complement to cross-linguistic theoretical and experimental work.

Acknowledgements

I am grateful to Mark Aronoff, Caleb Belth, Kenneth Hanson, Jeff Heinz, Sarah Payne, Charles Yang, and an audience at Stony Brook University for feedback they provided on drafts of this work.

References

Marco Baroni. 2005. 39 distributions in text. *Corpus Linguistics: An International Handbook Volume*, 2:803–822.

Caleb Belth, Sarah Payne, Deniz Beser, Jordan Kodner, and Charles Yang. 2021. The Greedy and Recursive Search for Morphological Productivity. In *Proceedings of the 43rd Annual Meeting of the Cognitive Science Society*, volume 43, pages 2869–2875.

Jean Berko. 1958. The child's learning of English morphology. *Word*, 14(2-3):150–177.

Sigríður Mjöll Björnsdóttir. 2021. Productivity and the acquisition of gender. *Journal of Child Language*.

Roger Brown. 1973. *A first language: The early stages*. Harvard University Press, Cambridge, MA.

Erwin Chan. 2008. *Structures and distributions in morphological learning*. Ph.D. thesis, University of Pennsylvania, Philadelphia, PA.

Harald Clahsen, Fraibet Aveledo, and Iggy Roca. 2002. The development of regular and irregular verb inflection in Spanish child language. *Journal of child language*, 29:591–622.

Bruce L Derwing and William J Baker. 1977. The psychological basis for morphological rules. In John Macnamara, editor, *Language learning and thought*, pages 85–110. Academic Press, New York.

Emeryse Emond and Rushen Shi. 2020. Infants' rule generalization is governed by the Tolerance Principle. In *45th Annual Boston University Conference on Language Development*.

Susan M Ervin and Wick R Miller. 1963. Language development. *Child Psychology*, pages 108–143.

Larry Fenson, Philip S Dale, J Steven Reznick, Elizabeth Bates, Donna J Thal, and Pethick. 1994. Variability in early communicative development. *Monographs of the society for research in child development*, 59(5).

Viviana Fratini, Joana Acha, and Itziar Laka. 2014. Frequency and morphological irregularity are independent variables. evidence from a corpus study of spanish verbs. *Corpus Linguistics and Linguistic Theory*, 10(2):289–314.

Ava Irani. 2019. *Learning from Positive Evidence: The Acquisition of Verb Argument Structure*. Ph.D. thesis, University of Pennsylvania.

Frederick Jelinek. 1997. *Statistical methods for speech recognition*. MIT press.

Jordan Kodner. 2019. Estimating child linguistic experience from historical corpora. *Glossa: A Journal of General Linguistics*, 4(1):122.

Jordan Kodner. 2020. *Language Acquisition in the Past*. Ph.D. thesis, University of Pennsylvania.

Jordan Kodner and Caitlin Richter. 2020. Transparent /ai/-raising as a contact phenomenon. In *Penn Working Papers in Linguistics: Selected Papers from NWAV*, volume 25, pages 61–70.

Elena Koulaguina and Rushen Shi. 2019. Rule generalization from inconsistent input in early infancy. *Language Acquisition*, 26(4):416–435.

William Labov. 1972. Some principles of linguistic methodology. *Language in society*, 1(1):97–120.

Sun Jae Lee and Jordan Kodner. 2020. Acquiring the Korean causatives. In *Proceedings of the Chicago Linguistics Society*, volume 54.

Constantine Lignos and Charles Yang. 2018. Morphology and language acquisition. *Cambridge handbook of morphology*, pages 765–791.

Brian MacWhinney. 2000. *The CHILDES project: The database*, volume 2. Psychology Press, Abingdon-on-Thames.

Gary F Marcus, Steven Pinker, Michael Ullman, Michelle Hollander, T John Rosen, Fei Xu, and Harald Clahsen. 1992. Overregularization in language acquisition. *Monographs of the society for research in child development*.

George A Miller. 1957. Some effects of intermittent silence. *The American journal of psychology*, 70(2):311–314.

Steven Pinker and Alan Prince. 1988. On language and connectionism: Analysis of a parallel distributed processing model of language acquisition. *Cognition*, 28(1-2):73–193.

Caitlin L. Richter. 2021. *Alternation-Sensitive Phone Learning: Implications for Children's Development and Language Change*. Ph.D. thesis, University of Pennsylvania.

Kathryn D Schuler. 2017. *The acquisition of productive rules in child and adult language learners*. Ph.D. thesis, Georgetown University.

Carson T. Schütze. 2005. Thinking about what we are asking speakers to do. In Stephan Kepser and Marga Reis, editors, *Linguistic evidence: Empirical, theoretical, and computational perspectives*, pages 457–485. Mouton de Gruyter, Berlin.

Betsy Sneller, Josef Fruehwald, and Charles Yang. 2019. Using the Tolerance Principle to predict phonological change. *Language Variation and Change*, 31(1):1–20.

Fei Xu and Steven Pinker. 1995. Weird past tense forms. *Journal of Child Language*, 22(3):531–556.

Charles Yang. 2013. Who's afraid of George Kingsley Zipf? or: Do children and chimps have language? *Significance*, 10(6):29–34.

Charles Yang. 2016. *The Price of Linguistic Productivity*. MIT Press, Cambridge, MA.

George Kingsley Zipf. 1949. *Human behavior and the principle of least effort: An introduction to human ecology*.

Predicting scalar diversity with context-driven uncertainty over alternatives

Jennifer Hu[1], Roger Levy[1], Sebastian Schuster[2]
[1]Department of Brain and Cognitive Sciences, Massachusetts Institute of Technology
[2]Department of Linguistics & Center for Data Science, New York University
jennhu@mit.edu, rplevy@mit.edu, schuster@nyu.edu

Abstract

Scalar implicature (SI) arises when a speaker uses an expression (e.g., *some*) that is semantically compatible with a logically stronger alternative on the same scale (e.g., *all*), leading the listener to infer that they did not intend to convey the stronger meaning. Prior work has demonstrated that SI rates are highly variable across scales, raising the question of what factors determine the SI strength for a particular scale. Here, we test the hypothesis that SI rates depend on the listener's confidence in the underlying scale, which we operationalize as uncertainty over the distribution of possible alternatives conditioned on the context. We use a T5 model fine-tuned on a text infilling task to estimate this distribution. We find that scale uncertainty predicts human SI rates, measured as entropy over the sampled alternatives and over latent classes among alternatives in sentence embedding space. Furthermore, we do not find a significant effect of the surprisal of the strong scalemate. Our results suggest that pragmatic inferences depend on listeners' context-driven uncertainty over alternatives.

1 Introduction

Human communication involves not only the transmission of linguistic signals, but also context-guided inference over the beliefs and goals of other conversational agents (e.g., Sperber and Wilson, 1986; Grice, 1975). One signature pattern of this pragmatic reasoning is scalar implicature (SI). The standard view is that SIs arise as a result of ordered relationships between linguistic items – when a weaker (less informative) item of a scale is uttered, then a listener can infer that the speaker did not have grounds to utter the stronger (more informative) item on that scale. For example, if Alice says "Some of the students passed the exam", Bob can draw the scalar inference that *not all* students passed the exam, even though Alice's utterance would still be semantically true in that scenario.

While this view predicts that SIs are context-independent and generally strong – known as the Homogeneity Assumption (Degen, 2015) – empirical studies have demonstrated a remarkable amount of variance in SI rates both within (Degen, 2015; Li et al., 2021) and across lexical scales (Doran et al., 2009; van Tiel et al., 2016; Gotzner et al., 2018; Pankratz and van Tiel, 2021). This raises the question of what factors determine the SI strength for a particular scale. In a landmark study, van Tiel et al. (2016) test two classes of potential predictors of SI strength: the availability of the strong scalemate given the weak scalemate, and the degree to which scalemates can be distinguished from each other. They demonstrate that availability is not a reliable predictor of SI strengths (but see Westera and Boleda 2020), while measures of scalemate distinctness, such as the boundedness of the scale, do robustly predict SI. More recent studies (e.g., Gotzner et al., 2018; Sun et al., 2018; Pankratz and van Tiel, 2021; Ronai and Xiang, 2022) have proposed a variety of other factors such as negative strengthening, polarity, and extremeness.

Here, we revisit the hypothesis that SI rates depend on the availability of the strong scalemate. While prior work has operationalized availability with measures of the strong scalemate such as word frequency or similarity/association with the weak scalemate (van Tiel et al., 2016; Westera and Boleda, 2020; Ronai and Xiang, 2022), we re-frame availability as the listener's *confidence in the underlying scale*. Upon hearing a scalar expression, listeners must determine the items on the scale as well as the ordering metric before inference proceeds (Hirschberg, 1985). If the listener is less certain about the scale, then they will be less likely to exclude the meaning of a particular strong scalemate. We operationalize scale uncertainty as uncertainty over the alternatives that could serve as a strong scalemate to the observed scalar expression. To estimate the alternatives predicted

Proceedings of the Workshop on Cognitive Modeling and Computational Linguistics, pages 68 - 74
May 26, 2022

by humans, we use a T5 model (Raffel et al., 2020) fine-tuned on a text infilling task. While prior studies have treated alternatives as linguistic forms, we also consider the idea that listeners reason about alternatives at a conceptual level (Buccola et al., 2021) by treating alternatives as latent classes in a conceptual space. Our results support the role of scale uncertainty in determining SI rates, and suggest a new way of testing conceptual theories of alternatives for scalar inference.

2 Human data

To obtain human SI strengths, we use the data from Experiment 2 by van Tiel et al. (2016). In our analyses, we only consider the adjectival scales from van Tiel et al.'s original materials, resulting in 32 scales. Each scale is a pair of adjectives ⟨[WEAK], [STRONG]⟩, where the meaning of [STRONG] entails the meaning of [WEAK] (e.g., ⟨*intelligent, brilliant*⟩). The experiment measures whether humans exclude the meaning of [STRONG] upon observing a speaker use [WEAK].

On each trial of the experiment, participants read a prompt of the form "John says: [NP] is [WEAK]", where [WEAK] is an adjective scalar item that may trigger a scalar inference, and [NP] is a noun phrase that sets the context for the scalar item. There were 3 such sentences per scale, which differ from each other only in the NP. For example, the weak scalar item *intelligent* is associated with the sentences "This student/That professor/The assistant is intelligent". Participants were then asked: "Would you conclude from this that, according to John, $[\text{NP}]_P$ is not [STRONG]?", where [STRONG] is the strong scalemate to [WEAK], and $[\text{NP}]_P$ is a pronominalized version of the [NP] in the speaker's original utterance (e.g., "she is not brilliant"). Participants marked their response as Yes or No. The SI rate for a scale is computed as the proportion of Yes responses averaged over participants and sentences.

3 Predictors

We use T5 (Raffel et al., 2020) to estimate all probabilities in our analyses. T5 is a sequence-to-sequence Transformer model (Vaswani et al., 2017) trained to represent language processing tasks as text-to-text problems. Our model is based on the pre-trained T5-base model from Huggingface Transformers (Wolf et al., 2020). Since the off-the-shelf T5 model is not optimized for text generation, we use a T5 model that has been fine-tuned on a text infilling task (Qian and Levy, 2022). The model is fine-tuned on a 10-million-token subset of the 2007 portion of the New York Times Corpus (Sandhaus, 2008). The supervision signal is generated by randomly masking some spans of words in a sentence to get the fragmentary context and a plausible completion. At inference time, the model decodes autoregressively via greedy sampling.

3.1 Predictability of strong scalemate

As a baseline, we first consider whether SI rates – i.e., the rate at which [WEAK] is taken to exclude the meaning of [STRONG] – are explained by the context-conditioned predictability of the tested strong scalemate. This is similar to production-based measures of availability, such as the tendency of humans to mention the strong scalemate in a Cloze task (van Tiel et al., 2016; Ronai and Xiang, 2022). However, these metrics are expensive to estimate, especially if we wish to estimate the full distribution of alternatives. We address this by using T5 as a proxy of human predictions, taking the view that humans maintain expectations about possible alternatives via a predictive language model optimized on the surface statistics of language.

To measure the predictability of a certain linguistic expression as a strong scalemate under T5, we leverage scalar constructions (Hearst, 1992; de Melo and Bansal, 2013; Pankratz and van Tiel, 2021). Scalar constructions are patterns such as *X, but not Y*, which indicate a scalar relationship between a weak item X and strong item Y. For each weak scalar item in our test materials, we construct a scalar template of the following form:

$$[\text{NP}] \text{ is } [\text{WEAK}], \text{ but not } \_\_\_\_\_ . \quad (1)$$

We have 3 such templates for each scale, where [NP] is given by the 3 sentences from van Tiel et al.'s materials. By embedding the weak scalar item within the *X, but not Y* construction, the model should set up expectations for a potential scalemate in the masked position. For each ⟨[WEAK], [STRONG]⟩ pair from van Tiel et al.'s items, we substitute the strong scalemate into the masked position and compute the surprisal (i.e., negative log probability) at that token under T5.[1] Language model surprisal has been shown to predict psychometric measures of human sentence processing (e.g., Smith and Levy, 2013; Goodkind and Bicknell, 2018; Wilcox et al., 2020), suggesting that

[1]When scalar items are split into multiple tokens, we obtain surprisals by summing over these sub-word tokens.

the distribution learned by these models captures expectations deployed by humans during real-time language comprehension.

3.2 Scale uncertainty

Next, we test the hypothesis that SI depends on the listener's uncertainty about the scale implied by the speaker's utterance. Depending on the context, a single word (e.g., *bad*) could lie on multiple scales – e.g., "The food is bad" might imply that the food is not rotten, whereas "The score is bad" might imply that the score is not failing. This uncertainty is not a function of a particular scalemate (unlike the availability measure described in Section 3.1 and in prior work), but rather a property of the scalar trigger and the context in which it is observed.

We operationalize scale uncertainty as uncertainty over the distribution of possible alternatives conditioned on the context. To obtain a set of candidate alternatives A, we sample $N = 100$ completions from the T5 infilling model given the scalar template in Equation (1).[2] During decoding, we restrict the maximum number of generated tokens to 5, and only keep the unique completions. We further process the outputs by removing punctuation and casing, and only keep the first word of the sequence (e.g., "always" and "always," would be collapsed into "always"). After this step, we also removed completions that consisted only of stopwords.[3] We performed these processing steps in order to reduce the sensitivity of the model-generated alternatives distribution to low-level features like punctuation, and to account for the model's tendency to output high-frequency function words.

3.3 Strings vs. concepts

For each of our surprisal and scale uncertainty measures, we consider two operationalizations that reflect differing theories of alternatives. The first assumes that surface-level linguistic forms (i.e., strings) are the alternatives driving SI. The second view is that listeners reason about alternatives at a conceptual level (Buccola et al., 2021), which we estimate using sentence embeddings.

String-based measures. We first consider the string-based view of alternatives. We obtain string-based surprisal by plugging the strong scalemate into the blank in Equation (1) (i.e., Y in the *X, but not Y* construction) and computing its context-conditioned surprisal under T5. Similarly, to obtain a string-based measure of scale uncertainty, we compute uncertainty over the strings that fill the masked position in the scalar template (Equation (1)). That is, we normalize the probabilities of each $a \in A$ to obtain a probability distribution over alternatives, and then compute the Shannon entropy over this distribution. We predict that lower surprisal reflects a more predictable alternative, and thus results in a stronger SI. Similarly, lower entropy reflects lower uncertainty over the underlying scale, and should lead to a stronger SI.

This method implicitly assumes that surface-level linguistic forms (i.e., strings) are the alternatives driving scalar inferences. As a single concept can be expressed with multiple forms, however, the surprisal over forms may not be a good estimate of the surprisal of the underlying concept. This motivates using hierarchical methods to identify latent classes among alternatives in some conceptual representation.

Hierarchical measures. An alternate view is that listeners do not reason about alternatives at the level of linguistic forms (i.e., strings), but instead a deeper conceptual level (Buccola et al., 2021). As a proxy for a conceptual representation of an alternative, we use sentence embeddings from Sentence-T5 (Ni et al., 2021). Prior work has shown that clustering over word embeddings has been shown to uncover latent topics, suggesting that there is usable conceptual information represented in the embedding spaces induced by large language models (e.g., Sia et al., 2020; Thompson and Mimno, 2020; Meng et al., 2022). For each sampled alternative $a \in A$, we substitute a into the masked position in the scalar template (Equation (1)) to obtain a full sentence, and then feed this as input to Sentence-T5 to obtain a 768-dimensional embedding of the entire sentence.[4] We assume sentences close in this space are more likely to reflect the same underlying scale, and distant sentences are likely to reflect different scales.

To formalize the idea of conceptual alternatives for scalar inference, we treat scales as latent classes that may give rise to multiple alternative strings. On this view, the surprisal of a strong scalemate is the surprisal of its underlying class, and scale uncer-

[2]The completions are not guaranteed to be scalar items, but we take this to be a first approximation. All results are averaged over 4 random seeds for the sampling of alternatives.

[3]https://gist.github.com/sebleier/554280

[4]We use the PyTorch implementation via SentenceTransformers (Reimers and Gurevych, 2019).

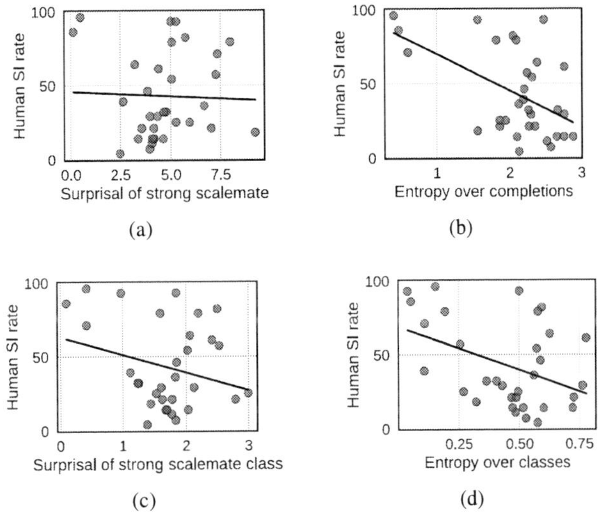

Figure 1: Best-fit linear relationship between human SI rates (van Tiel et al., 2016) and four predictors (Section 3): (a) String-based surprisal of the strong scalemate under T5. (b) Entropy over alternative strings sampled by T5. (c) Surprisal of latent class assigned to the strong scalemate by the Gaussian mixture model. (d) Entropy over probabilities of classes identified by the Gaussian mixture model.

tainty is uncertainty over these classes. To identify latent classes among alternative sentence embeddings, we fit a Gaussian mixture model (GMM) for each set of alternatives (i.e., one per weak scalar item, sentence template, and random seed). To determine the number of latent classes k, we fit a GMM for each $k \in \{1, 2, 3\}$ and chose the k that minimized the Bayesian information criterion (BIC) of the fitted model.[5]

After fitting a GMM on the alternative embeddings for each weak scalemate, we predict the class for each alternative. We obtain a score for each class by summing the probabilities assigned by T5 to each alternative within that class. We compute class-based surprisal as the negative log of the score assigned to the class containing the strong scalemate, and class-based scale uncertainty as the entropy over the normalized class scores. As before, we expect that lower surprisal and lower entropy should result in higher SI.

4 Results

We computed the four metrics described in Section 3 on the data from Experiment 2 of van Tiel et al. (2016), and evaluated the causal roles of each metric in predicting scalar inference rates across scales. For each of the four metrics, we fit a linear regression model to predict mean SI rates for each scale (averaged across trials). In all models, we included scale boundedness as an additional predictor, as it is the factor explaining the most variance in van Tiel et al.'s (2016) study.

Our first model tested string-based surprisal as a predictor of SI rates. In line with van Tiel et al.'s results, boundedness is a highly significant predictor ($p < 10^{-16}$). Furthermore, surprisal of the strong scalemate is not a significant predictor ($t = -0.09, p = 0.928$). Figure 1a shows the lack of relationship between in-context surprisal of the strong scalemate and SI rate. Each point represents a scale, with values averaged over the trials and sentence templates (three per scale) presented in van Tiel et al.'s Experiment 2. This lack of relationship concords with van Tiel et al.'s original finding that availability is not predictive of SI rate.

Our second model tested the predictive power of string-based scale uncertainty (i.e., the entropy over completions sampled from T5 in a scalar construction). We found string-based entropy to be a significant predictor of SI rate ($t = -3.28, p = 0.001$), suggesting that uncertainty over alternatives (as string forms) may play a role in scalar inference. Figure 1b shows the negative relationship between SI rates and string-based entropy.

Next, we turn to the hierarchical metrics, which treat alternatives as latent classes in sentence em-

[5]For speed of convergence, we assumed diagonal covariance matrices for each estimated class distribution.

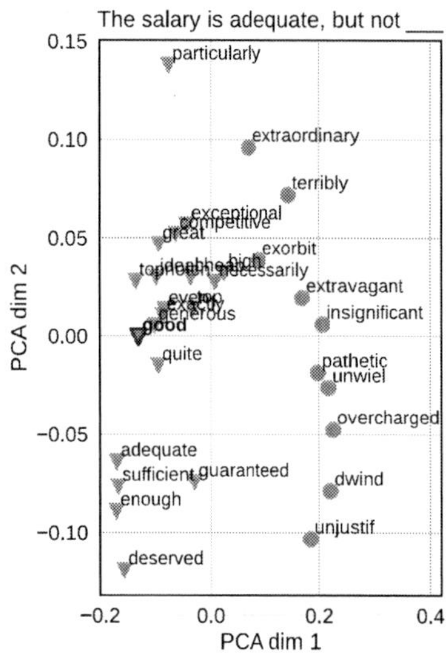

Figure 2: Example of classes (distinguished by color and marker) identified by Gaussian mixture model among alternatives in sentence embedding space. Sentence embeddings are projected into 2 dimensions via PCA for visualization.

bedding space. In general, the pattern mirrors what we found for the string-based metrics. Our third model did not find class-based surprisal to be a significant predictor of SI rates ($t = -1.33, p = 0.186$; Figure 1c), and our fourth model found class-based entropy to be a significant predictor ($t = -2.4, p = 0.01$; Figure 1d).

Finally, we performed a qualitative evaluation of the classes identified by the Gaussian mixture models (GMMs). Figure 2 shows the alternatives generated by T5 for the template "The salary is adequate, but not ____.", with each point obtained by projecting the Sentence-T5 embedding into 2-dimensional space via PCA. The BIC-minimizing GMM identifies two latent classes, distinguished by color and marker, among the alternatives generated by T5 for the weak scalar item *adequate*. First, we examine the cluster containing *good*, the strong scalemate tested in van Tiel et al.'s experiments (marked with boldface and outline). This cluster (indicated by blue triangles) contains *good* as well as semantically similar alternatives such as "great", "sufficient", and "enough". In general, the alternatives in this cluster appear to suggest a scale where high salaries are positive (e.g., from an employee's perspective), with strong scalar items like "generous", "ideal", and "competitive". In contrast, the second cluster (indicated by red circles) contains alternatives such as "extravagant" and "overcharged", capturing the potential of *adequate* to be on a scale where higher salaries are not always desirable (e.g., from an employer's perspective). While the model-generated alternatives and clusters are noisy, we take this to illustrate that a single weak scalar item (like *adequate*) can plausibly be interpreted as belonging to multiple scales.

5 Discussion

We tested the hypothesis that SI rates depend on the listener's confidence in the underlying scale, using two operationalizations of alternatives (surface-level string forms and latent classes in a sentence embedding space). Using data from a previously conducted experiment (van Tiel et al., 2016), we found that scale uncertainty was a significant predictor of SI rates: on average, when uncertainty over alternatives (i.e., entropy over sampled alternatives, or over classes of alternatives in sentence embedding space) is lower, humans are more likely to draw a scalar inference. On the other hand, the predictability of the strong scalemate (as measured by surprisal of the string form, or of its underlying cluster) was not a significant predictor of SI rates.

An open question is why scale uncertainty predicts SI rates, while strong scalemate surprisal and the availability measures from van Tiel et al. (2016) are poor predictors. We conjecture that the predictability of the strong scalemate may be shrouded by the paradigm used in experimental investigations of scalar diversity. In these experiments, the participant is explicitly asked to reason about the strong scalemate in the prompt (e.g., "John says: This student is intelligent. Would you conclude from this that, according to John, she is not brilliant?"). Thus, the effort required to retrieve the strong scalemate (e.g., "brilliant"), which may be captured by its in-context predictability, may no longer be relevant in this setting. We note, however, that our findings likely depend on the chosen clustering algorithm and conceptual representation of the alternatives. We intend to explore this space more broadly in future work.

Looking forward, our methods can be applied to scales that are ordered by ad-hoc relationships instead of entailment (Hirschberg, 1985). Beyond predicting scalar diversity, our approach suggests a way to derive quantitative behavioral predictions from non-linguistic alternatives (Buccola et al., 2021), and supports the idea that context-driven expectations may give rise to pragmatic behaviors.

References

Brian Buccola, Manuel Križ, and Emmanuel Chemla. 2021. Conceptual alternatives: Competition in language and beyond. *Linguistics and Philosophy*.

Gerard de Melo and Mohit Bansal. 2013. Good, Great, Excellent: Global Inference of Semantic Intensities. *Transactions of the Association for Computational Linguistics*, 1:279–290.

Judith Degen. 2015. Investigating the distribution of *some* (but not *all*) implicatures using corpora and web-based methods. *Semantics and Pragmatics*, 8(11):1–55.

Ryan Doran, Rachel E. Baker, Yaron McNabb, Meredith Larson, and Gregory Ward. 2009. On the Non-Unified Nature of Scalar Implicature: An Empirical Investigation. *International Review of Pragmatics*, 1(2):211 – 248. Place: Leiden, The Netherlands Publisher: Brill.

Adam Goodkind and Klinton Bicknell. 2018. Predictive power of word surprisal for reading times is a linear function of language model quality. In *Proceedings of the 8th Workshop on Cognitive Modeling and Computational Linguistics (CMCL 2018)*, pages 10–18, Salt Lake City, Utah. Association for Computational Linguistics.

Nicole Gotzner, Stephanie Solt, and Anton Benz. 2018. Scalar Diversity, Negative Strengthening, and Adjectival Semantics. *Frontiers in Psychology*, 9:1659.

Herbert P. Grice. 1975. Logic and Conversation. In Peter Cole and Jerry L. Morgan, editors, *Syntax and Semantics: Speech Acts*, volume 3, pages 41–58. Academic Press.

Marti A. Hearst. 1992. Automatic Acquisition of Hyponyms from Large Text Corpora. In *COLING 1992 Volume 2: The 14th International Conference on Computational Linguistics*.

Julia Bell Hirschberg. 1985. *A Theory of Scalar Implicature (Natural Languages, Pragmatics, Inference)*. PhD Thesis, University of Pennsylvania.

Elissa Li, Sebastian Schuster, and Judith Degen. 2021. Predicting Scalar Inferences From "Or" to "Not Both" Using Neural Sentence Encoders. In *Proceedings of the Society for Computation in Linguistics*, volume 4.

Yu Meng, Yunyi Zhang, Jiaxin Huang, Yu Zhang, and Jiawei Han. 2022. Topic Discovery via Latent Space Clustering of Pretrained Language Model Representations. In *The Web Conference*.

Jianmo Ni, Gustavo Hernández Ábrego, Noah Constant, Ji Ma, Keith B. Hall, Daniel Cer, and Yinfei Yang. 2021. Sentence-T5: Scalable Sentence Encoders from Pre-trained Text-to-Text Models.

Elizabeth Pankratz and Bob van Tiel. 2021. The role of relevance for scalar diversity: a usage-based approach. *Language and Cognition*, 13(4):562–594. Edition: 2021/08/16 Publisher: Cambridge University Press.

Peng Qian and Roger Levy. 2022. Flexible generation from fragmentary linguistic input. In *Proceedings of the 60th Annual Meeting of the Association for Computational Linguistics*. To appear.

Colin Raffel, Noam Shazeer, Adam Roberts, Katherine Lee, Sharan Narang, Michael Matena, Yanqi Zhou, Wei Li, and Peter J. Liu. 2020. Exploring the Limits of Transfer Learning with a Unified Text-to-Text Transformer. *Journal of Machine Learning Research*, 21(140):1–67.

Nils Reimers and Iryna Gurevych. 2019. Sentence-BERT: Sentence Embeddings using Siamese BERT-Networks. In *Proceedings of the 2019 Conference on Empirical Methods in Natural Language Processing*. Association for Computational Linguistics.

Eszter Ronai and Ming Xiang. 2022. Three factors in explaining scalar diversity. In *Proceedings of Sinn und Bedeutung 26*.

Evan Sandhaus. 2008. The New York Times Annotated Corpus (LDC2008T19).

Suzanna Sia, Ayush Dalmia, and Sabrina J. Mielke. 2020. Tired of Topic Models? Clusters of Pretrained Word Embeddings Make for Fast and Good Topics too! In *Proceedings of the 2020 Conference on Empirical Methods in Natural Language Processing (EMNLP)*, pages 1728–1736, Online. Association for Computational Linguistics.

Nathaniel J. Smith and Roger Levy. 2013. The effect of word predictability on reading time is logarithmic. *Cognition*, 128(3):302 – 319.

Dan Sperber and Deirdre Wilson. 1986. *Relevance: Communication and Cognition*. Wiley-Blackwell.

Chao Sun, Ye Tian, and Richard Breheny. 2018. A Link Between Local Enrichment and Scalar Diversity. *Frontiers in Psychology*, 9:2092.

Laure Thompson and David Mimno. 2020. Topic Modeling with Contextualized Word Representation Clusters.

Bob van Tiel, Emiel van Miltenburg, Natalia Zevakhina, and Bart Geurts. 2016. Scalar Diversity. *Journal of Semantics*, 33(1):137–175.

Ashish Vaswani, Noam Shazeer, Niki Parmar, Jakob Uszkoreit, Llion Jones, Aidan N Gomez, Łukasz Kaiser, and Illia Polosukhin. 2017. Attention is All you Need. In *Advances in Neural Information Processing Systems*, volume 30. Curran Associates, Inc.

Matthijs Westera and Gemma Boleda. 2020. A closer look at scalar diversity using contextualized semantic similarity. *Proceedings of Sinn und Bedeutung*, 24(2):439–454.

Ethan Wilcox, Jon Gauthier, Jennifer Hu, Peng Qian, and Roger Levy. 2020. On the predictive power of neural language models for human real-time comprehension behavior. In *Proceedings of the Cognitive Science Society*.

Thomas Wolf, Lysandre Debut, Victor Sanh, Julien Chaumond, Clement Delangue, Anthony Moi, Pierric Cistac, Tim Rault, Remi Louf, Morgan Funtowicz, Joe Davison, Sam Shleifer, Patrick von Platen, Clara Ma, Yacine Jernite, Julien Plu, Canwen Xu, Teven Le Scao, Sylvain Gugger, Mariama Drame, Quentin Lhoest, and Alexander Rush. 2020. Transformers: State-of-the-Art Natural Language Processing. In *Proceedings of the 2020 Conference on Empirical Methods in Natural Language Processing: System Demonstrations*, pages 38–45, Online. Association for Computational Linguistics.

Eye Gaze and Self-attention: How Humans and Transformers Attend Words in Sentences

Joshua Bensemann[*], **Alex Yuxuan Peng, Diana Benavides-Prado, Yang Chen, Neşet Özkan Tan, Paul Michael Corballis, Patricia Riddle,** and **Michael Witbrock**
University of Auckland

Abstract

Attention describes cognitive processes that are important to many human phenomena including reading. The term is also used to describe the way in which transformer neural networks perform natural language processing. While attention appears to be very different under these two contexts, this paper presents an analysis of the correlations between transformer attention and overt human attention during reading tasks. An extensive analysis of human eye tracking datasets showed that the dwell times of human eye movements were strongly correlated with the attention patterns occurring in the early layers of pre-trained transformers such as BERT. Additionally, the strength of a correlation was not related to the number of parameters within a transformer. This suggests that something about the transformers' architecture determined how closely the two measures were correlated.

1 Introduction

Attention is a process that is associated with both reading in humans and with Natural Language Processing (NLP) by state-of-the-art Deep Neural Networks (DNN) (Bahdanau et al., 2015). In both cases, it is the words within a sentence that are attended to during processing. In DNNs, attention results from mechanisms built into the network. Specifically, in the current state-of-the-art method Transformers (Vaswani et al., 2017), this attention process is the result of the dot product of two vectors that represent individual words in the text. For humans, attention processes are more complex as they can be broken into overt and covert attention (Posner, 1980). Overt attention is characterized by observable physical movements of which eye gaze is a well known example that is relevant to reading (Rayner, 2009). Covert attention, on the other hand, is characterized by mental shifts in focus and, therefore, not directly observable. For this study we have focused on the overt attention measure of eye gaze, with words at the center of an eye fixation being the words that we assume were being attended.

While attention in human reading processes and transformers appear to be completely different, this paper will present an analysis showing the relationship between the two[1]. Specifically, attention in well-known transformers such as BERT (Devlin et al., 2019), and its derivatives are closely related to humans' eye fixations during reading. We observed strong to moderate strength correlations between the dwell times of eyes over words and the self-attention in transformers such as BERT. We have explored some reasons for these different correlation levels and speculated on others.

This analysis is part of an ongoing research line where we attempt to overcome attention limits in transformers. When using transformers, both memory and computational requirements grow quadratically as the sequence length increases because every token attends to all other tokens. In previous work, we have used the attention mechanisms of pre-trained transformers as attention filters that can reduce a sequence length for a sentiment analysis task by 99% while still maintaining 70% accuracy (Tan et al., 2021). Our motivation for this paper was to explore the possibility of using models of eye gaze as an alternative filter. Strong correlations between the attentions produced by transformers and the overt attention of humans would suggest that models of eye movements could potentially be used in computationally inexpensive methods for approximating transformer attention. Alternatively we could use eye movements to train transformer attention towards overt attention patterns[2].

[*]Email: josh.bensemann@auckland.ac.nz

[1]Code and Full Results available at `https://github.com/Strong-AI-Lab/Eye-Tracking-Analysis`

[2]See appendix for a preliminary attempt.

Proceedings of the Workshop on Cognitive Modeling and Computational Linguistics, pages 75 - 87
May 26, 2022 ©2022 Association for Computational Linguistics

1.1 Transformers

Transformers (Vaswani et al., 2017) have dominated the leader boards for NLP tasks since their introduction to the deep learning community. Additionally, transformers have had an impact on computer vision (Dosovitskiy et al., 2021), including generative networks (Jiang et al., 2021). The general superior performance of transformers at these tasks is due to its attention mechanism:

$$\text{Attention}(\mathbf{Q}, \mathbf{K}, \mathbf{V}) = \text{softmax}\left(\frac{\mathbf{Q}\mathbf{K}^{\top}}{\sqrt{n}}\right)\mathbf{V} \tag{1}$$

where the word vectors representations of the text sequence **Q** are compared to those from sequence **K**. This is used to determine the amount of information word representations from the former should incorporate from the latter. If the query and key sequence are the same, as in a transformers encoder, it is called self-attention. The results of the attention process are then multiplied by sequence **V** to get the final outputs from the attention layer. **V** contains different representations for the words in **K**.

The more relevant a word in **K** is to those in **Q**, the more attention **Q** words allocate to that word. Research has examined the **Q** x **K** part of the attention mechanism to understand how transformers process information. Vaswani et al. (2017) showed that transformers could use words in **Q** to learn anaphora resolution by appropriately attending the word "its" in **K**.

The introduction of transformers was quickly followed by a proliferation of pre-trained models using the transformers architecture. Arguably, the most famous of these models is BERT, a.k.a. the Bidirectional Encoder Representations from Transformers model (Devlin et al., 2019). BERT was designed to encode information from whole passages of text into a single vector representation. Its bidirectional structure means that each word token is placed in the context of the entire sequence instead of just the tokens appearing before it. This structure provided an increase in performance on the GLUE benchmarks (Wang et al., 2019b) over mono-directional models such as the original GPT (Radford et al., 2018).

To ensure that the model learned to attend to the sequence as the whole, BERT was trained using Masked Language Modeling (MLM), a task inspired by the Cloze procedure (Taylor, 1953) from human reading comprehension studies. In MLM, random words from a sequence are hidden during input. The model then has to predict what word was hidden based on the context of surrounding words. BERT was also trained to perform Next Sentence Prediction (NSP) during MLM, forcing words from one sentence to attend to words in other sentences. BERT achieved state-of-the-art performance in multiple NLP benchmarks following this training regime, which led to its widespread adoption.

BERT's impact on the field can be seen in the number of subsequent models that are its direct descendants. Examples include models such as RoBERTa (Liu et al., 2019), which uses BERT's architecture but was trained via different methods. Other models, such as ALBERT (Lan et al., 2020), were created to condense BERT for faster performance with minimal accuracy loss. Even models such as XLNet (Yang et al., 2019) extended BERT's architecture to include recurrence mechanisms introduced in other models (Dai et al., 2019). In turn, some of these descendant models have been used to create other models. For example, BIGBIRD (Zaheer et al., 2020) was built using RoBERTa as its base.

1.2 Combining Transformers and Eye Gaze

There is a growing field of research that combines pre-trained transformers with eye-tracking data. Researchers have used outputs from BERT as features for machine learning models to predict eye fixations. In some instances, these outputs are combined with other features (Choudhary et al., 2021); in other instances, BERT itself is fine-tuned to predict eye fixations. For example Hollenstein et al. (2021a) have shown that BERT can be effective at predicting eye movements for texts written in multiple languages, including English, Dutch, German, and Russian.

Given the strong relationship between eye gaze and attention, it is unsurprising that there have been attempts to compare eye gaze to attention generated in transformers. Sood et al. (2020a) compared eye movements in reading comprehension task to three different neural networks, including XLNet. After fine-tuning XLNet, they compared attention from the last encoder layer to eye gaze and reported a non-significant correlation. However, their comparison only reported the correlation for the final attention layer of the network, while other studies comparing transformer attention to human metrics have indicated that the strength of an association can differ by layer (Toneva and Wehbe, 2019). Therefore, the present study calculated correlations with eye movements from all layers of the transformers. With that said, our results focused on the first layer as it generally produced the strongest correlations to eye gaze data.

Following the work of Sood et al. (2020a), the present study is a large-scale analysis of the relationship between attention in pre-trained transformers and human attention derived from eye gaze. We compared the self-attention values of 31 variants from 11 different transformers, including BERT, its descendants, and a few other state-of-the-art transformers (Table 1). No fine-tuning was performed; models were the same as those reported in their respective papers. Using the BERT-based models with their original parameter weights allowed us to investigate the effect that training regime had on how closely the attention was related to overt eye-based attention. Using non-BERT models allowed us to examine what effect model architecture had on this relationship. Finally, the different datasets enabled an exploration into how the human participants' task also affects this relationship. Results showed significant correlations between attention in the first layer of the transformers and total dwell time. These correlations were unrelated to the size of the model.

2 Related Work

There have been attempts to combine DNNs with eye data to perform various tasks. Some basic tasks include predicting how an eye will move across presented stimuli, whether text-based (Sood et al., 2020b) or images in general (Ghariba et al., 2020; Li and Yu, 2016; Harel et al., 2006; Huang et al., 2015; Tavakoli et al., 2017). These predictions can be used to create saliency maps that show what areas of a visual display are attractive to the eye.

In turn, saliency maps can be used to either understand biological visual processes or be incorporated as meta-data into machine learning models. The later endeavor has led to some improvements in task performance. In a recent example, Sood et al. (2020b) achieved state-of-the-art results in a text compression task by creating a Text Saliency Model (TSM) using a BiLSTM network that outputs embeddings into transformer self-attention layers. The TSM was pre-trained on synthetic data simulated by the E-Z reader model (Reichle et al., 1998) and fine-tuned on human eye-tracking data. The model's output was used to neuromodulate (Vecoven et al., 2020) a task-specific model via multiplicative attention.

Eye gaze data itself can be used to inspire new ways for neural networks to perform NLP tasks (Zheng et al., 2019). For example, it is well known that the human eye does not fixate on every word during reading (Duggan and Payne, 2011). Nevertheless, humans, until recently, performed well above machines in many NLP tasks (Fitzsimmons et al., 2014; He et al., 2021). These observations imply that the word skipping process is not detrimental to reading tasks. Some researchers have exploited this process by explicitly training their models to ignore words (Yu et al., 2017; Seo et al., 2018; Hahn and Keller, 2016). For example, Yu et al. (2017) trained LSTM models to predict the number of words to skip while performing sentiment analysis and found that the model could skip several words at a time and still be as accurate, if not more accurate, than the non-skipping models. Additionally, Hahn and Keller (2018) showed that the skipping processes could be modelled using actual eye movements and achieve the same result. These word skipping models exploit overt attention only, and it would be interesting to know what happens if skipping was modelled on covert attention instead.

Other research exploring the relationship between DNNs and human data has examined how closely the metrics used to measure eye movement are related to metrics used for machine language models. Studies of this type require identifying comparable processes between the two different systems and a suitable dataset. For example, Hao et al. (2020) compared model perplexity to psycholinguistic features.

There have even been comparisons of DNN attention to what humans attend to during reading tasks. Sen et al. (2020) compared the attention of humans during a sentiment analysis task to RNN models. Crowdsourced workers were asked to rate sentiments of YELP reviews and then highlight the important words for their decision-making process. They found correlations between the RNN outputs and human behavior. The strength of these correlations diminished as the length of the text increased.

Closely related to our study is the work of Sood et al. (2020a) who attempted to compare eye gaze to the attention mechanisms of three different neural network architectures. One of the models was the BERT-based transformer, XLNet (Yang et al., 2019). The other two networks were bespoke CNN and LSTM models. All models were trained on the MovieQA dataset (Tapaswi et al., 2016), and attention values were taken from the later levels of the networks. Several questions for the original dataset were selected for human testing, where the participants' eye gazes were tracked while they read and answered the questions. Sood et al. (2020a) observed that the attention scores from both the CNN and LSTM networks had strong negative correlations with the eye data. However, there was no significant correlation between eye gaze and XLNet.

Finally, there has been recent work using transformer representations to predict brain activity. For example, Toneva and Wehbe (2019) used layer representations of different transformers, including BERT and Transformer-XL, to predict activation in areas of the brain. They found that the middle layers best predict the activation as the context (sequence length) grew. Toneva and Wehbe (2019) tentatively suggested that this means there is a relationship between the layer and the type of processing occurring. To their surprise, they also found that modifying lower levels of BERT to produce uniform attention improved prediction performance.

Schrimpf et al. (2021) performed a similar analysis using many of the models included in the present study. They found that the output of some transformers could be used to predict their participants brain behavior to almost perfect accuracy. Prediction performance differed by model size and training regime, with GPT-2 performing best (Radford et al., 2019). Surprisingly, Schrimpf et al. (2021) found that untrained models also produced above chance prediction, leading them to suggest that the architecture of transformers captures important features of language before training occurs.

3 Analysis of Self-Attention Against Eye Gaze

All analyses used HuggingFace's (Wolf et al., 2020) version of the transformer and associated tokenizer. The models' weights were identical to those downloaded from HuggingFace; no fine-tuning was conducted. All analyses report Spearman correlations (Coefficient, 2008) to avoid data normality issues and provide a direct comparison to previously reported work.

3.1 Datasets

Six different datasets were used in our study. In all cases, eye-tracking data were captured from participants performing reading tasks in English.

The GECO Corpus (Cop et al., 2017) contains data from 19 Dutch bilingual and 14 English readers who read "The Mysterious Affair at Styles" by Agatha Christie across four sessions. Comprehension tests occurred between sessions. The bilingual participants completed two sessions in English and two in Dutch. We selected all English sessions for our analysis, regardless of the participant's bilingual status.

The PROVO Corpus (Luke and Christianson, 2018) contains 55 passages (average of 2.5 sentences). Passages were taken from online news articles, magazines, and works of fiction. Participants were 84 native English speakers instructed to read for comprehension.

The ZuCo Corpus (Hollenstein et al., 2018) is a combined reading, eye-tracking, and EEG dataset. Data was captured from 12 native English speakers who could read at their own pace with sentences presented one at a time. The participants completed three different tasks. Task 1 was a sentiment analysis task. Task 2 was a standard reading comprehension task where questions were presented after reading the text. Task 3 was also a reading comprehension task; however, the question appeared onscreen while the participant was reading.

We also used data from Sood et al. (2020a). They collected data from 32 passages taken from the MovieQA (Tapaswi et al., 2016) dataset. In Study 1, 18 participants answered questions from 16 passages under varying conditions such as multi-choice, free answer with text present, and free answer from memory. In Study 2, 4 participants answered multi-choice questions from the remaining 16 passages.

Additionally, we used data from Frank et al. (2013) where 48 participants read 205 sentences from unpublished novels for comprehension. The dataset contains eye movements from both native and non-native English speakers. Participants occasionally answered yes/no questions following a sentence.

The final dataset comes from Mishra et al. (2016) who conducted a sarcasm detection task. The

Table 1: List of models used in this paper

Model	Pre-trained models in Huggingface repository
ALBERT (Lan et al., 2020)	albert-base-v1, albert-base-v2, albert-large-v2, albert-xlarge-v2, albert-xxlarge-v2
BART (Lewis et al., 2020)	facebook-bart-base, facebook-bart-large
BERT (Devlin et al., 2019)	bert-base-uncased, bert-large-uncased, bert-base-cased, bert-large-cased, bert-base-multilingual-cased
BIGBIRD (Zaheer et al., 2020)	google-bigbird-roberta-base, google-bigbird-roberta-large
DeBERTa (He et al., 2021)	microsoft-deberta-base, microsoft-deberta-large, microsoft-deberta-xlarge, microsoft-deberta-v2-xlarge, microsoft-deberta-v2-xxlarge
DistilBERT (Sanh et al., 2019)	distilbert-base-uncased, distilbert-base-cased, distilbert-base-multilingual-cased
Muppet (Aghajanyan et al., 2021)	facebook-muppet-roberta-base, facebook-muppet-roberta-large
RoBERTa (Liu et al., 2019)	roberta-base, roberta-large
SqueezeBERT (Iandola et al., 2020)	squeezebert-squeezebert-uncased
XLM (Conneau et al., 2020)	xlm-roberta-base, xlm-roberta-large
XLNet (Yang et al., 2019)	xlnet-base-cased, xlnet-large-cased

dataset was taken from a wide variety of sources, all short passages containing a maximum of 40 words. Participants were non-native English speakers who were highly proficient in English.

3.2 Models

Table 1 lists the 31 variants from the 11 different bidirectional transformers models that we used. Our analysis method required all tokens to attend to all other tokens in a sequence. Therefore, unidirectional models such as GPT-2 (Radford et al., 2019) were excluded as they prevent tokens early in a sequence from attending tokens later in that sequence. We grouped the models into three types: 1) **Basic models** have the same architecture as BERT. 2) **Compact models** are those designed to be smaller versions of basic models. 3) **Alternative models** are those that greatly differ from the basic models.

3.2.1 Basic Models

BERT (Devlin et al., 2019): On release, BERT was state-of-the-art. It was trained using MLM, in which 15% of tokens were masked. Training also incorporated NSP by forcing the model to predict whether two sentences were contiguous or not. Our analysis includes a multilingual BERT and both the cased and uncased versions of English BERT.

RoBERTa (Liu et al., 2019): RoBERTa has an architecture identical to BERT but was trained for longer, with larger batch sizes and more data. The MLM examples were dynamically generated during a batch, unlike BERT which used the same mask patterns every time a sample was used. The NSP task was dropped as it did not affect performance.

We have also included the MUPPET version of RoBERTa (Aghajanyan et al., 2021), trained using multitask learning with tasks from four domains: classification, commonsense reasoning, reading comprehension, and summarization. Finally, we have included XLM-RoBERTa (Conneau et al., 2020), a multilingual version of RoBERTa.

3.2.2 Compact Models

ALBERT (Lan et al., 2020): A Lite BERT is a BERT-based model that uses two tricks to reduce the number of parameters and time taken required to train the model. 1) Factorized embedding parameterization - decomposing the large vocabulary embedding matrix into two small matrices; 2) Cross-layer sharing - parameters for all layers are shared.

DistilBERT (Sanh et al., 2019): This model used a Teacher – Student method for the distillation of knowledge (Buciluǎ et al., 2006; Hinton et al., 2015). Sanh et al. (2019) started with a full model and kept every second layer to create the student. The student was then trained on original training data. This procedure resulted in an almost as powerful model but half the size.

SqueezeBERT (Iandola et al., 2020): SqueezeBERT is Bert but with grouped convolutional layers instead of feed-forward layers. The model was trained using the same methods as ALBERT.

3.2.3 Alternative Attention Mechanisms

DeBERTa (He et al., 2021): DeBERTa differs from others on this list in that it decouples attention by word semantics from attention by word location. Version 2 of the model used a form of adversarial training to improve model generalization and surpassed human performance on Super GLUE benchmarks. We have used the RoBERTa based versions in this analysis.

One problem with transformers is the quadratic memory, and computational growth as sequence length increases because every token attends to all other tokens. Some have dealt with this problem by modifying the attention patterns to approximate this full attention pattern without requiring all of the attention comparisons. BIGBIRD (Zaheer et al., 2020) is an example that uses this attention approximation. The model uses a combination of global, sparse, and random attention. Again, we have used the RoBERTa based version of the model.

3.2.4 Alternative Architectures

XLNet (Yang et al., 2019): This model is a BERT extension using random permutations of word order during training. The model also incorporates the recurrence mechanism used in Transformer-XL (Dai et al., 2019).

BART (Lewis et al., 2020): BART is an encoder-decoder model that is to recover data from corrupted text input. BART has approximately 10% more parameters than comparable BERT models and no final feed-forward layer. Pre-training was based on corrupting the inputs using token masking, token deletion, token infilling, sentence permutation, and document rotation.

3.3 Analysis Method

The transformer data were created by converting the original texts into sentences and then tokenizing those sentences to create sequences. The next step was inputting tokenized sequences into the transformer and extracting the attention matrices produced for each attention head. In terms of Equation 1, we took the output of the softmax function before it was multiplied by $\mathbf{V}$ as that provided a normalized value indicating what proportion of attention each token payed to all others.

The attention value for each token was calculated by averaging across attention heads and matrix rows. This calculation produced a single vector representing the amount of attention allocated to each token by all others in the sentence. Our procedure differs from Sood et al. (2020a) who used the maximum attention from each word instead of the mean. Some preliminary analyses suggested that the mean attention values provided more stable results across datasets. The results using the maximum values are available on our GitHub repository for comparison purposes. If a word was tokenized into sub-words, those sub-words were also averaged to produce a single value. The special tokens [CLS] and [SEP] were used for the attention calculations but dropped from the final word-level attention vector. Finally, attention was normalized by sentence by calculating the proportion of attention allocated to each word.

Dwell time was used for the overt human attention data. Dwell time is a measurement of the total time that a participant's eye fixated on a word. This choice was necessary for consistency between analyses as it was the only measure to appear in all datasets. Dwell time data was extracted for each word in a sentence, with one sentence being produced for each participant in the original data. The dwell time data were also normalized by sentence by calculating the dwell time proportion for each word. The data from individual participants were then averaged to create one normalized sentence for each sentence in the text.

Data from the transformers and human participants were then matched so that each word in the text had a sentence normalized attention score from the transformers and the average participant. After matching, all the words from a text were pooled and used to calculate the Spearman correlation values. One-word sentences were removed as both scores were always 1.0, which inflated the correlation scores.

3.4 Results and Discussion

There were significant positive correlations between the total dwell time and the attention from all layers of the different models. This finding was an apparent departure from the results of Sood et al. (2020a) who reported a non-significant correlation of -.16 between the last layer of XLNet and their dataset. For comparison, we obtained a .428 correlation for their Study 1 data and .327 for their Study 2 data from XLNet's last layer. Although they did not directly specify the normalization they used, we suspect that the difference in results is due to us using sentence-level normalization and Sood et al. (2020a) using paragraph normalization. For comparison, we ran the same procedure using paragraph normalization and obtained non-significant correlations just as they did. In general, many of the correlations obtained using sentence normalization become much weaker when using the paragraph normalization. This finding corresponds well with the Sen et al. (2020) finding that attention for

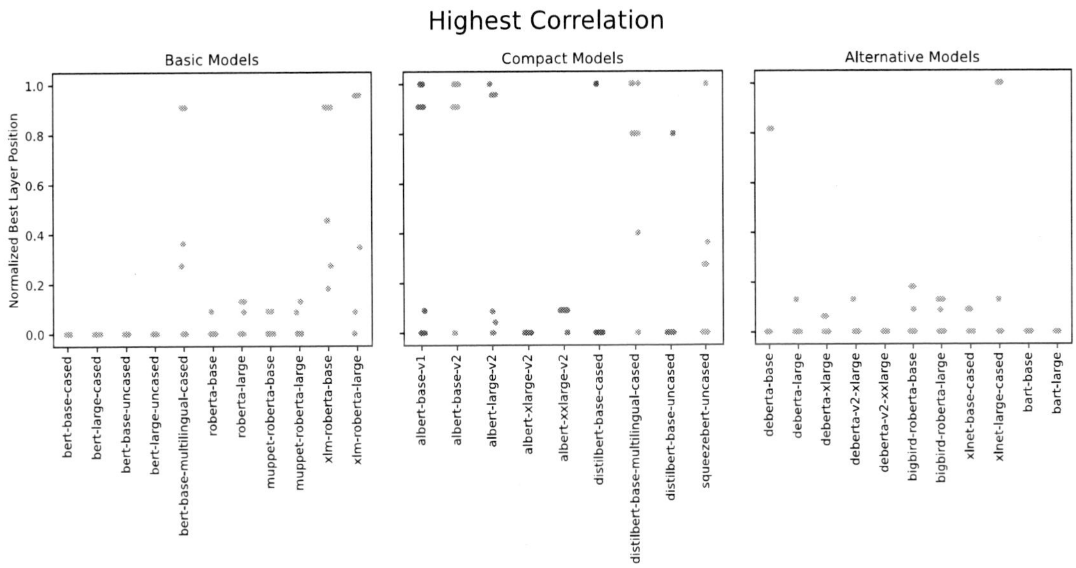

Figure 1: The relative position of the layer with the highest correlation. 0 is the first layer, 1 is the last layer. There are multiple dots for each model because each dot represents the highest correlation from a different dataset.

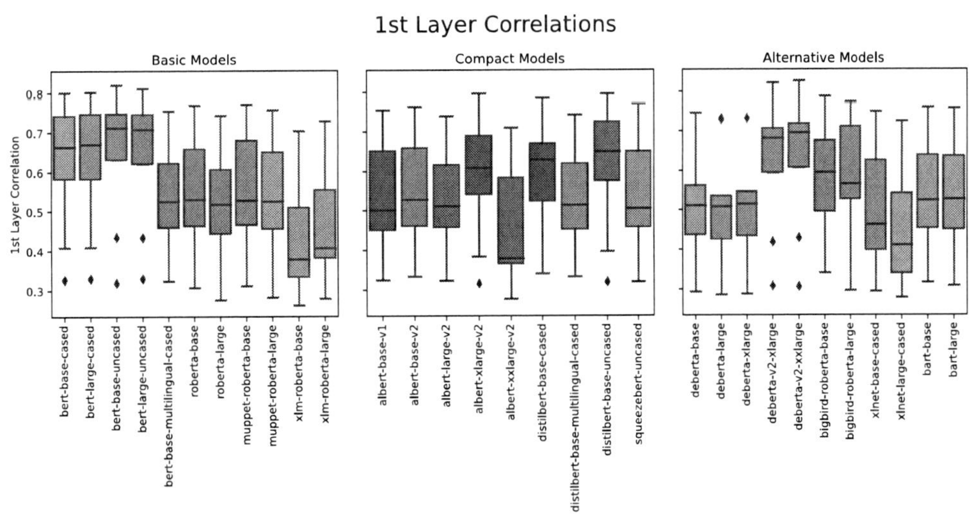

Figure 2: The correlations between the first layer attention patterns and eye gaze data from all models. The box plots represent the spread of correlation values across datasets.

non-transformer neural networks became less correlated with eye movements as the length of the text increased. All analyses presented here refer to sentence-level correlations. Paragraph-level analyses can be found in our GitHub repository.

Our first analysis investigated which attention layer was most closely correlated with the eye gaze data. Figure 1 shows the relative position of the layer with the highest correlation by model. In many cases, the highest correlation was produced by the earlier layers of each model, in 66.2% of cases this was the first layer (position 0). Notable exceptions to this rule are the multilingual versions of BERT and RoBERTa (i.e., XLM) and many compact models. Although further studies are needed, the finding that multilingual variants of models do not behave like monolingual variants is in line with some previously reported studies (Conneau et al., 2020; Hollenstein et al., 2021b; Vulić et al., 2020), where some studies report multilingual benefits and while others do not.

Further investigations found that when the first

Table 2: First layer correlations By dataset. Strongest correlations have been bolded.

Model	GECO	Mishra	Provo	Sood S1	Sood S2	ZuCo S1	ZuCo S2	ZuCo S3	Frank et al
albert-v1	0.744	0.754	0.497	0.450	0.326	0.501	0.580	0.325	0.652
albert-v2	0.748	0.739	0.492	0.460	0.329	0.503	0.585	0.326	0.637
bart	0.729	0.758	0.526	0.451	0.323	0.511	0.550	0.313	0.638
bert-cased	0.802	0.783	0.668	0.584	0.410	0.643	0.679	0.328	0.744
bert-multilingual-cased	0.753	0.727	0.525	0.459	0.338	0.489	0.622	0.324	0.603
bert-uncased	0.816	**0.791**	**0.710**	**0.626**	**0.434**	**0.693**	**0.722**	0.324	**0.746**
birdbird-roberta	0.775	0.774	0.600	0.511	0.363	0.582	0.565	0.319	0.693
deberta-v1	0.731	0.735	0.511	0.432	0.310	0.502	0.533	0.289	0.549
deberta-v2	**0.824**	0.770	0.708	0.601	0.423	0.688	0.712	0.306	0.660
distilbert-cased	0.786	0.772	0.623	0.523	0.378	0.629	0.632	0.341	0.670
distilbert-multilingual-cased	0.742	0.740	0.513	0.452	0.337	0.487	0.620	0.333	0.602
distilbert-uncased	0.796	0.780	0.649	0.576	0.396	0.649	0.678	0.319	0.725
roberta	0.709	0.755	0.523	0.453	0.329	0.504	0.537	0.291	0.632
roberta-muppet	0.712	0.763	0.527	0.460	0.329	0.501	0.542	0.297	0.665
squeezebert	0.730	0.769	0.505	0.458	0.320	0.499	0.549	**0.348**	0.650
xlm	0.690	0.715	0.391	0.358	0.271	0.379	0.476	0.313	0.532
xlnet	0.678	0.736	0.436	0.369	0.287	0.408	0.470	0.297	0.584

layer did not produce the highest correlation, the first-layer correlation value was on average, 0.055 lower than the best correlation value. In 75% of cases, this difference was less than 0.082. Therefore, the first layer value appears to be a good representation of the correlation between the model and the eye gaze data. An extreme example of this were the ALBERT variants, which, likely due to weight sharing during training, have virtually identical correlations from attention values from each of its levels (Figure 3). Due to its general best performance, the first layer results have been used at the best performance for all models. Analyses using the actual best performance can be observed in our GitHub repository, although those results are highly similar to those reported here.

Our next analysis compared performance across models based on the first layer correlations. Figure 2 shows that, in general, the size of the model does not determine the correlation between the human eye and transformer attention. Evidence for this can be seen in minor differences between various-sized variants of the same model. For example, the cased and uncased versions of BERT-base and BERT-large are very similar, despite the large variant containing 340 million parameters compared to the base variants' 110 million. Similar observations can be observed across the other models, especially DeBERTa, where the largest variants have 1.5 billion parameters, and the smaller ones contain less than 1/3 of that number. This observation was confirmed with a non-significant sign test (p = *.090*) that compared each variant to the next smallest variant in its model type. Due to this similarity, results in Table 2 reports a single value per model type that is an average for each size variant. Table 3 shows the highest correlation by dataset. In most cases, this model was either BERT-uncased or DeBERTa-V2.

While the number of parameters is not what determines the correlations, comparing across models in Figure 2 suggests that training is essential for determining those relationships. For example, the BERT models have identical architectures to various RoBERTa models, yet Table 2 shows that the BERT correlations were consistently higher than the RoBERTa based models. The other clear examples of training effects can be seen in the differences between DeBERTa V1 and V2, where V2 models use the Scale-invariant-Fine-Tuning (SiFT) algorithm introduced in the original paper. Interestingly, the addition of the SiFT algorithm allowed DeBERTa V2 to surpass human performance on the SuperGLUE benchmarks (Wang et al., 2019a), and Table 3 shows that this model was often the second-highest correlated model. While it would be great to find a direct relationship between how human-like a model's performance is and how correlated its attention patterns are to eye movements, that is not the case. Excluding the compact models, the BERT descendants outperform it on many of the benchmarks, yet only DeBERTA comes close to having stronger correlations to human eye movements. In most cases, attention patterns less correlated with overt human attention produced better overall performance on NLP tasks.

Tables 2 and 3 show the rankings by correlation are similar between datasets, with BERT-uncased

Table 3: The three models with strongest correlation to eye-tracking data for each dataset. The uncased version of BERT produced the strongest correlation in 7 out of 9 cases.

	GECO	Mishra	Provo	Sood S1	Sood S2	ZuCo S1	ZuCo S2	ZuCo S3	Frank-et-al
1	deberta-v2	bert-uncased	bert-uncased	bert-uncased	bert-uncased	bert-uncased	bert-uncased	squeezebert	bert-uncased
2	bert-uncased	bert-cased	deberta-v2	deberta-v2	deberta-v2	deberta-v2	deberta-v2	distilbert-cased	bert-cased
3	bert-cased	distilbert-uncased	bert-cased	bert-cased	bert-cased	distilbert-uncased	bert-cased	distilbert-multilingual	distilbert-uncased

producing the highest correlation in all but two cases. In one of the exceptions, the GECO dataset, BERT-uncased, was ranked second. In the other exception, ZuC0 Task 3, the ranking was much lower. In general, the correlations from ZuCo Task 3 differ greatly from the other datasets. The correlations are lower for all models, and the model rankings are very different, with two of the compact models, SqueezeBERT and DistillBERT, ranking highest, and BERT-uncased, ninth. Task 3's participants were the same as Tasks 1 and 2. Those first two tasks produced results closer to the other datasets, meaning Task 3's lower correlations were likely due to the task itself.

Interestingly, in Task 3, the participants were presented with the question on the screen, allowing them to direct their eye gaze to find the information they required. This contrasts with most of the other datasets where the questions about the data were presented after reading. The only exceptions to this were some tasks by Sood et al. (2020a) where the question appeared on screen in Study 2 and in 2/3s of the tests in Study 1. Furthermore, the correlations from Sood et al. (2020a) Studies 2 and 1 were also the second and third lowest of the datasets, respectively (Table 2). While further study is needed, the lower correlations from SOOD et al. and ZuCo Task 3 may indicate that while transformer attention patterns produce strong correlations when reading typically, the relationship drops when the reader actively searches for information.

Our final analysis looked at correlations across levels of BERT (Figure 3). The results of Toneva and Wehbe (2019) suggest that the middle layers of BERT provided the best features for predicting brain activity in humans. They speculated that these relationships could mean that the middle layers of BERT could be related to the kinds of processing that occurs in those brain levels. Our results show that the attention patterns from BERT's first layer were closely related to eye gaze data. Again, while speculative, our results combined with Toneva and Wehbe (2019) would suggest that for BERT at least, the lower levels correspond best

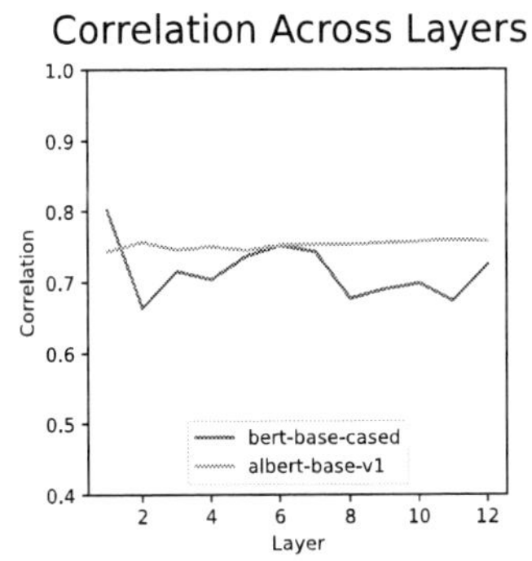

Figure 3: The average correlations across layers for bert-base-cased and albert-base-v1.

to text information entering the eyes. In contrast, the middle layers correspond to specific processing. With that said, not all transformers produced the strongest correlations from their first layer. For example, as mentioned above, Figure 3 shows the data from ALBERT-V1 where the correlations from all levels were relatively the same.

4 Conclusion

This paper analyzed the correlations between attention in pre-trained transformers and human attention derived from eye gaze. We found correlations between the two that were generally stronger in the earlier layers of the model and, in most cases, strongest in the first layer. These correlations were unaffected by the model's size, as different sized variants of models produced similar correlations. The training the models received did appear to matter, although the present study cannot determine the full extent of that relationship. We found that correlations were weaker from eye-tracking studies where the participants could actively guide their reading towards seeking the information they needed than when presented with questions after reading. While we found a relationship between overt human attention and attention in some pre-trained transformers, additional research would be required before models of eye gaze could be used to replace attention in transformers.

References

Armen Aghajanyan, Anchit Gupta, Akshat Shrivastava, Xilun Chen, Luke Zettlemoyer, and Sonal Gupta. 2021. Muppet: Massive multi-task representations with pre-finetuning. In *Proceedings of the 2021 Conference on Empirical Methods in Natural Language Processing*, pages 5799–5811, Online and Punta Cana, Dominican Republic. Association for Computational Linguistics.

Dzmitry Bahdanau, Kyunghyun Cho, and Yoshua Bengio. 2015. Neural machine translation by jointly learning to align and translate. In *3rd International Conference on Learning Representations, ICLR 2015, San Diego, CA, USA, May 7-9, 2015, Conference Track Proceedings*.

Cristian Buciluă, Rich Caruana, and Alexandru Niculescu-Mizil. 2006. Model compression. In *Proceedings of the 12th ACM SIGKDD international conference on Knowledge discovery and data mining*, pages 535–541.

Shivani Choudhary, Kushagri Tandon, Raksha Agarwal, and Niladri Chatterjee. 2021. Mtl782_iitd at cmcl 2021 shared task: Prediction of eye-tracking features using bert embeddings and linguistic features. In *Proceedings of the Workshop on Cognitive Modeling and Computational Linguistics*, pages 114–119.

Spearman Rank Correlation Coefficient. 2008. The concise encyclopedia of statistics.

Alexis Conneau, Kartikay Khandelwal, Naman Goyal, Vishrav Chaudhary, Guillaume Wenzek, Francisco Guzmán, Edouard Grave, Myle Ott, Luke Zettlemoyer, and Veselin Stoyanov. 2020. Unsupervised cross-lingual representation learning at scale. In *Proceedings of the 58th Annual Meeting of the Association for Computational Linguistics*, pages 8440–8451, Online. Association for Computational Linguistics.

Uschi Cop, Nicolas Dirix, Denis Drieghe, and Wouter Duyck. 2017. Presenting geco: An eyetracking corpus of monolingual and bilingual sentence reading. *Behavior research methods*, 49(2):602–615.

Zihang Dai, Zhilin Yang, Yiming Yang, Jaime Carbonell, Quoc Le, and Ruslan Salakhutdinov. 2019. Transformer-XL: Attentive language models beyond a fixed-length context. In *Proceedings of the 57th Annual Meeting of the Association for Computational Linguistics*, pages 2978–2988, Florence, Italy. Association for Computational Linguistics.

Jacob Devlin, Ming-Wei Chang, Kenton Lee, and Kristina Toutanova. 2019. BERT: pre-training of deep bidirectional transformers for language understanding. In *Proceedings of the 2019 Conference of the North American Chapter of the Association for Computational Linguistics: Human Language Technologies, NAACL-HLT 2019, Minneapolis, MN, USA, June 2-7, 2019, Volume 1 (Long and Short Papers)*, pages 4171–4186. Association for Computational Linguistics.

Alexey Dosovitskiy, Lucas Beyer, Alexander Kolesnikov, Dirk Weissenborn, Xiaohua Zhai, Thomas Unterthiner, Mostafa Dehghani, Matthias Minderer, Georg Heigold, Sylvain Gelly, Jakob Uszkoreit, and Neil Houlsby. 2021. An image is worth 16x16 words: Transformers for image recognition at scale. In *9th International Conference on Learning Representations, ICLR 2021, Virtual Event, Austria, May 3-7, 2021*. OpenReview.net.

Geoffrey B Duggan and Stephen J Payne. 2011. Skim reading by satisficing: evidence from eye tracking. In *Proceedings of the SIGCHI conference on human factors in computing systems*, pages 1141–1150.

Gemma Fitzsimmons, Mark J. Weal, and Denis Drieghe. 2014. Skim reading: an adaptive strategy for reading on the web. In *ACM Web Science Conference, WebSci '14, Bloomington, IN, USA, June 23-26, 2014*, pages 211–219. ACM.

Stefan L Frank, Irene Fernandez Monsalve, Robin L Thompson, and Gabriella Vigliocco. 2013. Reading time data for evaluating broad-coverage models of english sentence processing. *Behavior research methods*, 45(4):1182–1190.

Bashir Muftah Ghariba, Mohamed S Shehata, and Peter McGuire. 2020. A novel fully convolutional network for visual saliency prediction. *PeerJ computer science*, 6:e280.

Michael Hahn and Frank Keller. 2016. Modeling human reading with neural attention. In *Proceedings of the 2016 Conference on Empirical Methods in Natural Language Processing*, pages 85–95.

Michael Hahn and Frank Keller. 2018. Modeling task effects in human reading with neural attention. *arXiv preprint arXiv:1808.00054*.

Yiding Hao, Simon Mendelsohn, Rachel Sterneck, Randi Martinez, and Robert Frank. 2020. Probabilistic predictions of people perusing: Evaluating metrics of language model performance for psycholinguistic modeling. *arXiv preprint arXiv:2009.03954*.

Jonathan Harel, Christof Koch, and Pietro Perona. 2006. Graph-based visual saliency. In *Advances in Neural Information Processing Systems 19, Proceedings of the Twentieth Annual Conference on Neural Information Processing Systems, Vancouver, British Columbia, Canada, December 4-7, 2006*, pages 545–552. MIT Press.

Pengcheng He, Xiaodong Liu, Jianfeng Gao, and Weizhu Chen. 2021. Deberta: decoding-enhanced bert with disentangled attention. In *9th International Conference on Learning Representations, ICLR 2021, Virtual Event, Austria, May 3-7, 2021*.

Geoffrey Hinton, Oriol Vinyals, and Jeff Dean. 2015. Distilling the knowledge in a neural network. *arXiv preprint arXiv:1503.02531*.

Nora Hollenstein, Federico Pirovano, Ce Zhang, Lena Jäger, and Lisa Beinborn. 2021a. Multilingual language models predict human reading behavior. In *Proceedings of the 2021 Conference of the North American Chapter of the Association for Computational Linguistics: Human Language Technologies*, pages 106–123, Online. Association for Computational Linguistics.

Nora Hollenstein, Federico Pirovano, Ce Zhang, Lena Jäger, and Lisa Beinborn. 2021b. Multilingual language models predict human reading behavior. In *Proceedings of the 2021 Conference of the North American Chapter of the Association for Computational Linguistics: Human Language Technologies*, pages 106–123.

Nora Hollenstein, Jonathan Rotsztejn, Marius Troendle, Andreas Pedroni, Ce Zhang, and Nicolas Langer. 2018. Zuco, a simultaneous eeg and eye-tracking resource for natural sentence reading. *Scientific data*, 5(1):1–13.

Xun Huang, Chengyao Shen, Xavier Boix, and Qi Zhao. 2015. Salicon: Reducing the semantic gap in saliency prediction by adapting deep neural networks. In *Proceedings of the IEEE international conference on computer vision*, pages 262–270.

Forrest Iandola, Albert Shaw, Ravi Krishna, and Kurt Keutzer. 2020. SqueezeBERT: What can computer vision teach NLP about efficient neural networks? In *Proceedings of SustaiNLP: Workshop on Simple and Efficient Natural Language Processing*, pages 124–135, Online. Association for Computational Linguistics.

Yifan Jiang, Shiyu Chang, and Zhangyang Wang. 2021. Transgan: Two pure transformers can make one strong gan, and that can scale up. *Advances in Neural Information Processing Systems*, 34.

Zhenzhong Lan, Mingda Chen, Sebastian Goodman, Kevin Gimpel, Piyush Sharma, and Radu Soricut. 2020. ALBERT: A lite BERT for self-supervised learning of language representations. In *8th International Conference on Learning Representations, ICLR 2020, Addis Ababa, Ethiopia, April 26-30, 2020*.

Mike Lewis, Yinhan Liu, Naman Goyal, Marjan Ghazvininejad, Abdelrahman Mohamed, Omer Levy, Veselin Stoyanov, and Luke Zettlemoyer. 2020. BART: denoising sequence-to-sequence pre-training for natural language generation, translation, and comprehension. In *Proceedings of the 58th Annual Meeting of the Association for Computational Linguistics, ACL 2020, Online, July 5-10, 2020*, pages 7871–7880. Association for Computational Linguistics.

Guanbin Li and Yizhou Yu. 2016. Visual saliency detection based on multiscale deep cnn features. *IEEE transactions on image processing*, 25(11):5012–5024.

Yinhan Liu, Myle Ott, Naman Goyal, Jingfei Du, Mandar Joshi, Danqi Chen, Omer Levy, Mike Lewis, Luke Zettlemoyer, and Veselin Stoyanov. 2019. Roberta: A robustly optimized bert pretraining approach. *arXiv preprint arXiv:1907.11692*.

Steven G Luke and Kiel Christianson. 2018. The provo corpus: A large eye-tracking corpus with predictability norms. *Behavior research methods*, 50(2):826–833.

Abhijit Mishra, Diptesh Kanojia, and Pushpak Bhattacharyya. 2016. Predicting readers' sarcasm understandability by modeling gaze behavior. In *Proceedings of the AAAI Conference on Artificial Intelligence*, volume 30.

Michael I Posner. 1980. Orienting of attention. *Quarterly journal of experimental psychology*, 32(1):3–25.

Alec Radford, Karthik Narasimhan, Tim Salimans, and Ilya Sutskever. 2018. Improving language understanding with unsupervised learning.

Alec Radford, Jeffrey Wu, Rewon Child, David Luan, Dario Amodei, Ilya Sutskever, et al. 2019. Language models are unsupervised multitask learners. *OpenAI blog*, 1(8):9.

Keith Rayner. 2009. The 35th sir frederick bartlett lecture: Eye movements and attention in reading, scene perception, and visual search. *Quarterly journal of experimental psychology*, 62(8):1457–1506.

Erik D Reichle, Alexander Pollatsek, Donald L Fisher, and Keith Rayner. 1998. Toward a model of eye movement control in reading. *Psychological review*, 105(1):125.

Victor Sanh, Lysandre Debut, Julien Chaumond, and Thomas Wolf. 2019. Distilbert, a distilled version of bert: smaller, faster, cheaper and lighter. *arXiv preprint arXiv:1910.01108*.

Martin Schrimpf, Idan Asher Blank, Greta Tuckute, Carina Kauf, Eghbal A Hosseini, Nancy Kanwisher, Joshua B Tenenbaum, and Evelina Fedorenko. 2021. The neural architecture of language: Integrative modeling converges on predictive processing. *Proceedings of the National Academy of Sciences*, 118(45).

Cansu Sen, Thomas Hartvigsen, Biao Yin, Xiangnan Kong, and Elke Rundensteiner. 2020. Human attention maps for text classification: Do humans and neural networks focus on the same words? In *Proceedings of the 58th Annual Meeting of the Association for Computational Linguistics*, pages 4596–4608.

Min Joon Seo, Sewon Min, Ali Farhadi, and Hannaneh Hajishirzi. 2018. Neural speed reading via skim-rnn. In *6th International Conference on Learning Representations, ICLR 2018, Vancouver, BC, Canada, April 30 - May 3, 2018, Conference Track Proceedings*.

Ekta Sood, Simon Tannert, Diego Frassinelli, Andreas Bulling, and Ngoc Thang Vu. 2020a. Interpreting attention models with human visual attention in machine reading comprehension. In *Proceedings of the 24th Conference on Computational Natural Language Learning*, pages 12–25, Online. Association for Computational Linguistics.

Ekta Sood, Simon Tannert, Philipp Müller, and Andreas Bulling. 2020b. Improving natural language processing tasks with human gaze-guided neural attention. *Advances in Neural Information Processing Systems*, 33:6327–6341.

Neset Özkan Tan, Joshua Bensemann, Diana Benavides-Prado, Yang Chen, Mark Gahegan, Lia Lee, Alex Yuxuan Peng, Patricia Riddle, and Michael Witbrock. 2021. An explainability analysis of a sentiment prediction task using a transformer-based attention filter. In *Proceedings of the Ninth Annual Conference on Advances in Cognitive Systems*.

Makarand Tapaswi, Yukun Zhu, Rainer Stiefelhagen, Antonio Torralba, Raquel Urtasun, and Sanja Fidler. 2016. Movieqa: Understanding stories in movies through question-answering. In *Proceedings of the IEEE conference on computer vision and pattern recognition*, pages 4631–4640.

Hamed R Tavakoli, Ali Borji, Jorma Laaksonen, and Esa Rahtu. 2017. Exploiting inter-image similarity and ensemble of extreme learners for fixation prediction using deep features. *Neurocomputing*, 244:10–18.

Wilson L Taylor. 1953. "cloze procedure": A new tool for measuring readability. *Journalism quarterly*, 30(4):415–433.

Mariya Toneva and Leila Wehbe. 2019. Interpreting and improving natural-language processing (in machines) with natural language-processing (in the brain). *Advances in Neural Information Processing Systems*, 32:14954–14964.

Ashish Vaswani, Noam Shazeer, Niki Parmar, Jakob Uszkoreit, Llion Jones, Aidan N Gomez, Łukasz Kaiser, and Illia Polosukhin. 2017. Attention is all you need. In *Advances in neural information processing systems*, pages 5998–6008.

Nicolas Vecoven, Damien Ernst, Antoine Wehenkel, and Guillaume Drion. 2020. Introducing neuromodulation in deep neural networks to learn adaptive behaviours. *PloS one*, 15(1):e0227922.

Ivan Vulić, Simon Baker, Edoardo Maria Ponti, Ulla Petti, Ira Leviant, Kelly Wing, Olga Majewska, Eden Bar, Matt Malone, Thierry Poibeau, et al. 2020. Multi-simlex: A large-scale evaluation of multilingual and crosslingual lexical semantic similarity. *Computational Linguistics*, 46(4):847–897.

Alex Wang, Yada Pruksachatkun, Nikita Nangia, Amanpreet Singh, Julian Michael, Felix Hill, Omer Levy, and Samuel R Bowman. 2019a. Superglue: a stickier benchmark for general-purpose language understanding systems. In *Proceedings of the 33rd International Conference on Neural Information Processing Systems*, pages 3266–3280.

Alex Wang, Amanpreet Singh, Julian Michael, Felix Hill, Omer Levy, and Samuel R. Bowman. 2019b. GLUE: A multi-task benchmark and analysis platform for natural language understanding. In *7th International Conference on Learning Representations, ICLR 2019, New Orleans, LA, USA, May 6-9, 2019*.

Thomas Wolf, Lysandre Debut, Victor Sanh, Julien Chaumond, Clement Delangue, Anthony Moi, Pierric Cistac, Tim Rault, Remi Louf, Morgan Funtowicz, Joe Davison, Sam Shleifer, Patrick von Platen, Clara Ma, Yacine Jernite, Julien Plu, Canwen Xu, Teven Le Scao, Sylvain Gugger, Mariama Drame, Quentin Lhoest, and Alexander Rush. 2020. Transformers: State-of-the-art natural language processing. In *Proceedings of the 2020 Conference on Empirical Methods in Natural Language Processing: System Demonstrations*, pages 38–45, Online. Association for Computational Linguistics.

Zhilin Yang, Zihang Dai, Yiming Yang, Jaime Carbonell, Russ R Salakhutdinov, and Quoc V Le. 2019. Xlnet: Generalized autoregressive pretraining for language understanding. *Advances in neural information processing systems*, 32.

Adams Wei Yu, Hongrae Lee, and Quoc Le. 2017. Learning to skim text. In *Proceedings of the 55th Annual Meeting of the Association for Computational Linguistics (Volume 1: Long Papers)*, pages 1880–1890.

Manzil Zaheer, Guru Guruganesh, Kumar Avinava Dubey, Joshua Ainslie, Chris Alberti, Santiago Ontañón, Philip Pham, Anirudh Ravula, Qifan Wang, Li Yang, and Amr Ahmed. 2020. Big bird: Transformers for longer sequences. In *Advances in Neural Information Processing Systems 33: Annual Conference on Neural Information Processing Systems 2020, NeurIPS 2020, December 6-12, 2020, virtual*.

Yukun Zheng, Jiaxin Mao, Yiqun Liu, Zixin Ye, Min Zhang, and Shaoping Ma. 2019. Human behavior inspired machine reading comprehension. In *Proceedings of the 42nd International ACM SIGIR Conference on Research and Development in Information Retrieval*, pages 425–434.

A Investigating the Effect of Injecting Eye Gaze Bias During Training

As a preliminary experiment, we investigated the effect of injecting human eye gaze bias during training on test accuracy. We used the BERT model (Devlin et al., 2019) and the sarcasm-detection dataset published in Mishra et al. (2016) as a case study.

A.1 Method

The Mishra et al. (2016) dataset was originally proposed to predict non-native English speakers' understanding of sarcasm by using eye-tracking information. The dataset contains information on the fixation duration of each word for each participant. We injected the eye-gazing bias during training by optimising the following loss function:

$$L = H(y, \hat{y}) + \alpha H(p, \hat{p}) \tag{2}$$

where $H(y, \hat{y})$ is the cross-entropy loss of the binary classification task of sarcasm detection, and $H(p, \hat{p})$ computes the divergence of the first-layer attention values from the distribution of the normalised fixation duration values given a sentence. The hyperparameter α controls the weight of the second term in the loss function.

Our experiments only used the fixation duration values from Participant 6 because they had the highest overall accuracy for sarcasm detection (90.29%). All the hyperparameters were tuned on a validation set extracted from the training set before being applied to the entire training set.

A.2 Results

The results are plotted in Figure 4. As expected, the models fine-tuned from pre-trained BERT models had significantly better test accuracy on both the small and large training sets than models trained from scratch on the Mishra et al. (2016) dataset.

A t-test confirmed that when the models were trained on the large training set without pre-training, an eye gaze bias injection during training hurt the performance (*p* < *.05*). With pre-training, both models in Figure 4(b) performed better than the best participant in the Mishra et al. (2016) dataset. The bias injection still lowered the mean accuracy, although the difference was no longer statistically significant. When the small training set was used to train the models, we found no significant difference after the bias injection.

Comparing our results to Sood et al. (2020b) suggests that training a model to predict eye gaze improves text compression performance, whereas using eye gaze data to regulate sarcasm detection decreased performance. It is unknown whether the difference in results is due to our task choice or to our method of using human data.

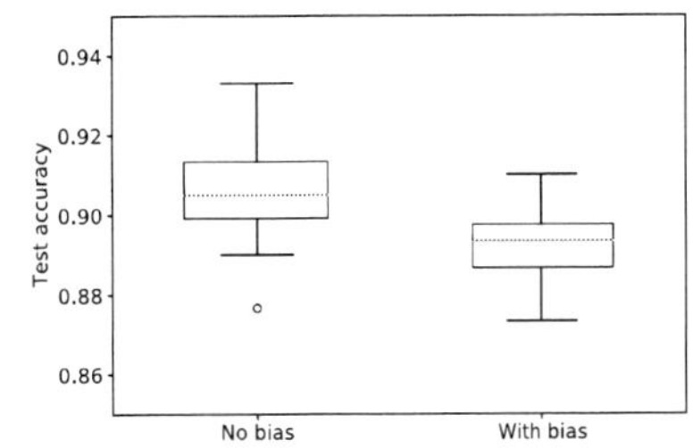

(a) Large training set without pre-training

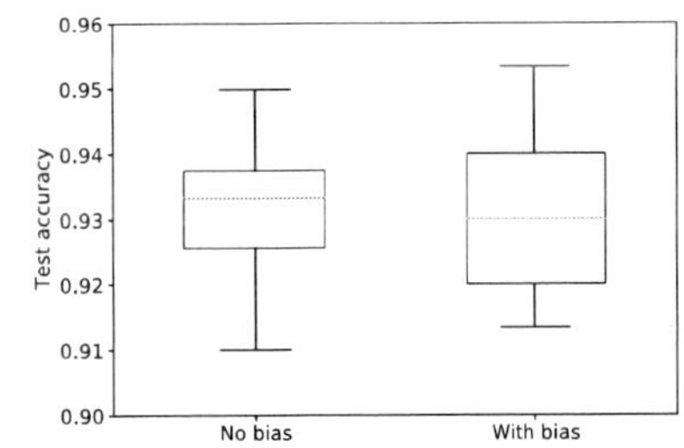

(b) Large training set with pre-training

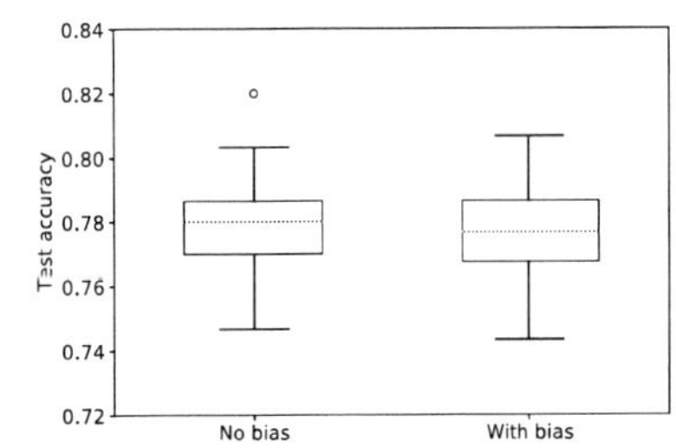

(c) Small training set without pre-training

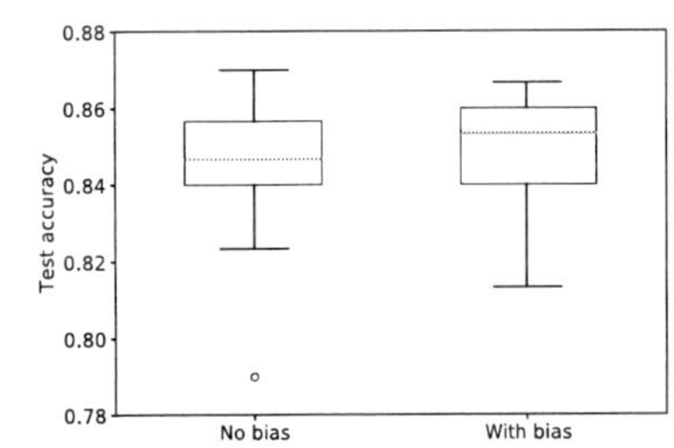

(d) Small training set with pre-training

Figure 4: Comparison of the BERT models trained with eye gaze bias against the models trained without in terms of test accuracy. Models in plots (a) and (b) were trained on 693 examples, and the results were obtained after 20 runs. Models in plots (c) and (d) were trained on only 70 examples, and the experiments were repeated 50 times. The same test set (300 examples) was used for all the experiments.

About Time: Do *Transformers* Learn Temporal Verbal Aspect?

Eleni Metheniti ① ③
① IRIT (CNRS)
Université Toulouse - Paul Sabatier (UT3)
31400 Toulouse, France

Tim Van de Cruys ① ②
② KU Leuven
Faculty of Arts
Department of Linguistics
Leuven.AI institute
B-3000 Leuven, Belgium

Nabil Hathout ③
③ CLLE-CNRS
Université Toulouse - Jean Jaurès (UT2J)
Maison de la Recherche
31058 Toulouse, France

firstname.lastname@{univ-tlse2.fr, irit.fr, kuleuven.be}

Abstract

Aspect is a linguistic concept that describes how an action, event, or state of a verb phrase is situated in time. In this paper, we explore whether different transformer models are capable of identifying aspectual features. We focus on two specific aspectual features: telicity and duration. Telicity marks whether the verb's action or state has an endpoint or not (telic/atelic), and duration denotes whether a verb expresses an action (dynamic) or a state (stative). These features are integral to the interpretation of natural language, but also hard to annotate and identify with NLP methods. We perform experiments in English and French, and our results show that transformer models adequately capture information on telicity and duration in their vectors, even in their non-finetuned forms, but are somewhat biased with regard to verb tense and word order.

1 Introduction

Aspect is a linguistic concept that characterizes how an action, event, or state (expressed by a verb phrase) relates to time, beyond the scope of the verb's tense; via aspect, information such as frequency, duration, and completion is conveyed. Some verbs express events or actions that have or do not have a clearly-defined endpoint because of their meaning (lexical aspect or *aktionsart*), while others can express different temporal properties in different contexts and forms (grammatical aspect). Languages may express aspect in various ways, e.g. by using grammatical verb tense (incomplete actions with continuous/progressive, perfect progressive and imperfect, complete actions with perfect), morphemes (e.g. Finnish, Czech) or with aspect markers (e.g. Mandarin Chinese). However, certain aspectual features cannot simply be deduced from morphosyntax and require some degree of semantic knowledge. In this paper, we focus on two of these aspectual features: telicity and duration. **Telicity** is related to the goal-oriented nature of the verb phrase. The verb's action is said to be *telic* if it has an endpoint; for example, verbs which demonstrate an action such as *kick, eat* ("I kicked the ball.", "I eat an apple.") are *telic*, because the action described has a perceived ending. When the verb denotes a state, e.g. *exist*, or when the completion of the verb's action is either indefinite, impossible or irrelevant, e.g. *agree, stay* ("I agree with you.", "We stayed at the hotel."), then the verb phrase is characterized as *atelic*. **Duration** is another aspectual feature, different from telicity: it distinguishes between verbs that describe a state (*stative*, e.g. *occupy, lie*) or an action (*durative*, e.g. *run, knock*) regardless of whether they have a perceived endpoint or not. The perception of telicity and duration is the outcome of the entire verbal phrase, and not solely the verb's features (Krifka, 1998). Besides, the context can also place constraints on the aspectual class of a verb (Siegel, 1998). Therefore, making sound judgments on aspectual features such as telicity and duration, especially in a morphologically-poor language like English, is not always an easy task—our datasets in Section 4.1 provide some examples of sentences where these features are hard to assess, even for a human. Aspect has been exploited for tasks where semantic knowledge is necessary, since it provides information on temporal relations (Costa and Branco, 2012), textual entailment (Hosseini et al., 2018; Kober et al., 2019) and event ordering (Chambers et al., 2014).

In recent years, transformer-based models have shown great success in NLP tasks which traditionally require in-depth language analysis and complex strategies on capturing dependencies, semantic information, and world knowledge. However, it remains unclear whether the success of these models is due to a genuine capability to accurately model linguistic meaning, or whether the models are just very good at picking up statistical correlations, but fail to capture fine-grained semantic distinctions (Ettinger, 2020). With this

Proceedings of the Workshop on Cognitive Modeling and Computational Linguistics, pages 88 - 101
May 26, 2022 ©2022 Association for Computational Linguistics

research question in mind, our goal is to investigate whether transformer-based architectures (both with and without fine-tuning) are able to capture the semantic information related to telicity and duration. To do so, we make use of two datasets annotated for telicity and duration (Friedrich and Gateva, 2017; Alikhani and Stone, 2019), and we conduct a range of experiments using several pretrained transformer architectures in two languages (English and French). We extend our experiments from Metheniti et al. (2021), where we only made use of the Friedrich and Gateva dataset and only in English. We aim to explore the capabilities of transformer architectures in classifying aspect beyond mere quantitative evaluation: we made custom qualitative datasets in order to observe how complex context, verb tense and prepositional phrases affect classification.[1]

We find that classification with fine-tuned models is very successful—both for telicity and duration—and this success can be largely attributed to the knowledge built up during pre-training, as contextual word embeddings by themselves are already quite capable of capturing this information. We noticed that complex cases where the context was conflicting with the verbal aspect were harder for the models to classify, and we provide evidence that misclassification in complex sentences is related to verb tense and word order. Finally, comparing the two languages we investigate, even though the French models show lower accuracy, they were more successful in classifying more difficult cases of telicity and duration, because of the properties of verbal tense in French.

2 Acquisition of telicity and duration

Before examining how transformer models handle telicity and duration, it is important to briefly present how humans learn to identify and express these concepts. Complex semantic features are learned by humans with the use of multiple exemplars in the speaker's L1 (mother language), in order to create constructions which encapsulate abstract concepts, such as the perceived duration of an action and the presence or absence of an outcome (Christiansen and Chater, 2001). Frequency (Ellis, 2002) and distributional bias (Andersen, 1993) are crucial for the acquisition of a language's specific patterns of expressing these concepts, however, their semantics and lexical properties are separate from the grammar of the language and interact with it, to understand and express concepts.

Focusing on lexical aspect, Shirai (1991) and Shirai and Andersen (1995) present the *aspect hypothesis*, claiming that children associate past and perfective marking to telic verbs (applying it to activity, accomplishment and achievement verbs in this order) and avoid such marking with stative verbs. Wulff et al. (2009) confirm this hypothesis experimentally, showing that there is a strong negative correlation between telicity and progressivity (e.g. speakers will mostly avoid using progressive tenses with telic verbs). Todorova et al. (2000) observed, in a self-paced reading experiment, that the combination of aspectually conflicting predicate and temporal modifiers in sentences produced a delay in processing – this suggests that humans have some preferred temporal association with verbs and modifiers, and when there is contradicting context, there is a need for reassessment of the given structure. Proctor et al. (2004) also conducted experiments of self-paced reading, with sentences with verbs whose telicity degree depends—to some extent—on the verb's object (e.g. consumption verbs with a finite/infinite object), and observed that there was no time cost in the processing of these sentences (also pointed out by Todorova et al.), which leads to the conclusion that the processing of a predicate, even with conflicting telicity marking, is simpler than the additional information of a temporal preposition. However, Van Hout (1998) claims that prepositions are mentally learned as markers of telicity earlier in life than the presence of bound/unbound objects (in experiments with Dutch as L1), meaning that some function words are also considered important for the final telicity degree of an utterance.

Regarding duration, in earlier stages of language acquisition, it has been observed that children may erroneously assign stativity to an action without immediate change at the time of utterance (Rocca, 2002), and such mistakes also occur in L2 learners of English (i.e. people who are learning as a foreign language). Wen (1997) also noted that L2 learners of Chinese acquired the perfectivity markers before the duration markers. Such findings further support the *aspect hypothesis*, showing that the perception of time requires a significant amount of processing and contextualizing for humans, and that the lexi-

[1] Our code and hand-crafted datasets are made available at `https://github.com/lenakmeth/telicity_classification/`.

cal aspect of a verb (and therefore, the telicity and duration of its presented action/state) is eventually learned and preferred, but can be overwritten (intentionally, in complex cases, at a computational cost, or erroneously, in earlier stages of language acquisition).

3 Previous Work

Siegel and McKeown (2000) were the first to propose natural language processing methods for aspectual classification; they used decision trees, genetic programming, and logistic regression to locate linguistic indicators of stativity and completeness, and observed that there was an improvement on the classification of these features, especially with supervised methods, compared to unsupervised classification.

Friedrich and Palmer (2014) use a semi-supervised approach for learning lexical aspect, combining linguistic and distributional features, in order to predict a verb's stativity/duration, and also released two datasets of annotated sentences for stativity. Friedrich and Pinkal (2015) extended this approach by classifying verbal lexical aspect into multiple categories of duration, habitual/episodic/static, and Friedrich et al. (2016) expanded their datasets and categories, achieving 76% accuracy on supervised classification compared to the 80% of their human baseline. In their most recent work, Friedrich and Gateva (2017) have released two datasets in English with gold and silver annotations of telicity and duration (gold is human annotated; silver is obtained from parallel English–Czech corpora where aspectual features were extracted from Czech morphological markers). With these datasets and an L1-regularized multi-class logistic regression model, they report significant improvement on automatic telicity classification.

Loáiciga and Grisot (2016) exploit telicity in order to improve on French–English machine translation; they are using verb classification of telicity (defined as *boundedness*) and notice improvement on the translation of tense. Falk and Martin (2016) also use a machine learning approach, alongside morpho-syntactic and semantic annotations, to predict the aspect of French verbs in different contexts (*verb readings*). Moving away from hard-coded annotations and lexical aspect, Peng (2018) uses two different compositional models to classify aspect, exploring the entire clause and not only the verb, with the use of distributional vectors and without annotated linguistic features, and highlights the importance of the verbal phrase and the verb's dependents in the interpretation of telicity. Kober et al. (2020) propose modeling aspect of English verbs in context, with the use of compositional distributional models, and confirm that a verb's context and closed-class words of tense are strong features for aspect classification.

4 Methodology

4.1 English Datasets

Telicity and duration-annotated sentences will be used as two separate datasets for our experiments. The two datasets from which we are sourcing sentences are constructed by Friedrich and Gateva (2017) and by Alikhani and Stone (2019).

Friedrich and Gateva's dataset[2] includes gold- and silver-annotations of telicity (telic/atelic) and duration (stative/durative). The gold annotations are based on the MASC dataset (Ide et al., 2008), while the silver annotations were crafted on the basis of the InterCorp parallel corpus of English and Czech (Čermák and Rosen, 2012), extracting the annotations from the Czech morphological markers of telicity and duration and applying them to the English translations. Each annotation corresponds to a specific verb in each sentence and not the entire clause.

The "Captions" dataset[3] by Alikhani and Stone (2019) was created from five image–text corpora, in order to study inferential connections in sentences. It has been annotated for telicity (telic/atelic) and duration (stative/durative/punctual) based on the verb's aspect. Even though the focus of the original work was on the head verb of each sentence, the verbs were not separately annotated, therefore we used dependency parsing with spaCy (Honnibal et al., 2020) in order to extract the verb and its position for our experiments. We noticed some inconsistencies in annotation, which we corrected, and we also excluded the sentences annotated with the *punctual* label, since there were too few sentences to warrant a third category or to combine with the *durative* label.

In Table 1 we present the sizes of the datasets and our final dataset. We split this dataset in training, validation and test sets with a ratio of 80-10-10%.

We also created some smaller datasets for testing

[2] `https://github.com/annefried/telicity`

[3] `https://github.com/malihealikhani/Captions`

purposes, in order to observe specific phenomena in our models. First, we created forty sentences annotated for telicity, and forty for duration, a sample of which can be found in Table 2. We also crafted "minimal pairs" of sentences with telicity annotations, where each pair includes the same verb but in a context that has a different degree of telicity (see examples in Table 3). We also created variations for some of these sentences, moving prepositional phrases to different positions in the sentence or changing the verb tense without changing the meaning or the degree of telicity, in order to test whether the models are sensitive not only to specific verbs but also word position and tenses (see Table 4).

4.2 Verb position

Aspect is generally attributed to the verb; we therefore want to indicate the position of the verb in the sentence. To do so, we make use of a binary mask that indicates the position of the verb form without auxiliaries (or multiple positions, when the verb is split into subwords by the model tokenizer). Technically, we implement the binary mask by making use of so-called `token_type_ids` vectors. These vectors' intended use is to mark tokens of different segments (when performing classification tasks for pairs of sentences)—but since our input consists of a single sentence, we can employ them for specifying the position of the verb. An example is shown in Table 5. Unfortunately, RoBERTa based models (RoBERTa and CamemBERT) do not support the use of `token_type_ids` vectors; we will therefore use these models without an explicit indication of verb position.

4.3 Transformer models

Transformers are neural network models which assign weighted attention to the different parts of the input with a sequence of alternating neural feed-forward layers and self-attention layers. These models have proven to be very successful in a variety of NLP tasks, and they have been shown to implicitly capture syntactic and semantic information and dependencies. In this work, we are using pretrained transformer models provided by the `transformers` library (Wolf et al., 2020).

BERT (Devlin et al., 2019) is a transformer-based bi-directional encoder, which is trained by randomly masking words in the input sequence and learning to fill the word in the masked position,

Type	Label	Friedrich	Captions	Current	Total
telicity	telic	1,831	785	2,885	**6,173**
	atelic	2,661	1,256	3,288	
duration	stative	1,860	419	2,036	
	durative	38	1,843	2,045	**4,081**

Table 1: Number of sentences and annotations in each dataset, and our final dataset sizes.

label	sentence
telic	I ate a fish for lunch.
telic	John built a house in a year.
telic	The cat drank all the milk.
atelic	John watched TV.
atelic	I always spill milk when I pour it in my mug.
atelic	Cork floats on water.
stative	Bread consists of flour, water and yeast.
stative	This box contains a cake.
stative	I have disliked mushrooms for years.
durative	She plays tennis every Friday.
durative	The snow melts every spring.
durative	The boxer is hitting his opponent.

Table 2: A sample from our qualitative dataset.

label	sentence
telic	I will receive new stock on Friday.
atelic	I will receive new stock on Fridays.
telic	The boy is eating an apple.
atelic	The boy is eating apples.
telic	I drank the whole bottle.
atelic	I drank juice.
telic	The Prime Minister made that declaration yesterday.
atelic	The Prime Minister made that declaration for months.

Table 3: A sample of minimal pairs for telicity.

label	sentence
telic	John built a house in a year.
telic	John had built a house in a year.
telic	In a year, John built a house.
telic	In a year, John had built a house.
atelic	We swim in the lake in the afternoons.
atelic	We swim in the lake each afternoon.
atelic	In the afternoons, we swim in the lake.
atelic	Each afternoon, we swim in the lake.

Table 4: A sample of variations of tense and word order.

tokens	He	worked	well	and	earned	much	.		
vector	0	1	0	0	0	0	0		
tokens	He	work	###ed	well	and	earn	###ed	much	.
vector	0	1	1	0	0	0	0	0	0

Table 5: Sentence tokens and the corresponding `token_type_ids` vectors, depending on tokenization. Each sequence also includes the model's special tokens and padding.

while also learning to predict the next sentence given the first sentence.

RoBERTa (Liu et al., 2019) has the same model architecture as BERT, but focuses only on the masked language modeling objective, and expands BERT's use of subwords from unseen words to almost all tokens. The model modifies key hyperparameters in BERT, has been trained with much larger mini-batches and learning rates, and has improved results on the masked language modeling objective and on downstream task performance.

XLNet (Yang et al., 2019) is an auto-regressive pretraining model which introduces permutation language modeling, where all tokens are predicted but in random order (unlike BERT, which predicts only the masked tokens). This method allows the model to better learn dependencies and relations between words. XLNet reportedly outperforms BERT on tasks such as question answering, sentiment analysis, and document ranking.

ALBERT (Lan et al., 2019) is a transformer architecture, based on BERT but using fewer parameters more efficiently; the vocabulary is decomposed into two small matrices and the size of the hidden layer embeddings (which learn context-dependent representations) is separated from the vocabulary embeddings (which learn context-independent representations). ALBERT has managed to outperform BERT on tasks such as reading comprehension, proving that better exploitation of contextual representations could be more beneficial than larger training and parameter sizes.

4.4 Fine-tuning & binary classification

One of our experiments explores the process of fine-tuning a transformer model for binary sequence classification of telicity and duration (separately), and testing the fine-tuned model's accuracy on predicting the telicity or duration annotated label of a sentence. Fine-tuning is the strategy of adapting a pretrained model to a specific task, by adding an extra layer on top of the existing ones and specializing it on the given task. Thus, we can exploit the existing model's knowledge from its contextual word embeddings, and further specialize the model on a specific task without the need for large specialized resources, large computational power and long training times; in many tasks, fine-tuned transformer models have consistently provided state-of-the-art results (Sun et al., 2019).

In order to perform binary classification of telicity (telic/atelic) or duration (stative/durative), we first fine-tune the pretrained models on some annotated examples of telicity and duration. The input is entire sentences, with or without the verb position information (presented in Section 4.2), and their label of telicity or duration. We fine-tune the models as Devlin et al. (2019) have recommended, with some modifications; we use a batch size of 32 and a learning rate of 2×10^{-5}. We apply dropout with probability p = 0.1 and weight decay with $\lambda = 0.01$. We use the PyTorch's ADAM as our optimizer (AdamW) without bias correction. We fine-tune each model for a maximum of 4 epochs, following the recommendation of Devlin et al. (2019) to train for 2-4 epochs when fine-tuning on a specific task. For `base` models each training epoch took ~3 minutes and for `large` models ~7 minutes, on one GPU system of a computing cluster, with CUDA acceleration.

As baselines, we make use of two standard binary classification models trained and tested on the same sets: a simple bag-of-words logistic regression model, implemented with the Python library *scikit-learn* (Pedregosa et al., 2011) with default parameters and data scaling, and a one-layer convolutional neural network model (CNN) implemented with `Pytorch` (Paszke et al., 2019) and trained for 50 epochs, which is commonly used for text classification tasks (Kim, 2014). The CNN model is trained with the fastText 300-dimensional embeddings (Bojanowski et al., 2017), embedding dimension of 300, filter size of $[3, 4, 5]$, 100 filters per dimension, dropout rate of 0.5, learning rate of 0.01 and the Adadelta optimizer.

4.5 Classification with layer embeddings and logistic regression

Pretrained models already contain linguistic information in their contextualized word embeddings, which we can extract and use with task-specific models for classification. The process of extracting the knowledge of a transformer model's embeddings has been explored since the popularization of contextual word embeddings with ELMo (Peters et al., 2018), since it allows for faster computations with results comparable to fine-tuned transformer models (Tang et al., 2019). We equally conduct an experiment without any finetuning, where we apply a logistic regression to the contextual embeddings of each layer as provided by the pre-trained model. We extract the contextual word embeddings (for the annotated verb) from each layer of a transformer model, and we train a logistic regression model (using `scikit-learn`) to classify telicity and duration, in order to examine how much information relevant to telicity and duration has been learned by each layer.

4.6 Classification in French

We also wanted to examine whether telicity and duration were classifiable in a different language with transformer models. We chose French, as it differs from English in the way verb tenses are formed (conjugation, compound tenses) and used (present continuous is morphologically the same as present simple), but it does not have a dedicated morpheme to expressing telicity such as Finnish and Czech. We are using the two monolingual French transformer models available from the `transformers` library, CamemBERT (Martin et al., 2020) and FlauBERT (Le et al., 2020). CamemBERT is built based on the RoBERTa architecture and trained on monolingual data. FlauBERT is a BERT-based model trained with multiple, heterogeneous corpora, and a more extensive tokenization procedure.

Since there are no available annotations of telicity and duration in French, we translated our English datasets with the DeepL translator[4] and reviewed manually a portion of the datasets (200 sentences) for translation accuracy and annotation correctness. Our average score for the accuracy of the machine-translated sentences was 88% and for the accuracy of the annotated labels was 73.5%. We also extracted the verb-head word of each sentence with the spaCy dependency parser to train with/without verb position, but we are not entirely confident in the results, therefore we are not testing the models' verb embeddings per layer and the unseen verbs of the test set, as we did in English. We use the resulting datasets to fine-tune the FlauBERT and CamemBERT models, and assess their abilities on aspectual classification. In addition, we manually translated our qualitative test sets and made appropriate changes (when verb tense did not convey the desired telicity, for example), and in lieu of the 80 sentences on variations of word order and verb tense, we created more minimal pairs with variations on prepositional phrases.

[4] `https://www.deepl.com/translator`

5 Results for English

5.1 Quantitative analysis

During the fine-tuning process, we were able to identify via validation which models were most and least successful in predicting binary tags. The results for validation are presented in Table 6 for telicity and Table 7 for duration. In Appendix A.1 we are comparing the probability distributions for the binary labels, for the most successful model (in terms of accuracy).

On classifying **telicity**, the best performing model was `bert-large-cased`. Overall, BERT models outperformed the other architectures, but all models achieved accuracy of > 0.80. When trained with the extra information of verb position in the sentence, accuracy improved for all models and sets $(+0.01 - 0.04)$. Examining the probability distribution of the two labels, we observed that the BERT models, both `base` and `large`, with the use of the verb position, were the most confident in assigning a label to a sentence (with the probability of each label being > 0.9) while the `large` versions of other models were the ones whose probability distribution included more cases with lower label probability. The models were overall more confident with correct predictions, and only very slightly less confident (with a few labels closer to $0.4 - 0.6$, but still the majority above > 0.9) for wrong predictions.

Our findings on classifying **duration** were similar to the ones on telicity, with the models performing overall better on this classification task despite the dataset being smaller. The BERT models were the most successful ones, achieving accuracy of up to 0.96, however all models achieved accuracy of > 0.93. The effect of the use of the verb position information is not apparent in this classification task, since we notice an improvement or deterioration of 0.01 in most models. Examining the probability distribution of the two labels, all models were very confident in classifying sentences, regardless of their accuracy, and high confidence in both right and wrong predictions (erroneously).

In both cases, the fine-tuned transformers models outperformed the baselines we have established.

5.2 Qualitative analysis

As mentioned, we also created our own annotated datasets of telicity and duration, in order to study aspectual properties beyond the scope of classification metrics. We took a closer look at the correct

Model	Verb	Acc.	Prec.	Rec.	F1
`bert-base-uncased`	yes	0.86	0.86	0.86	0.86
	no	0.81	0.81	0.81	0.81
`bert-base-cased`	yes	0.87	0.87	0.87	0.87
	no	0.81	0.80	0.80	0.80
`bert-large-uncased`	yes	0.86	0.86	0.86	0.86
	no	0.81	0.80	0.80	0.80
`bert-large-cased`	yes	**0.88**	**0.87**	**0.87**	**0.87**
	no	0.81	0.81	0.80	0.80
`roberta-base`	no	0.84	0.84	0.84	0.84
`roberta-large`	no	0.80	0.81	0.79	0.79
`xlnet-base-cased`	yes	0.82	0.82	0.82	0.82
	no	0.81	0.81	0.81	0.80
`xlnet-large-cased`	yes	0.82	0.82	0.82	0.82
	no	0.80	0.80	0.80	0.80
`albert-base-v2`	yes	0.84	0.84	0.84	0.84
	no	0.81	0.80	0.80	0.80
`albert-large-v2`	yes	0.80	0.80	0.80	0.80
	no	0.82	0.81	0.81	0.81
CNN (50 epochs)	no	0.75	0.75	0.75	0.75
Log. Regr. BoW	no	0.61	0.61	0.61	0.61

Table 6: Results of classification accuracy on the telicity test set. 'Verb' refers to training the model with the added information of the verb position.

Model	Verb	Acc.	Prec.	Rec.	F1
`bert-base-uncased`	yes	**0.96**	**0.96**	**0.96**	**0.96**
	no	0.94	0.94	0.94	0.94
`bert-base-cased`	yes	**0.96**	**0.96**	**0.96**	**0.96**
	no	0.96	0.95	0.96	0.96
`bert-large-uncased`	yes	**0.96**	**0.96**	**0.96**	**0.96**
	no	0.95	0.95	0.94	0.94
`bert-large-cased`	yes	**0.96**	**0.96**	**0.96**	**0.96**
	no	0.95	0.95	0.95	0.95
`roberta-base`	no	0.95	0.95	0.95	0.95
`roberta-large`	no	0.95	0.95	0.95	0.95
`xlnet-base-cased`	yes	0.94	0.94	0.94	0.94
	no	0.95	0.95	0.95	0.95
`xlnet-large-cased`	yes	0.94	0.94	0.94	0.94
	no	0.95	0.95	0.95	0.95
`albert-base-v2`	yes	0.95	0.95	0.95	0.95
	no	0.95	0.95	0.95	0.95
`albert-large-v2`	yes	**0.96**	**0.96**	**0.96**	**0.96**
	no	**0.96**	**0.96**	**0.96**	**0.96**
CNN (50 epochs)	no	0.88	0.88	0.88	0.88
Log. Regr. BoW	no	0.70	0.70	0.69	0.69

Table 7: Results of classification accuracy on the duration test set. 'Verb' refers to training the model with the added information of the verb position.

and incorrect predictions of the models, in order to determine which cases were easier or more difficult for models to classify. For the sake of brevity, we are presenting only a few examples of successes and failures; our goal was to manually examine the strengths and weaknessess of the models in difficult and conflicting cases of classification, hence the smaller qualitative datasets and the presentation of the most interesting examples.

For **telicity**, overall, models were quite successful in classifying the sentences of our qualitative dataset.For example, all models were able to identify that sentences with statements are atelic, such as *Cork floats on water.* and *The Earth revolves around the Sun.*, and sentences with an action were correctly classified almost all the time: *I spilled the milk.* was correctly classified as *telic*, and *I always spill milk when I pour it in my mug.* was also correctly classified as *atelic* (except for the `xlnet` models).

For the majority of the models, the errors in classification could be located in some specific sentences, where the verb or the verbal phrase would be considered (a)telic, but part of the context defines the temporal aspect of the sentence in the opposite way, either a prepositional phrase (e.g. *I eat a fish for lunch on Fridays.*; *eat* with an object would be considered telic, but the prepositional phrase *on Fridays* shows an action without perceived ending) or a grammatical tense (e.g. *The inspectors are always checking every document very carefully.*; even though the action should have a perceived ending, the continuous tense and the presence of the adverb *always* render this sentence atelic).

Moving to our minimal pairs of telic-atelic sentences, we observe that, in most cases, most models are able to classify correctly a sentence based both on the verb action and the context; *I drank the whole bottle.* and *I drank juice.* were correctly classified as *telic* and *atelic* respectively, despite of the presence of the same verb and tense. However, in our qualitative dataset, we noticed that the sentence *The cat drank all the milk.* was incorrectly classified as *atelic* by all the models. Another interesting mistake we noticed was the classification of the pair *The boy is eating an apple.* and *The boy is eating apples.* as both atelic; in the former sentence, the action is telic for pragmatic reasons (one apple that will be finished), but the tense is continuous.

In order to observe specific tenses, word positions and context more extensively, we can examine the variations of a sentence and see whether the models classified them all with the same label or not. The telic sentence *I ate a fish for lunch at noon.* has confused some of the models, whether the prepositional phrase *at noon* was at the beginning or the end. However, the same sentences regardless of the phrase's position, with past perfect tense *had eaten* is always classified as telic. In some complex cases, such as the sentence *The Prime*

Minister made that declaration for months. we notice that most models fail to classify it as atelic in all its variations, except for when the prepositional phrase is at the start and the tense is present perfect continuous (*has been making*). We noticed that even sentences with a more obvious degree of telicity (*John Wilkes Booth killed Lincoln on 1865.* – telic) were sometimes labeled incorrectly, when the prepositional phrase was at the end rather than the start.

Regarding **duration**, the models were less successful at classifying stative sentences than durative; even some sentences with intransitive verbs, such as *Bread consists of flour, water and yeast.* and *This cookbook includes a recipe for bread.* were classified as durative. However, stative sentences with animate subjects such as *I disagree with you.* were correctly classified. Durative sentences, despite of verb tense and context, were always correctly classified, e.g. *She plays tennis every Friday.* and *She's playing tennis right now.*.

5.3 Layer verb embeddings

By extracting the contextual word embeddings for the verb of each sentence, from each layer, and training a logistic regression model with these embeddings, we were able to examine how much information on telicity and duration is learned by each layer. In Appendix, Figure 3, we present the accuracy for each layer of the *base* models. Models achieved accuracy of up to 79% for telicity classification and up to 90% for duration classification, which is comparable to the performance of the finetuned models. Improvement of accuracy is not proportional as we move to higher layers; we notice that for telicity, some models achieve high accuracy in the middle layers, and again in the final layers, with accuracy sometimes dropping in the last layer.

5.4 Unseen verbs

In our training and test datasets, there was a large variety of verb-head words, which allowed us to test the classification success on sentences where the verb has not been observed by the model. For telicity, 267 verb forms which were the head of their phrase were not "seen" by the model in the training set (and 146 of them were not split in subwords), and for duration, 117 verbs (and 80 intact). We tested which of the corresponding sentences were marked incorrectly, and the models' average probability of the assigned label. Overall, few sentences were labeled incorrectly (see results in Table 10), with labels of either category for both classification tasks. This suggests that the context plays an important role for the models' choices, even when the verb form has not been observed by the model.

6 Results for French

6.1 Quantitative analysis

The results of the classification for telicity and duration are presented in Tables 8 and 9. Accuracy is overall lower than English, and the CNN classifier baseline performed equally well or sometimes outperformed some models. We questioned whether this was a problem of the machine translation process, but since all sets were created in the same way, we consider this unlikely. However, the fact that the additional verb position information was almost always detrimental is probably a problem caused by parsing, since French makes use of compound tenses more often than English.

Model	Verb	Acc.	Prec.	Rec.	F1
`camembert-base`	no	**0.77**	0.77	0.78	0.77
`camembert-large`	no	0.76	0.77	0.77	0.77
`flaubert-small-cased`	yes	0.69	0.70	0.70	0.69
	no	0.73	0.73	0.73	0.72
`flaubert-base-uncased`	yes	0.74	0.75	0.74	0.72
	no	0.76	0.76	0.76	0.75
`flaubert-base-cased`	yes	0.76	0.76	0.77	0.76
	no	0.77	0.78	0.78	0.78
`flaubert-large`	yes	0.73	0.74	0.74	0.72
	no	0.75	0.76	0.76	0.74
CNN (50 epochs)	no	0.71	0.69	0.65	0.65
Log. Regr. BoW	no	0.61	0.59	0.59	0.59

Table 8: Accuracy metrics for telicity classification with French transformer models.

Model	Verb	Acc.	Prec.	Rec.	F1
`camembert-base`	no	0.82	0.82	0.82	0.82
`camembert-large`	no	**0.87**	0.87	0.87	0.87
`flaubert-small-cased`	yes	0.79	0.79	0.79	0.79
	no	0.81	0.81	0.81	0.8
`flaubert-base-uncased`	yes	0.80	0.81	0.80	0.80
	no	0.84	0.84	0.84	0.84
`flaubert-base-cased`	yes	0.81	0.82	0.82	0.81
	no	0.83	0.83	0.83	0.83
`flaubert-large`	yes	0.81	0.81	0.81	0.80
	no	0.87	0.87	0.87	0.87
CNN (50 epochs)	no	0.80	0.82	0.82	0.82
Log. Regr. BoW	no	0.68	0.68	0.67	0.67

Table 9: Accuracy metrics for duration classification with French transformer models.

6.2 Qualitative analysis

We notice that for French, the fine-tuned models performed better on the qualitative sets than their English counterparts, avoiding common mistakes such as classifying the atelic sentence *Je mange un poisson à midi le vendredi.* ("I eat a fish for lunch of Fridays.") as telic. However, there were (fewer, but some) common mistakes through the models which did not exist for English, e.g. *Je renverse toujours le lait quand je le verse dans ma tasse.* ("I always spill milk when I pour it in my mug." – atelic) and *Jenny a travaillé comme médecine toute sa vie.* ("Jenny worked as a doctor her whole life." – atelic) in which the context affects telicity more than the verb. Comparing minimal pairs, we notice that, unlike in English, the sentence *J'ai bu du jus de fruit.* ("I drank juice." – atelic) was frequently marked as telic by the models, and so did its pair *J'ai bu toute la bouteille.* ("I drank the whole bottle." – telic). And unlike the common mistake of marking both sentences as telic in English, the French models marked the sentences *Le garçon mange [une pomme / des pommes].* ("The boy is eating [an apple / apples]) both as atelic.

For the duration classification, as in English, we observe that stative sentences were the ones which were occasionally or always incorrectly classified by the models; sentences with statements such as *Le pain est composé de farine, d'eau et de levure.* ("Bread consists of flour, water and yeast.") or *J'aime le chocolat.* ("I love chocolate.") were labeled incorrectly.

7 Discussion

Transformer models were quite successful in the classification tasks, outperforming our baselines to a large extent, and they proved to be quite successful even without fine-tuning. Contextual embeddings proved to be an efficient way to encode the aspectual information of a verb and its interaction with its context, and this knowledge is probably already learned in the pretraining process.

The superior performance of the duration classification with fine-tuned models did raise a question: from our datasets, most stative questions came from the Friedrich dataset and most durative sentences from the Captions dataset; did the models learn to classify duration or to identify the different corpora? With our qualitative analysis on two languages, we can conclude that the models are indeed able to classify duration and were successful because of the little overlap between stative and durative verbs and contexts. However, the models struggled with sentences for which world knowledge is crucial, which is a known issue (Rogers et al., 2021).

From our experiment with verb tenses and prepositional phrases, we noticed that perfect and continuous tenses are beneficial to classification by the models, and leading a sentence with a prepositional phrase of time sometimes improved predictions. However, conflicting context will almost always confuse the models.

In addition, our findings on the French datasets showed that, even with our lower-performing models, the syntactic and semantic choices that a language makes in expressing aspect did affect the models' capabilities of classifying aspect.The differences in classification errors and successes that we observed, between the qualitative datasets of the two languages, may also indicate that there is a different way in which languages are semantically represented by transformer models, even with different model architectures.

8 Conclusion

In this study, we conducted several experiments that test the capability of transformer models to grasp aspectual categories, viz. telicity and duration. We tested this capability using a binary classification setting. Using two annotated datasets for telicity and duration (Friedrich and Gateva, 2017; Alikhani and Stone, 2019), we fine-tuned transformer models of different architectures and in two languages and found that transformer models were very successful on the classification of aspect even when trained on small datasets. Providing the verb position as additional information improved performance in both telicity and duration classification for English. The pretrained transformer models also possess knowledge of aspect even without fine-tuning (when looking at layerwise contextual word embeddings). However, our qualitative analysis also revealed weaknesses; for complex sentences, where the verbal aspect contradicted the temporal information in the context (e.g. telic verb with an atelic prepositional phrase, resulting in an overall atelic sentence), the models classified based on verb rather than context, meaning that they are able to distinguish the most important part of the sequence but not capture more fine-grained information when it is necessary.

Acknowledgements

This work has been funded by CNRS (80|PRIME-2019 project MoDiCLI). Experiments were carried out with the OSIRIM platform[5] which is administered by IRIT and supported by CNRS, the Region Midi-Pyrénées, the French Government, and ERDF. We would like to thank our reviewers for their insightful comments and suggestions.

References

Malihe Alikhani and Matthew Stone. 2019. "Caption" as a Coherence Relation: Evidence and Implications. In *Proceedings of the Second Workshop on Shortcomings in Vision and Language*, pages 58–67.

Roger W Andersen. 1993. Input distribution as explanations for underdeveloped and mature morphological systems. *Progression and regression in language: Sociocultural, neuropsychological and linguistic perspectives*, page 309.

Piotr Bojanowski, Edouard Grave, Armand Joulin, and Tomas Mikolov. 2017. Enriching word vectors with subword information. *Transactions of the Association for Computational Linguistics*, 5:135–146.

Nathanael Chambers, Taylor Cassidy, Bill McDowell, and Steven Bethard. 2014. Dense Event Ordering with a Multi-Pass Architecture. In *Transactions of the Association for Computational Linguistics*, volume 2, pages 273–284.

Morten H Christiansen and Nick Chater. 2001. Connectionist psycholinguistics: Capturing the empirical data. *Trends in Cognitive Sciences*, 5(2):82–88.

Francisco Costa and António Branco. 2012. Aspectual Type and Temporal Relation Classification. In *Proceedings of the 13th Conference of the European Chapter of the Association for Computational Linguistics*, pages 266–275, Avignon, France. Association for Computational Linguistics.

Jacob Devlin, Ming-Wei Chang, Kenton Lee, and Kristina Toutanova. 2019. Bert: Pre-training of Deep Bidirectional Transformers for Language Understanding. In *Proceedings of the 2019 Conference of the North American Chapter of the Association for Computational Linguistics: Human Language Technologies, Volume 1 (Long and Short Papers)*, pages 4171–4186, Minneapolis, Minnesota. Association for Computational Linguistics.

Nick C Ellis. 2002. Frequency effects in language processing: A review with implications for theories of implicit and explicit language acquisition. *Studies in second language acquisition*, 24(2):143–188.

[5] `https://osirim.irit.fr/`

Allyson Ettinger. 2020. What bert is not: Lessons from a new suite of psycholinguistic diagnostics for language models. *Transactions of the Association for Computational Linguistics*, 8:34–48.

Ingrid Falk and Fabienne Martin. 2016. Automatic identification of aspectual classes across verbal readings. In *Proceedings of the Fifth Joint Conference on Lexical and Computational Semantics*, pages 12–22.

Annemarie Friedrich and Damyana Gateva. 2017. Classification of telicity using cross-linguistic annotation projection. In *Proceedings of the 2017 Conference on Empirical Methods in Natural Language Processing*, pages 2559–2565.

Annemarie Friedrich and Alexis Palmer. 2014. Automatic prediction of aspectual class of verbs in context. In *Proceedings of the 52nd Annual Meeting of the Association for Computational Linguistics (Volume 2: Short Papers)*, pages 517–523.

Annemarie Friedrich, Alexis Palmer, and Manfred Pinkal. 2016. Situation entity types: automatic classification of clause-level aspect. In *Proceedings of the 54th Annual Meeting of the Association for Computational Linguistics (Volume 1: Long Papers)*, pages 1757–1768.

Annemarie Friedrich and Manfred Pinkal. 2015. Automatic recognition of habituals: a three-way classification of clausal aspect. In *Proceedings of the 2015 Conference on Empirical Methods in Natural Language Processing*, pages 2471–2481.

Matthew Honnibal, Ines Montani, Sofie Van Landeghem, and Adriane Boyd. 2020. spaCy: Industrial-strength Natural Language Processing in Python.

Mohammad Javad Hosseini, Nathanael Chambers, Siva Reddy, Xavier R. Holt, Shay B. Cohen, Mark Johnson, and Mark Steedman. 2018. Learning Typed Entailment Graphs with Global Soft Constraints. In *Transactions of the Association for Computational Linguistics*, volume 6, pages 703–717.

Nancy Ide, Collin Baker, Christiane Fellbaum, Charles Fillmore, and Rebecca Passonneau. 2008. MASC: the Manually Annotated Sub-Corpus of American English. In *Proceedings of the Sixth International Conference on Language Resources and Evaluation (LREC'08)*, Marrakech, Morocco. European Language Resources Association (ELRA).

Yoon Kim. 2014. Convolutional neural networks for sentence classification. *CoRR*, abs/1408.5882.

Thomas Kober, Malihe Alikhani, Matthew Stone, and Mark Steedman. 2020. Aspectuality Across Genre: A Distributional Semantics Approach. In *Proceedings of the 28th International Conference on Computational Linguistics*, pages 4546–4562, Barcelona, Spain (Online). International Committee on Computational Linguistics.

Thomas Kober, Sander Bijl de Vroe, and Mark Steedman. 2019. Temporal and Aspectual Entailment. In *Proceedings of the 13th International Conference on Computational Semantics - Long Papers*, pages 103–119, Gothenburg, Sweden. Association for Computational Linguistics.

Manfred Krifka. 1998. The origins of telicity. In *Events and grammar*, pages 197–235. Springer.

Zhenzhong Lan, Mingda Chen, Sebastian Goodman, Kevin Gimpel, Piyush Sharma, and Radu Soricut. 2019. ALBERT: A lite BERT for self-supervised learning of language representations. *arXiv preprint arXiv:1909.11942*.

Hang Le, Loïc Vial, Jibril Frej, Vincent Segonne, Maximin Coavoux, Benjamin Lecouteux, Alexandre Allauzen, Benoit Crabbé, Laurent Besacier, and Didier Schwab. 2020. Flaubert: Unsupervised language model pre-training for french. In *Proceedings of the 12th Language Resources and Evaluation Conference*, pages 2479–2490.

Yinhan Liu, Myle Ott, Naman Goyal, Jingfei Du, Mandar Joshi, Danqi Chen, Omer Levy, Mike Lewis, Luke Zettlemoyer, and Veselin Stoyanov. 2019. RoBERTa: A robustly optimized BERT pretraining approach. *arXiv preprint arXiv:1907.11692*.

Sharid Loáiciga and Cristina Grisot. 2016. Predicting and Using a Pragmatic Component of Lexical Aspect of Simple Past Verbal Tenses for Improving english-to-french Machine Translation. In *Linguistic Issues in Language Technology, Volume 13, 2016*. CSLI Publications.

Louis Martin, Benjamin Muller, Pedro Javier Ortiz Suárez, Yoann Dupont, Laurent Romary, Éric Villemonte De La Clergerie, Djamé Seddah, and Benoît Sagot. 2020. Camembert: a tasty french language model. In *Proceedings of the 58th Annual Meeting of the Association for Computational Linguistics*, pages 7203–7219.

Eleni Metheniti, Tim Van de Cruys, and Nabil Hathout. 2021. Prédire l'aspect linguistique en anglais au moyen de transformers. In *Traitement Automatique des Langues Naturelles (TALN 2021)*, pages 209–218, Lille, France. ATALA.

Adam Paszke, Sam Gross, Francisco Massa, Adam Lerer, James Bradbury, Gregory Chanan, Trevor Killeen, Zeming Lin, Natalia Gimelshein, Luca Antiga, Alban Desmaison, Andreas Kopf, Edward Yang, Zachary DeVito, Martin Raison, Alykhan Tejani, Sasank Chilamkurthy, Benoit Steiner, Lu Fang, Junjie Bai, and Soumith Chintala. 2019. Pytorch: An imperative style, high-performance deep learning library. In H. Wallach, H. Larochelle, A. Beygelzimer, F. d'Alché-Buc, E. Fox, and R. Garnett, editors, *Advances in Neural Information Processing Systems 32*, pages 8024–8035. Curran Associates, Inc.

F. Pedregosa, G. Varoquaux, A. Gramfort, V. Michel, B. Thirion, O. Grisel, M. Blondel, P. Prettenhofer, R. Weiss, V. Dubourg, J. Vanderplas, A. Passos, D. Cournapeau, M. Brucher, M. Perrot, and E. Duchesnay. 2011. Scikit-learn: Machine Learning in Python. *Journal of Machine Learning Research*, 12:2825–2830.

Qiwei Peng. 2018. *Towards aspectual classification of clauses in a large single-domain corpus*. School of Informatics, University of Edinburgh, Edingburgh, UK.

Matthew E Peters, Mark Neumann, Mohit Iyyer, Matt Gardner, Christopher Clark, Kenton Lee, and Luke Zettlemoyer. 2018. Deep contextualized word representations. In *Proceedings of NAACL-HLT*, pages 2227–2237.

Andrea S Proctor, Michael Walsh Dickey, and Lance J Rips. 2004. The time-course and cost of telicity inferences. In *Proceedings of the Annual Meeting of the Cognitive Science Society*, volume 26.

Sonia Rocca. 2002. Lexical aspect in child second language acquisition of temporal morphology. *The L2 acquisition of tense-aspect morphology*.

Anna Rogers, Olga Kovaleva, and Anna Rumshisky. 2021. A Primer in BERTology: What we know about how BERT works. In *Transactions of the Association for Computational Linguistics*, volume 8, pages 842–866. MIT Press.

Yasuhiro Shirai. 1991. Primacy of aspect in language acquisition: Simplified input and prototype.

Yasuhiro Shirai and Roger W. Andersen. 1995. The acquisition of tense-aspect morphology: A prototype account. *Language*, 71(4):743–762.

Eric V. Siegel and Kathleen R. McKeown. 2000. Learning Methods to Combine Linguistic Indicators:Improving Aspectual Classification and Revealing Linguistic Insights. In *Computational Linguistics*, volume 26, pages 595–627.

Eric Victor Siegel. 1998. *Linguistic Indicators for Language Understanding: Using machine learning methods to combine corpus-based indicators for aspectual classification of clauses*. Columbia University. Ph.D. thesis.

Chi Sun, Xipeng Qiu, Yige Xu, and Xuanjing Huang. 2019. How to fine-tune BERT for text classification? In *China National Conference on Chinese Computational Linguistics*, pages 194–206. Springer.

Raphael Tang, Yao Lu, Linqing Liu, Lili Mou, Olga Vechtomova, and Jimmy Lin. 2019. Distilling task-specific knowledge from bert into simple neural networks. *arXiv preprint arXiv:1903.12136*.

Marina Todorova, Kathy Straub, William Badecker, and Robert Frank. 2000. Aspectual coercion and the online computation of sentential aspect. In *Proceedings of the Annual Meeting of the Cognitive Science Society*, volume 22.

Angeliek Van Hout. 1998. On the role of direct objects and particles in learning telicity in dutch and english. In *Proceedings of the 22nd Annual Boston University Conference on Language Development*, volume 2, pages 397–408. Cascadilla Press Somerville, MA.

Xiaohong Wen. 1997. Acquisition of chinese aspect: An analysis of the interlanguage of learners of chinese as a foreign language. *ITL-International Journal of Applied Linguistics*, 117(1):1–26.

Thomas Wolf, Lysandre Debut, Victor Sanh, Julien Chaumond, Clement Delangue, Anthony Moi, Pierric Cistac, Tim Rault, Rémi Louf, Morgan Funtowicz, Joe Davison, Sam Shleifer, Patrick von Platen, Clara Ma, Yacine Jernite, Julien Plu, Canwen Xu, Teven Le Scao, Sylvain Gugger, Mariama Drame, Quentin Lhoest, and Alexander M. Rush. 2020. Transformers: State-of-the-Art Natural Language Processing. In *Proceedings of the 2020 Conference on Empirical Methods in Natural Language Processing: System Demonstrations*, pages 38–45, Online.

Stefanie Wulff, Nick C. Ellis, Ute Römer, Kathleen Bardovi-Harlig, and Chelsea J. Leblanc. 2009. The acquisition of tense–aspect: Converging evidence from corpora and telicity ratings. *The Modern Language Journal*, 93(3):354–369.

Zhilin Yang, Zihang Dai, Yiming Yang, Jaime Carbonell, Russ R Salakhutdinov, and Quoc V Le. 2019. XLNet: Generalized autoregressive pretraining for language understanding. *Advances in Neural Information Processing Systems*, 32:5753–5763.

František Čermák and Alexandr Rosen. 2012. The Case of InterCorp, a multilingual parallel corpus. In *International Journal of Corpus Linguistics*, volume 13, pages 411–427.

A Additional figures

A.1 Probability distributions (English)

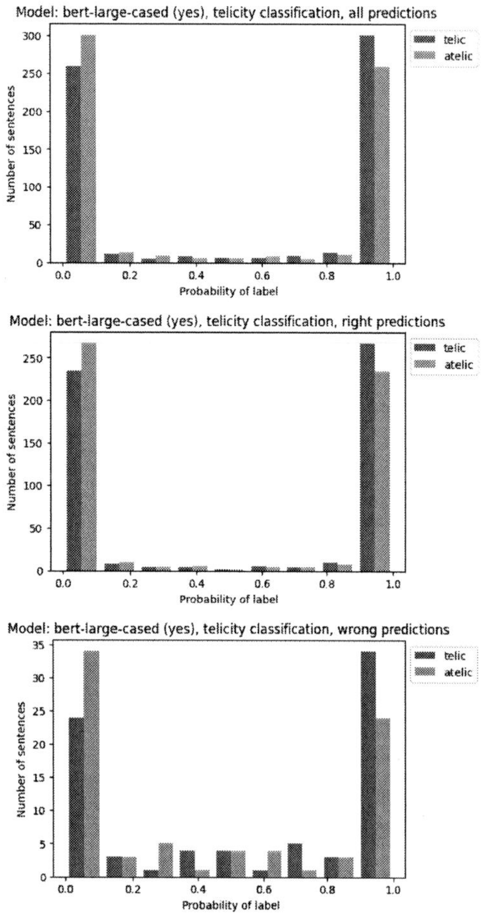

Figure 1: Probability distribution for the telicity labels, for the most successful model (bert-large-cased with verb position).

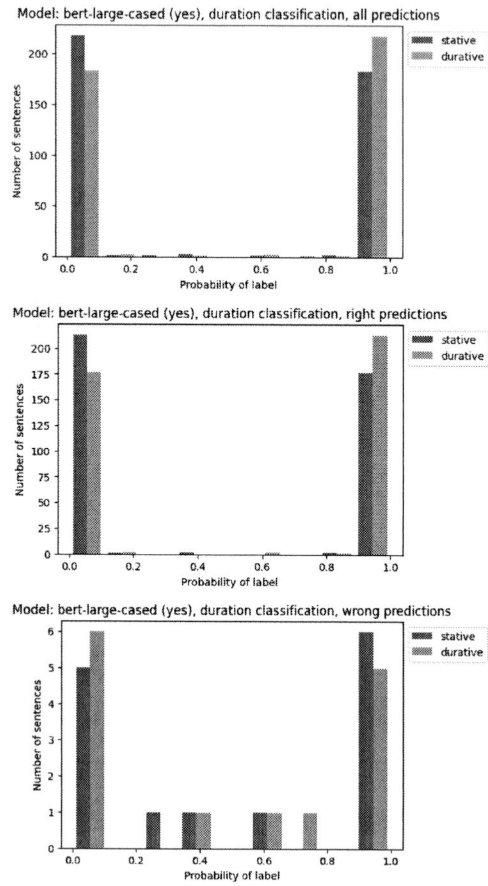

Figure 2: Probability distribution for the duration labels, for the most successful model (bert-large-cased with verb position).

A.2 Correct label predictions on unseen verbs in test set (English)

Model	Verb	Telicity						Duration					
		Seen verbs			Unseen Verbs			Seen verbs			Unseen Verbs		
		Correct	Wrong	Acc.	Correct	Wrong	Acc.	Correct	Wrong	Acc.	Correct	Wrong	Acc.
`bert-base-uncased`	yes	1286	240	0.84	180	41	0.81	681	26	0.96	142	6	0.96
	no	1194	336	0.78	170	50	0.77	678	29	0.96	143	5	**0.97**
`bert-base-cased`	yes	1290	218	**0.86**	169	31	**0.85**	665	17	**0.98**	129	5	0.96
	no	1169	342	0.77	162	37	0.81	661	21	0.97	128	6	0.96
`bert-large-uncased`	yes	1292	234	0.85	190	31	0.86	687	20	0.97	142	6	0.96
	no	1191	339	0.78	177	43	0.8	688	19	0.97	143	5	**0.97**
`bert-large-cased`	yes	1308	200	0.87	168	32	0.84	666	16	**0.98**	128	6	0.96
	no	1167	344	0.77	153	46	0.77	667	15	**0.98**	127	7	0.95
`roberta-base`	no	1243	291	0.81	185	41	0.82	662	19	0.97	126	8	0.94
`roberta-large`	no	1157	377	0.75	176	50	0.78	667	14	**0.98**	127	7	0.95
`xlnet-base-cased`	yes	1196	327	0.79	174	43	0.8	651	30	0.96	127	8	0.94
	no	1175	350	0.77	171	45	0.79	656	25	0.96	129	6	0.96
`xlnet-large-cased`	yes	1190	333	0.78	174	43	0.8	653	28	0.96	127	8	0.94
	no	1182	343	0.78	169	47	0.78	652	29	0.96	125	10	0.93
`albert-base-v2`	yes	1281	271	0.83	186	44	0.81	698	16	**0.98**	138	5	**0.97**
	no	1194	362	0.77	187	42	0.82	696	18	0.97	137	6	0.96
`albert-large-v2`	yes	1204	348	0.78	174	56	0.76	690	24	0.97	137	6	0.96
	no	1212	344	0.78	184	45	0.8	698	16	**0.98**	137	6	0.96

Table 10: The results on the test set, for sentences with seen/unseen verbs in the training set, for telicity and duration. The ratio of correct/incorrect labels is similar, with seen and unseen verbs, both for telicity and duration.

A.3 Classification with pretrained word embeddings and logistic regression (English)

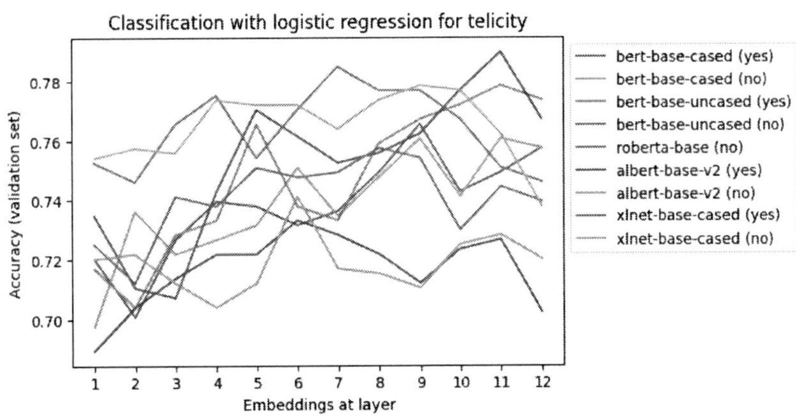

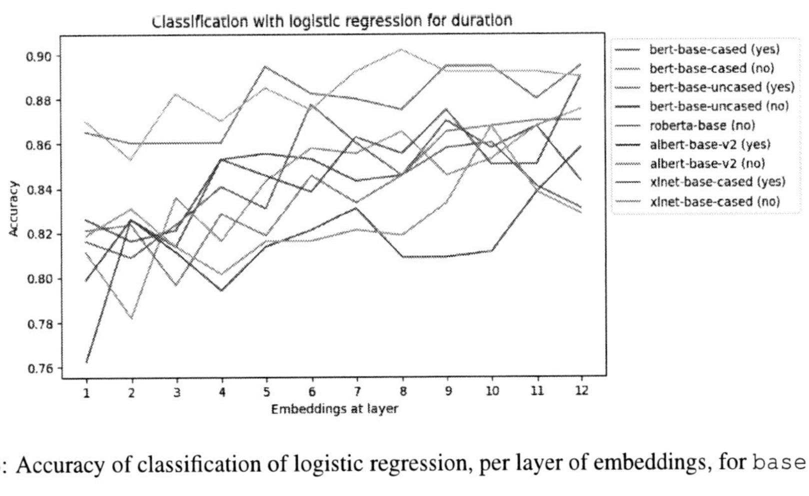

Figure 3: Accuracy of classification of logistic regression, per layer of embeddings, for `base` models.

Poirot at CMCL 2022 Shared Task: Zero Shot Crosslingual Eye-Tracking Data Prediction using Multilingual Transformer Models

Harshvardhan Srivastava
Oracle India , Bengaluru
Indian Institute of Technology, Kharagpur
harshvardhan.srivastava@oracle.com

Abstract

Eye tracking data during reading is a useful source of information to understand the cognitive processes that take place during language comprehension processes. Different languages account for different cognitive triggers, however there seems to be some uniform indicators across languages. In this paper, we describe our submission to the CMCL 2022 shared task on predicting human reading patterns for multilingual dataset. Our model uses text representations from transformers and some hand engineered features with a regression layer on top to predict statistical measures of mean and standard deviation for 2 main eye-tracking features. We train an end-to-end model to extract meaningful information from different languages and test our model on two separate datasets. We compare different transformer models and show ablation studies affecting model performance. Our final submission ranked 4th place for SubTask-1 and 1st place for SubTask-2 for the shared task.

1 Introduction

Eye tracking provides an accurate millisecond record of where people are looking while reading and is useful for descriptive study of language processing and understanding of the cognitive processing of brain related to reading. Eye movements are many times language-specific because they depend on structure and ordering of words which are language dependent, however some features tend to be stable and universal and can be observed in all languages. Modeling of human reading has been widely explored in psycholinguistics. The ability to accurately predict eye tracking between languages pushes this field forward, facilitating comparisons between models and analysis of their various functions.

In this paper, we compare our eye-tracking prediction results with some simple baselines using token-level features, which we improve upon with our zero shot cross lingual model which we have described in section 3.

2 Task Description

2.1 Problem Statement

In this section we briefly describe the task at hand which is the challenge of predicting eye-tracking features recorded during sentence processing of multiple languages. This task is more complex as compared to previous editions of the shared task due to changes made compared to the previous edition (Hollenstein et al., 2021); (i) **Multilingual data**: We use an eye movement dataset with sentences from six languages (Chinese, Dutch, English, German, Hindi, Russian) and (ii) **Eye-tracking features**: To take into account the individual differences between readers, the task is not limited to predict the mean eye tracking features across readers, but also the standard deviation of the feature values. The task details can be found in Hollenstein et al. (2022).

We formulate the task as a regression task to predict 2 eye-tracking features and the corresponding standard deviation across readers. The targets are briefly described here: **first fixation duration (FFDAvg)**, the duration of the first fixation on the prevailing word; **standard deviation (FFDStd)** across readers; **total reading time (TRTAvg)**, the sum of all fixation durations on the current word, including regressions; **standard deviation (TRT-Std)** across readers.

The shared task is modelled as two related subtasks of increasing complexity :

Subtask 1: Predict eye-tracking features for sentences of the 6 provided languages

Subtask 2: Predict eye-tracking features for sentences from a new surprise language

2.2 Related Work

Multiple deep learning approaches have been explored in the past on cognitive modelling with lin-

Proceedings of the Workshop on Cognitive Modeling and Computational Linguistics, pages 102 - 107
May 26, 2022 ©2022 Association for Computational Linguistics

Name	Abbreviation	Language	Subjects	Training Set Sentences	Training Set Tokens	Dev Set Sentences	Dev Set Tokens	Test Set Sentences	Test Set Tokens	Source
Beijing Sentence Corpus	BSC	ZH	60	120	1355	7	82	23	248	Pan et al. (2021)
Postdam-Allahabad Hindi Eye-tracking Corpus	PAHEC	HI	30	122	2021	7	142	24	433	Husain et al. (2015)
Russian Sentence Corpus	RSC	RU	84	115	1140	7	59	22	218	Laurinavichyute et al. (2019)
Provo Corpus	Provo	EN	30	107	2067	6	152	21	440	Luke and Christianson (2018)
ZuCo 1.0 Corpus (NR)	ZuCo1	EN	12	240	5235	15	269	45	994	Hollenstein et al. (2018)
ZuCo 2.0 Corpus (NR)	ZuCo2	EN	18	279	5398	17	303	53	1127	Hollenstein et al. (2019)
GECO Corpus (Dutch L1 part)	GECO-NL	NL	18	640	7462	40	405	120	1475	Cop et al. (2017)
Potsdam Textbook Corpus	PoTeC	DE	75	80	1463	5	139	16	293	Jäger et al. (2021)
Copenhagen Corpus	CopCo	DA	-	-	-	-	-	402	6767	-

Table 1: Overview of the selected datasets

guistic perspective on English datasets ZuCo (Hollenstein et al., 2018, 2019) and Provo(Luke and Christianson, 2018). Salicchi and Lenci (2021) uses cosine similarity and surprisal within regression architecture to model the surprisal characteristic of a new word. Li and Rudzicz (2021); Yu et al. (2021) use the transformer methods to extract the linguistic embeddings; the former applying ensembling methods while the latter using surface, linguistic and behavioral features in combination with the linguistic embeddings.

2.3 Dataset

The dataset comprises of the eye-tracking data recorded during natural reading from 8 datasets in 6 languages. The training data contains 1703 sentences, the development set contains 104 sentences, and the test set 324 sentences. The data provided contains scaled features in the range between 0 and 100 to facilitate evaluation via the mean absolute average (MAE). The eye-tracking feature values are averaged over all readers.

The detailed dataset information about the number of sentences in each datasource and the tokenwise information is shown in table 1.

3 Our Approach

Our models heavily use contextualised embeddings extracted from the pretrained models based on transformer architecture (Vaswani et al., 2017). We experiment on the training dataset with multilingual transformer models which are briefly described below :

mBERT (Devlin et al., 2019) a deep contextual representation based on a series of transformers trained by a self-supervised objective with data from Wikipedia in 104 languages. It has been trained with masked language modelling objective and training makes no use of explicit cross-lingual signal.

XLM (Lample and Conneau, 2019) is a Transformer-based model that, like BERT, is trained with the masked language modeling (MLM) objective. Additionally, XLM is trained with a Translation Language Modeling (TLM) objective in an attempt to force the model to learn similar representations for different languages.

XLM-RoBERTa (Conneau et al., 2020) uses self-supervised training techniques to achieve state-of-the-art performance in cross-lingual understanding. It is trained on unlabeled text in 100 languages extracted from CommonCrawl datasets.

These transformer methods use either WordPiece or BytePair model for tokenization, due to which we use only the first token embedding of the tokenized word by these methods. We use the above three tranformer models and attach the extracted output embeddings from these models to the manually constructed features which we have described in 3.1. The entire model architecture is explained in Figure 1.

3.1 Features

Along with the encoder representations from the multilingual transformer models, we use 3 additional features, which we use to help us provide information to our embeddings. We discard other features like `POS-Tag` and `word_freq`, due to non-uniformity in cross-lingual setting and unavailability of reliable and enormous word-frequency list for some of the languages which could reduce the performance and create bias for some languages during training time.

The first two length based features use word division information and the word length information. During neurological processing of language, brain takes up dual pathways to process a word as shown

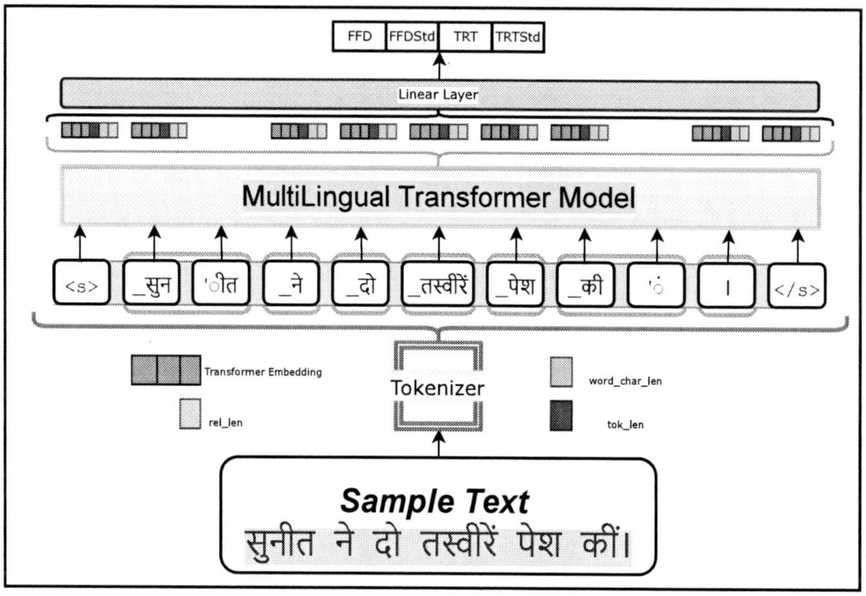

Figure 1: Model Representation

in MacGregor and Shtyrov (2013). The third feature is based on the relative length of the word as compared to preceding word.

tok_len : This feature is length of the parts of words when the word is tokenized measured in number of parts, which focuses on the complexity of the word based on length as cognitively longer words as processed.

word_char_len : This second feature is based on the apparent space taken up by the word evaluated by the number of characters it takes up when represented in `UTF-8` format. This feature is inspired by studies shown in Joseph et al. (2009).

rel_len: The third feature is the relative length of the word as compared to its preceding word. This can capture a sense of ease in reading a short word immediately after reading a word with great character length. For starting words of the sentence, we take the previous word length as zero.

3.2 Baselines

We start by implementing some simple baselines using token-level features using length based ideas as word-length is a commonality which can be found in multilingual settings which we described in section 3.1. We start with a median baseline model which takes the median of all the training token labels, instead of using an average baseline to prevent offsetting the predictions by a language with higher or lower valued variables. Along with the median baseline , we also use 5 commonly used machine learning regression models (i) Linear Regression *(lr)* ,(ii) Support Vector Regression *(svr)*,(iii) Gradient Boosting Methods *(lgbm, xgboost)* , (iv) Multi-Layer Perceptron *(MLPRegressor)* as our baselines. These baselines do not contain any contextual information.

3.3 Implementation and Hyperparameter Details

The models were trained with *MSE*(mean squared error) as loss function and the final evaluation was done using *MAE*(Mean Absolute Error) measure. For the baseline, models were trained taking each label as a regression target variable to remove label correlation if a regressor performs poorly in a multi output regression setting, while when using transformer based models, we trained a single model with a 4 length output regressor head which corresponded each to the final output target variables. Before the final regression layer, we used a hidden linear layer after the embedding output. The model evaluation for task submission was done using dev set after every epoch to measure the performance improvement and prevent overfitting. The implementation can be found here [1].

The details of the hyperparameters used for the training are given in table 4.

[1] `https://github.com/hvarS/CMCL-2022`

	Dev Set					Test Set - SubTask1					Test Set - SubTask2				
Model	**FFDAvg**	**FFDStd**	**TRTAvg**	**TRTStd**	**Overall**	**FFDAvg**	**FFDStd**	**TRTAvg**	**TRTStd**	**Overall**	**FFDAvg**	**FFDStd**	**TRTAvg**	**TRTStd**	**Overall**
Baseline$_{median}$	5.931	2.578	8.999	5.886	5.848	5.448	2.440	8.361	5.661	5.478	3.459	2.436	6.524	5.857	4.569
Baseline$_{lr}$	5.615	2.570	8.574	5.768	5.632	5.243	2.465	8.289	5.750	5.437	4.755	3.002	8.721	7.252	5.932
Baseline$_{svr}$	5.203	2.492	8.118	5.650	5.366	4.848	2.356	7.700	5.465	5.092	3.580	2.399	6.588	5.798	4.591
Baseline$_{lgbm}$	5.209	2.528	8.004	5.534	5.319	4.835	2.415	7.869	5.584	5.176	4.390	2.966	8.407	7.127	5.723
Baseline$_{MLPRegressor}$	5.268	2.531	8.195	5.701	5.423	4.914	2.418	7.972	5.734	5.260	4.315	2.904	8.136	7.328	5.671
Baseline$_{xgboost}$	5.210	2.532	8.050	5.566	5.340	4.834	2.413	7.871	5.591	5.178	4.302	2.942	8.337	7.106	5.672
mBERT$_{uncased}$	5.014	2.512	7.981	5.523	5.257	4.795	**2.325**	**7.267**	5.409	4.949	3.756	3.012	5.578	5.841	4.546
mBERT$_{cased}$	5.025	2.492	8.011	5.498	5.369	4.801	2.413	7.342	**5.124**	4.920	3.754	3.056	5.579	5.764	4.538
XLM$_{100}$	4.914	2.584	8.134	5.512	5.286	4.902	2.425	7.814	5.414	5.138	3.331	2.944	5.448	5.798	4.380
XLM-RoBERTa$_{base}$	4.892	2.486	8.231	5.504	5.278	4.745	2.327	7.321	5.738	5.031	3.214	2.987	5.556	5.666	4.355
XLM-RoBERTa$_{large}$	4.845	2.482	7.943	5.491	5.215	**4.738**	2.364	7.268	5.223	**4.898**	**2.945**	**2.726**	**5.602**	**5.654**	**4.232**

Table 2: MAE results on the dev and test set. **Bold** entries are the best performing models for that particular target

	SubTask-1				SubTask-2			
Model Version	**FFDAvg**	**FFDStd**	**TRTAvg**	**TRTStd**	**FFDAvg**	**FFDStd**	**TRTAvg**	**TRTStd**
XLM-RoBERTa$_{large}$	4.738	2.364	7.268	5.223	2.945	2.726	5.602	5.654
- tok_len	4.746	2.486	7.314	5.463	2.944	2.692	5.605	5.640
- word_char_len	4.976	2.484	7.454	5.478	3.014	2.696	5.712	5.642
- rel_len	4.787	2.486	7.457	5.466	3.121	2.703	6.241	5.644
- tok_len,word_char_len	5.012	2.427	7.785	5.421	3.154	2.710	6.785	5.546
- tok_len,rel_len	5.097	2.497	7.854	5.601	3.564	2.731	6.645	5.645
- word_char_len,rel_len	5.124	2.492	7.771	5.671	3.452	2.722	6.621	5.664
- tok_len,word_char_len,rel_len	5.465	2.488	8.370	5.684	4.371	2.744	7.186	5.678

Table 3: Feature Importance Ablation Study. The best performing model XLM-RoBERTa is taken for ablation

Parameter	**Value**
Optimizer	AdamW
Warm-Up Steps (%)	10%
epochs	100
learning rate	5e-2
weight decay	1e-2
dropout	0.5
batch size	64
hidden layer size	1024

Table 4: Hyperparameter Details

4 Results and Discussion

Table 2 shows the evaluation results on the dev set and the two test sets for SubTask-1 and SubTask-2 respectively based on MAE on the 4 target variables. Our transformer based models strongly outperformed the baseline approaches. The best performing model was XLM-RoBERTa$_{large}$ model, edging over the transformer models. mBERT model performed better than the XLM model on SubTask-1, but XLM outperforms the former on SubTask-2, suggesting better zero shot performance of XLM for this subtask. Also, the large models tended to perform better than their base counterpart implying higher parameter count resulted in better cross-lingual and zero shot cross-lingual performance. Also since originally the XLM-RoBERTa, mBERT and XLM models were trained for masked language modelling purpose, they have inherent inner representations of over 100 languages which helps in cross-lingual downstream tasks. One possible reason that mBERT performs better than XLM on SubTask-1 could be that XLM models are used for general sentence representations which mBERT identifies language from context and infers accordingly. For the same mentioned reason, it is possible that XLM performs better in zero shot setting.

4.1 Feature Importance

To evaluate the effectiveness of the engineered features ; `tok_len`, `word_char_len` and `rel_len`, an ablation study was conducted using the best performing model. We employ the strategy similar to used in Oh (2021); the three input features were ablated by simply replacing them with zeros during inference, which allowed us to effectively analyse the influence of these additional features. Table 3 shows the effects of model performance without the permutation of the engineered features.

Ablations on the external features show that these features affect the mean (μ) feature values, specifically the *FFDAvg* and the *TRTAvg*, indicating that these external features influence the final model performance for target mean values while the contextualised embedding portion takes care of the standard deviation (σ) of the targets. It can be observed that the `word_char_len` feature affects the target FFDAvg value to a large extent, while `rel_len` clearly affects the model performance on SubTask-2. One of the possible reasons could be the infusion of previous word contextual knowledge captured by `rel_len`. Also, the feature `tok_len` in combination with other features also improves the model performance, which may indicate it being not a very strong sole indicator.

5 Conclusion and Future Work

In this paper, we presented our approach to the CMCL 2022 Shared Task on eye-tracking data prediction. Our models use the fusion model that involve using the multilingual contextualized token representations using transformer architecture and attaching input features that we created that aid the model performance in predicting eye tracking features. This approach helped us become language agnostic which essentially helped the model to perform well in the zero shot cross-lingual setting in Subtask-2. Our best model based on XLM-RoBERTa outperforms the baseline and is also competitive with other systems submitted to the shared for both SubTask-1 and SubTask-2. Although the embeddings from large language models as shown previously work fairly well as they consider the context of the sentence into consideration as well, possibly they can be improved further if take into consideration the surprisal index which would positively correlate with the reading time and fixation duration as shown in Salicchi and Lenci (2021). In future, we aim to use more etymological features based on shared language history and also use the cross language lexical similarity index when predicting in cross lingual setting .

References

Alexis Conneau, Kartikay Khandelwal, Naman Goyal, Vishrav Chaudhary, Guillaume Wenzek, Francisco Guzmán, Edouard Grave, Myle Ott, Luke Zettlemoyer, and Veselin Stoyanov. 2020. Unsupervised cross-lingual representation learning at scale.

Uschi Cop, Nicolas Dirix, Denis Drieghe, and Wouter Duyck. 2017. Presenting geco: An eyetracking corpus of monolingual and bilingual sentence reading. *Behavior research methods*, 49(2):602–615.

Jacob Devlin, Ming-Wei Chang, Kenton Lee, and Kristina Toutanova. 2019. Bert: Pre-training of deep bidirectional transformers for language understanding.

Nora Hollenstein, Emmanuele Chersoni, Cassandra L. Jacobs, Yohei Oseki, Laurent Prévot, and Enrico Santus. 2021. CMCL 2021 shared task on eye-tracking prediction. In *Proceedings of the Workshop on Cognitive Modeling and Computational Linguistics*, pages 72–78, Online. Association for Computational Linguistics.

Nora Hollenstein, Emmanuelle Chersoni, Cassandra Jacobs, Yohei Oseki, Laurent Prévot, and Enrico Santus. 2022. Cmcl 2022 shared task on multilingual and cross lingual prediction of human reading behavior. In *Proceedings of the Workshop on Cognitive Modeling and Computational Linguistics*.

Nora Hollenstein, Jonathan Rotsztejn, Marius Troendle, Andreas Pedroni, Ce Zhang, and Nicolas Langer. 2018. Zuco, a simultaneous eeg and eye-tracking resource for natural sentence reading. *Scientific data*, 5(1):1–13.

Nora Hollenstein, Marius Troendle, Ce Zhang, and Nicolas Langer. 2019. Zuco 2.0: A dataset of physiological recordings during natural reading and annotation. *arXiv preprint arXiv:1912.00903*.

Samar Husain, Shravan Vasishth, and Narayanan Srinivasan. 2015. Integration and prediction difficulty in hindi sentence comprehension: Evidence from an eye-tracking corpus. *Journal of Eye Movement Research*, 8.

Lena A Jäger, Thomas Kern, and Patrick Haller. 2021. Potsdam textbook corpus (potec).

Holly S.S.L. Joseph, Simon P. Liversedge, Hazel I. Blythe, Sarah J. White, and Keith Rayner. 2009. Word length and landing position effects during reading in children and adults. *Vision Research*, 49(16):2078–2086.

Guillaume Lample and Alexis Conneau. 2019. Cross-lingual language model pretraining.

Anna K Laurinavichyute, Irina A Sekerina, Svetlana Alexeeva, Kristine Bagdasaryan, and Reinhold Kliegl. 2019. Russian sentence corpus: Benchmark measures of eye movements in reading in russian. *Behavior research methods*, 51(3):1161–1178.

Bai Li and Frank Rudzicz. 2021. TorontoCL at CMCL 2021 shared task: RoBERTa with multi-stage fine-tuning for eye-tracking prediction. In *Proceedings of the Workshop on Cognitive Modeling and Computational Linguistics*, pages 85–89, Online. Association for Computational Linguistics.

Steven G Luke and Kiel Christianson. 2018. The provo corpus: A large eye-tracking corpus with predictability norms. *Behavior research methods*, 50(2):826–833.

Lucy J. MacGregor and Yury Shtyrov. 2013. Multiple routes for compound word processing in the brain: Evidence from eeg. *Brain and Language*, 126(2):217–229.

Byung-Doh Oh. 2021. Team Ohio State at CMCL 2021 shared task: Fine-tuned RoBERTa for eye-tracking data prediction. In *Proceedings of the Workshop on Cognitive Modeling and Computational Linguistics*, pages 97–101, Online. Association for Computational Linguistics.

Jinger Pan, Ming Yan, Eike Richter, Hua Shu, and Reinhold Kliegl. 2021. The beijing sentence corpus: A chinese sentence corpus with eye movement data and predictability norms. *Behavior Research Methods*.

Lavinia Salicchi and Alessandro Lenci. 2021. PIHKers at CMCL 2021 shared task: Cosine similarity and surprisal to predict human reading patterns. In *Proceedings of the Workshop on Cognitive Modeling and Computational Linguistics*, pages 102–107, Online. Association for Computational Linguistics.

Ashish Vaswani, Noam Shazeer, Niki Parmar, Jakob Uszkoreit, Llion Jones, Aidan N. Gomez, Lukasz Kaiser, and Illia Polosukhin. 2017. Attention is all you need.

Qi Yu, Aikaterini-Lida Kalouli, and Diego Frassinelli. 2021. KonTra at CMCL 2021 shared task: Predicting eye movements by combining BERT with surface, linguistic and behavioral information. In *Proceedings of the Workshop on Cognitive Modeling and Computational Linguistics*, pages 120–124, Online. Association for Computational Linguistics.

NU HLT at CMCL 2022 Shared Task: Multilingual and Crosslingual Prediction of Human Reading Behavior in Universal Language Space

Joseph Marvin Imperial
Human Language Technology Lab (NU HLT)
National University
Manila, Philippines
jrimperial@national-u.edu.ph

Abstract

In this paper, we present a unified model that works for both multilingual and crosslingual prediction of reading times of words in various languages. The secret behind the success of this model is in the preprocessing step where all words are transformed to their universal language representation via the International Phonetic Alphabet (IPA). To the best of our knowledge, this is the first study to favorably exploit this phonological property of language for the two tasks. Various feature types were extracted covering basic frequencies, n-grams, information theoretic, and psycholinguistically-motivated predictors for model training. A finetuned Random Forest model obtained best performance for both tasks with 3.8031 and 3.9065 MAE scores for mean first fixation duration (FFDAvg) and mean total reading time (TRTAvg) respectively[1].

1 Introduction

Eye movement data has been one of the most used and most important resource that has pushed various interdisciplinary fields such as development studies, literacy, computer vision, and natural language processing research into greater heights. In a technical point of view, correctly determining theoretically grounded and cognitively plausible predictors of eye movement will allow opportunities to make computational systems leveraging on these properties to be more human-like (Sood et al., 2020).

Common human reading prediction works make use of the standard Latin alphabet as it is internationally used. However, investigating eye movement and reading patterns in other non-Anglocentric writing systems such as Chinese and Bengali is as equally as important (Share, 2008; Liversedge et al., 2016). Fortunately, there is a growing number of previous works exploring multilinguality in eye tracking prediction both in data collection and novel prediction approaches. The study of Liversedge et al. (2016) was the first to explore potential crosslinguality of Chinese, English and Finnish which differ in aspects of visual density, spacing, and orthography to name a few. The results of the study favorably support possible *universality of representation* in reading. In the same vein, Hollenstein et al. (2021) was the first to try use of large finetuned multilingual language models like BERT (Devlin et al., 2019) and XLM (Conneau and Lample, 2019) in a crosslingual setting to predict eye tracking features across English, Dutch, German, and Russian. Data-wise, the published works of Siegelman et al. (2022) for MECO, Pynte and Kennedy (2006) for the Dundee corpus, and Cop et al. (2017) for GECO have made significant impact in the field where they covered curation and collection of eye-tracking corpus for other languages in addition to English.

2 Task Definition and Data

The CMCL 2022 Shared Task (Hollenstein et al., 2022)[2] describes two challenges: predicting eye-tracking features in a **multilingual** and **crosslingual setup**. The eye movement dataset for this Shared Task contains sentences written in six languages: Mandarin Chinese (Pan et al., 2021), Hindi (Husain et al., 2015), Russian (Laurinavichyute et al., 2019), English (Luke and Christianson, 2018; Hollenstein et al., 2018, 2020), Dutch (Cop et al., 2017), and German (Jäger et al., 2021). The mean first fixation duration (FFDAvg) and mean total reading time (TRTAvg) as well as their corresponding standard deviations (FFDStd and TRTStd) are the four main eye-tracking features that need to be predicted by the participants through proposed computational means. For the multilingual task,

[1] https://github.com/imperialite/cmcl2022-unified-eye-tracking-ipa

[2] https://cmclorg.github.io/shared_task

Proceedings of the Workshop on Cognitive Modeling and Computational Linguistics, pages 108 - 113
May 26, 2022 ©2022 Association for Computational Linguistics

the training, validation, and testing datasets conform to the identified six languages. While for the crosslingual task, a surprise language (Danish) is provided as the test dataset.

3 Eye-Tracking Prediction in Universal Language Space

The proposed solution in this work is inspired by both classical and recent previous works in speech recognition systems (Schultz and Waibel, 1998, 2001; Dalmia et al., 2019) with multilingual and crosslingual capabilities through the transformation of words or similar sounding units in one global shared space using the International Phonetic Alphabet (IPA). This functionality allows models to generalize and adapt parameters to new languages while maintaining a stable vocabulary size for character representation. By definition, the IPA contains 107 characters for consonants and vowels, 31 for diacritics for modifying said consonants and vowels, and 17 signs to emphasize suprasegmental properties of phonemes such as stress and intonation (Association et al., 1999).

Figure 1 describes the unified methodology used for tackling both the multilinguality and crosslinguality challenge of the Shared Task. The backbone of this proposed solution lies with the phonetic transcription preprocessing step to convert the raw terms from the data written in Mandarin Chinese, Hindi, Russian, English, Dutch, and German to their IPA form. We used Epitran by Mortensen et al. (2018) for this process. The surprise language for the crosslingual task, Danish, is not currently supported by Epitran. We instead resorted to use Automatic Phonetic Transcriber[3], a paid transcription service that caters the Danish language. The transcription cost of the Danish test data is €15.

3.1 Feature Extraction

After obtaining the phonetic transcriptions, a total of fourteen features based on various types were extracted spanning general frequencies, n-grams, based on information theory, and based on motivations from psycholinguistics.

Frequency and Length Features. The simplest features are frequency and length-based predictors. Studies have shown that the length of words correlate with fixation duration as long words would obviously take time to read (Rayner, 1977; Hollenstein and Beinborn, 2021). For this study, we extracted the (a) word length (`word_len`), (b) IPA length (`ipa_len`), (c) IPA vowels count per term (`ipa_count`), and (d) normalized IPA vowel count per term over length (`ipa_norm`).

N-Gram Features. Language model-based features is a classic in eye-tracking prediction research as they capture word probabilities through frequency. We extracted raw count of unique n-grams per word (`bigram_count`, `trigram_count`), raw count of total n-grams per term (`bigram_sum`, `trigram_sum`), and normalized counts over word length (`bigram_norm`, `trigram_norm`) for character bigrams and trigrams in IPA form guided by the general formula for n-gram modelling below:

$$P(w_n \mid w_{n-N+1}^{n-1}) = \frac{C(w_{n-N+1}^{n-1} w_n)}{C(w_{n-N+1}^{n-1})} \quad (1)$$

Psycholinguistially-Motivated Features. Features with theoretical grounding are more practical to use when invetigating phenomena in human reading. In line with this, we extracted two psycholinguistically-motivated features: **imageability** and **concreteness**. When reading, humans tend to visualize words and scenarios as they are formed in context. This measure of ease of how words or phrases can easily be visualized in the min from a verbal material is quantified as imageability (Lynch, 1964; Richardson, 1976). On the other hand, concreteness is a measure of lexical organization where words are easily perceived by the senses. In the example of Schwanenflugel et al. (1988), words such as *chair* or *computer* are better understood than abstract words like *freedom*. Words with high concreteness scores are better recalled from the mental lexicon than abstract words as they have better representation in the imaginal system (Altarriba et al., 1999). We use these two features as we posit that the visualization and retrieval process of imageability and concreteness respectively can contribute to the reading time in milliseconds.

For this task, we used the crosslingual word embedding-based approximation for all the seven languages present in the dataset from the the work of Ljubešić et al. (2018).

Information Theoretic Features. Features inspired by information theory such as the concept

[3] http://tom.brondsted.dk/text2phoneme/

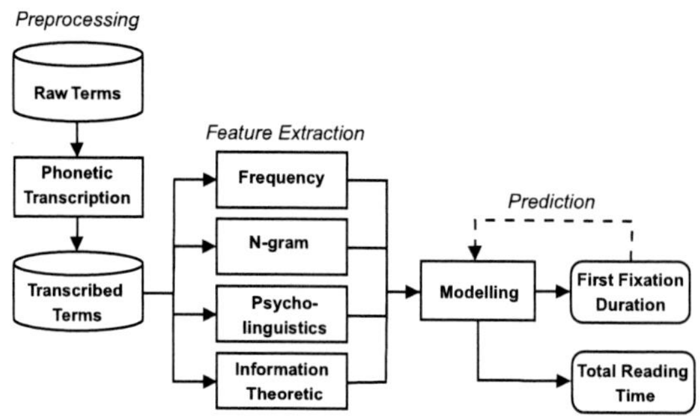

Figure 1: The proposed **unified** approach to multilingual and crosslingual human reading pattern prediction in universal language space via IPA.

of surprisal have thoroughly used in human reading pattern prediction (Hale, 2001; Levy, 2008; Demberg and Keller, 2008, 2009; Goodkind and Bicknell, 2018). Surprisal describes that processing time of a word to be read is proportional to its negative log based on a probability given by context as shown below:

$$\text{surprisal}(w_i) = -\log_2 P(w_i \mid w_1 ... w_{i-1}) \quad (2)$$

Thus, if a word is more likely to occur in its context, it is read more quickly (Shannon, 1948). For this task, since words are converted to a universal language space, the correct terminology in this case is bits per phoneme or **phonotactic complexity** as coined by Pimentel et al. (2020).

While surprisal quantifies the word's predictability or processing cost during reading, we also obtain the **entropy** H of each word x from the corpus. The entropy quantifies the expected value of information from an event as shown in the formula below:

$$H(X) = -\sum_{i=1}^{n} (\frac{count_i}{N}) \log_2 (\frac{count_i}{N}) \quad (3)$$

where $count_i$ is the count of character n_i and each word N consists of n characters. With this measure, a higher entropy score entails higher uncertainty for a word, thus, leading to increased reading time at the millisecond level.

3.2 Model Training Setup

We used four machine learning algorithms via WEKA (Witten and Frank, 2002) for modelling the features with FFDAvg and TRTAvg: linear regression (**LinReg**), multilayer perceptron (**MLP**), random forest (**RF**), and k-Nearest Neighbors (**kNN**). We only used the finetuned RF model for the prediction of FFDAvg and TRTAvg. Meanwhile, FFDStd and TRTStd are obtained by using the top models of all the four algorithms, re-running them to get FFDAvg and TRTAvg, and calculating the standard deviation. For TRTAvg, we added the predicted FFDAvg from the best model as an additional feature as we posit that the first fixation duration is a contributor to the overall reading time.

4 Results

Table 1 describes the main results of the experiments for predicting FFDAvg and TRTAvg using multiple finetuned supervised techniques evaluated through mean absolute error (MAE) and root mean squared error (RMSE). As mentioned previously, since the methodology used in this study cuts across multilingual and crosslingual tasks, the results reported in this applied are applicable to both. From the Table, the RF models outperformed the other three models in predicting FFDAVg and TRTAvg using 100% and 75% random selected features respectively and across 100 iterations. The RF model's effectivity can be attributed to its structure of multiple decision trees which normalize overfitting (Ho, 1995). Following RF in performance is kNN using Euclidean distance observing the same pattern as RF with different hyperparameter values such as 5 and 20 for the nearest neighbor for predicting FFDAvg and TRTAvg. On the other hand, both LinReg and MLP have no improvements regardless of hyperparameter values. For LinReg, using an M5 feature selection only provides extremely minor improvement in performances for FFDAvg and TRTAvg prediction. For MLP, using

Model	FFDAvg		TRTAvg	
	MAE	RMSE	MAE	RMSE
LinReg (k=10, M5)*†	**5.2361**	**6.7267**	**4.3419**	**7.0546**
LinReg (k=10, greedy)	5.2361	6.7267	4.3420	7.0545
LinReg (k=10, none)	5.2363	6.7274	4.3429	7.0594
MLP (k=10, lr=0.005, m=0.2)*†	**4.9898**	**6.4169**	**4.1744**	**6.2140**
MLP (k=10, lr=0.5, m=0.2)	6.7916	8.3791	4.8475	7.0840
MLP (k=10, lr=0.005, m=0.002)	5.0018	6.4299	4.1862	6.2177
MLP (k=10, lr=0.5, m=0.002)	6.4447	8.0110	4.9528	6.9668
MLP (k=10, lr=0.0005, m=0.0002)	5.5024	7.0474	4.2956	6.3823
RF (k=10, iters = 100)*	**3.8031**	**5.2750**	3.9600	5.8446
RF (k=10, iters = 100, 50% feats)	3.8045	5.2766	3.9094	5.8015
RF (k=10, iters = 100, 75% feats†)	3.8056	5.2762	**3.9065**	**5.8006**
kNN (k=10, nn=5, dist=euc)*	**4.3335**	**5.9651**	4.2953	6.3741
kNN (k=10, nn=10, dist=euc)	4.4263	6.0133	4.2053	6.2436
kNN (k=10, nn=20, dist=euc)†	4.5646	6.1284	**4.1793**	**6.2432**

Table 1: Results of predicting mean first fixation duration (FFDAvg) and mean total reading time (TRTAvg) using hyperparameter-tuned traditional supervised models over cross-fold validation of k=10. The tuned Random Forest (RF) model achieved the best performance which was used for both tasks of multilingual and crosslingual prediction. Top performing models from the four algorithm class were used for predicting the held-out test data to get the standard deviation of FFDAvg (*) and TRTAvg (†).

FFDAvg		TRTAvg	
bigram_norm	-0.1751	FFDAvg	0.8068
trigram_norm	-0.1393	bigram_count	0.2219
word_len	-0.1334	trigram_count	0.2156
bigram_sum	-0.1304	phonetic_comp	-0.2107
trigram_sum	-0.1101	ipa_ent	0.1925
imageability	0.1101	ipa_len	0.1921
concreteness	0.1044	trigram_norm	-0.1886

Table 2: Top 7 predictors for FFDAvg and TRTAvg with the highest absolute correlation coefficients.

default values in WEKA for momentum and learning rate obtained the best performance similarly for for FFDAvg and TRTAvg prediction.

4.1 Feature Importance

Viewing the results in a correlation analysis perspective, Table 2 shows the top 50% of the predictors, total 7, which are significantly correlated with FFDAvg and TRTAvg respectively. Only one predictor is common for both values, the normalized trigrams in IPA space which is fairly high in FFDAvg along with normalized bigrams than in TRTAvg. This may hint that normalized n-gram features may be plausible features of eye movement only for first passes over the word and not with the total accumulated time of fixations. Likewise, the psycholinguistically-motivated features, imageability and concreteness, were only seen in the FFDAvg section as well proving their potential plausibility for the same observation. All the length-based features such as word, IPA, bigram, and trigram-based counts were considered as top predictors for FFDAvg and TRTAvg. This unsurprisingly supports the results from the classical work of Rayner (1977) on correlation of lengths with fixations. Lastly, the strong correlation of first fixation duration with the total reading time with a score of r = 0.8068 proves the theoretical grounding of the proposed methodology as stated in Figure 1 albeit in post-hoc.

5 Conclusion

Precise eye movement datasets in multiple languages are considered one of the most important contributions that benefit various interdisciplinary fields such as psycholinguistics, developmental studies, behavioral studies, computer vision, and natural language processing. In this paper, we present a novel method of transforming multilingual eye-tracking data (English, Mandarin, Hindi, Russian, German, Dutch, and Danish) to their IPA equivalent, enforcing a single vocabulary space which allows competitive results for both multilingual and crosslingual tasks in a regression analysis setup. Future directions of this paper can explore more cognitively and theoretically plausible features that can be extracted as well as deeper interpretation studies of the predictive models trained.

References

Jeanette Altarriba, Lisa M Bauer, and Claudia Benvenuto. 1999. Concreteness, context availability, and imageability ratings and word associations for abstract, concrete, and emotion words. *Behavior Research Methods, Instruments, & Computers*, 31(4):578–602.

International Phonetic Association, International Phonetic Association Staff, et al. 1999. *Handbook of the International Phonetic Association: A guide to the use of the International Phonetic Alphabet*. Cambridge University Press.

Alexis Conneau and Guillaume Lample. 2019. Crosslingual language model pretraining. *Advances in Neural Information Processing Systems*, 32.

Uschi Cop, Nicolas Dirix, Denis Drieghe, and Wouter Duyck. 2017. Presenting geco: An eyetracking corpus of monolingual and bilingual sentence reading. *Behavior Research Methods*, 49(2):602–615.

Siddharth Dalmia, Xinjian Li, Alan W Black, and Florian Metze. 2019. Phoneme level language models for sequence based low resource asr. In *ICASSP 2019-2019 IEEE International Conference on Acoustics, Speech and Signal Processing (ICASSP)*, pages 6091–6095. IEEE.

Vera Demberg and Frank Keller. 2008. Data from eyetracking corpora as evidence for theories of syntactic processing complexity. *Cognition*, 109(2):193–210.

Vera Demberg and Frank Keller. 2009. A computational model of prediction in human parsing: Unifying locality and surprisal effects. In *Proceedings of the Annual Meeting of the Cognitive Science Society*, volume 31.

Jacob Devlin, Ming-Wei Chang, Kenton Lee, and Kristina Toutanova. 2019. BERT: Pre-training of deep bidirectional transformers for language understanding. In *Proceedings of the 2019 Conference of the North American Chapter of the Association for Computational Linguistics: Human Language Technologies, Volume 1 (Long and Short Papers)*, pages 4171–4186, Minneapolis, Minnesota. Association for Computational Linguistics.

Adam Goodkind and Klinton Bicknell. 2018. Predictive power of word surprisal for reading times is a linear function of language model quality. In *Proceedings of the 8th Workshop on Cognitive Modeling and Computational Linguistics (CMCL 2018)*, pages 10–18, Salt Lake City, Utah. Association for Computational Linguistics.

John Hale. 2001. A probabilistic earley parser as a psycholinguistic model. In *Second Meeting of the North American Chapter of the Association for Computational Linguistics*.

Tin Kam Ho. 1995. Random decision forests. In *Proceedings of 3rd International Conference on Document Analysis and Recognition*, volume 1, pages 278–282. IEEE.

Nora Hollenstein and Lisa Beinborn. 2021. Relative importance in sentence processing. In *Proceedings of the 59th Annual Meeting of the Association for Computational Linguistics and the 11th International Joint Conference on Natural Language Processing (Volume 2: Short Papers)*, pages 141–150, Online. Association for Computational Linguistics.

Nora Hollenstein, Emmanuel Chersoni, Cassandra Jacobs, Yohei Oseki, Laurent Prévot, and Enrico Santus. 2022. CMCL 2022 Shared Task on Multilingual and Crosslingual Prediction of Human Reading Behavior. In *Proceedings of the Workshop on Cognitive Modeling and Computational Linguistics*.

Nora Hollenstein, Federico Pirovano, Ce Zhang, Lena Jäger, and Lisa Beinborn. 2021. Multilingual language models predict human reading behavior. In *Proceedings of the 2021 Conference of the North American Chapter of the Association for Computational Linguistics: Human Language Technologies*, pages 106–123, Online. Association for Computational Linguistics.

Nora Hollenstein, Jonathan Rotsztejn, Marius Troendle, Andreas Pedroni, Ce Zhang, and Nicolas Langer. 2018. ZuCo, a simultaneous EEG and eye-tracking resource for natural sentence reading. *Scientific Data*, 5(1):1–13.

Nora Hollenstein, Marius Troendle, Ce Zhang, and Nicolas Langer. 2020. ZuCo 2.0: A dataset of physiological recordings during natural reading and annotation. In *Proceedings of the 12th Language Resources and Evaluation Conference*, pages 138–146, Marseille, France. European Language Resources Association.

Samar Husain, Shravan Vasishth, and Narayanan Srinivasan. 2015. Integration and prediction difficulty in hindi sentence comprehension: Evidence from an eye-tracking corpus. *Journal of Eye Movement Research*, 8(2).

Lena A Jäger, Thomas Kern, and Patrick Haller. 2021. Potsdam Textbook Corpus (potec).

Anna K Laurinavichyute, Irina A Sekerina, Svetlana Alexeeva, Kristine Bagdasaryan, and Reinhold Kliegl. 2019. Russian sentence corpus: Benchmark measures of eye movements in reading in russian. *Behavior Research Methods*, 51(3):1161–1178.

Roger Levy. 2008. Expectation-based syntactic comprehension. *Cognition*, 106(3):1126–1177.

Simon P Liversedge, Denis Drieghe, Xin Li, Guoli Yan, Xuejun Bai, and Jukka Hyönä. 2016. Universality in eye movements and reading: A trilingual investigation. *Cognition*, 147:1–20.

Nikola Ljubešić, Darja Fišer, and Anita Peti-Stantić. 2018. Predicting concreteness and imageability of words within and across languages via word embeddings. In *Proceedings of The Third Workshop on Representation Learning for NLP*, pages 217–222, Melbourne, Australia. Association for Computational Linguistics.

Steven G Luke and Kiel Christianson. 2018. The provo corpus: A large eye-tracking corpus with predictability norms. *Behavior Research Methods*, 50(2):826–833.

Kevin Lynch. 1964. *The image of the city*. MIT press.

David R Mortensen, Siddharth Dalmia, and Patrick Littell. 2018. Epitran: Precision g2p for many languages. In *Proceedings of the Eleventh International Conference on Language Resources and Evaluation (LREC 2018)*.

Jinger Pan, Ming Yan, Eike M Richter, Hua Shu, and Reinhold Kliegl. 2021. The beijing sentence corpus: A chinese sentence corpus with eye movement data and predictability norms. *Behavior Research Methods*, pages 1–12.

Tiago Pimentel, Brian Roark, and Ryan Cotterell. 2020. Phonotactic complexity and its trade-offs. *Transactions of the Association for Computational Linguistics*, 8:1–18.

Joel Pynte and Alan Kennedy. 2006. An influence over eye movements in reading exerted from beyond the level of the word: Evidence from reading english and french. *Vision Research*, 46(22):3786–3801.

Keith Rayner. 1977. Visual attention in reading: Eye movements reflect cognitive processes. *Memory & cognition*, 5(4):443–448.

John TE Richardson. 1976. Imageability and concreteness. *Bulletin of the Psychonomic Society*, 7(5):429–431.

Tanja Schultz and Alex Waibel. 1998. Multilingual and crosslingual speech recognition. In *Proc. DARPA Workshop on Broadcast News Transcription and Understanding*, pages 259–262. Citeseer.

Tanja Schultz and Alex Waibel. 2001. Language-independent and language-adaptive acoustic modeling for speech recognition. *Speech Communication*, 35(1-2):31–51.

Paula J Schwanenflugel, Katherine Kip Harnishfeger, and Randall W Stowe. 1988. Context availability and lexical decisions for abstract and concrete words. *Journal of Memory and Language*, 27(5):499–520.

Claude Elwood Shannon. 1948. A mathematical theory of communication. *The Bell system technical journal*, 27(3):379–423.

David L Share. 2008. On the anglocentricities of current reading research and practice: the perils of overreliance on an" outlier" orthography. *Psychological Bulletin*, 134(4):584.

Noam Siegelman, Sascha Schroeder, Cengiz Acartürk, Hee-Don Ahn, Svetlana Alexeeva, Simona Amenta, Raymond Bertram, Rolando Bonandrini, Marc Brysbaert, Daria Chernova, et al. 2022. Expanding horizons of cross-linguistic research on reading: The multilingual eye-movement corpus (meco). *Behavior Research Methods*, pages 1–21.

Ekta Sood, Simon Tannert, Philipp Müller, and Andreas Bulling. 2020. Improving natural language processing tasks with human gaze-guided neural attention. *Advances in Neural Information Processing Systems*, 33:6327–6341.

Ian H Witten and Eibe Frank. 2002. Data mining: practical machine learning tools and techniques with java implementations. *Acm Sigmod Record*, 31(1):76–77.

HkAmsters at CMCL 2022 Shared Task: Predicting Eye-Tracking Data from a Gradient Boosting Framework with Linguistic Features

Lavinia Salicchi
The Hong Kong Polytechnic University
lavinia.salicchi@connect.polyu.hk

Rong Xiang
The Hong Kong Polytechnic University
xiangrong0302@gmail.com

Yu-Yin Hsu
The Hong Kong Polytechnic University
yyhsu@polyu.edu.hk

Abstract

Eye movement data are used in psycholinguistic studies to infer information regarding cognitive processes during reading. In this paper, we describe our proposed method for the Shared Task of Cognitive Modeling and Computational Linguistics (CMCL) 2022 - Subtask 1, which involves data from multiple datasets on 6 languages. We compared different regression models using features of the target word and its previous word, and target word surprisal as regression features. Our final system, using a gradient boosting regressor, achieved the lowest mean absolute error (MAE), resulting in the best system of the competition.

1 Introduction

This year's Cognitive Modeling and Computational Linguistics (CMCL) workshop proposed a Shared Task focused on eye-tracking data prediction (Hollenstein et al., 2022). Differently from the last edition (Hollenstein et al., 2021), the 2022 Shared Task includes two subtasks: "Predict eye-tracking features for sentences of the 6 provided languages" and "Predict eye-tracking features for sentences from a new surprise language". In this paper, we present our proposed method for the first subtask.

In this task, the teams were asked to predict 4 eye-tracking features for 6 different languages (Chinese, Dutch, English, German, Hindi, and Russian); the features were: first fixation duration (FFD, which refers to the duration of the first fixation on the prevailing word), the standard deviation of the FFD across readers, total reading time (TRT, which refers to the sum of all fixation durations on the current word, including regressions), and the standard deviation of TRT across readers.

One of the challenging aspects of this task is the substantially different nature of these languages; they belong to different language families or different branches within the same family (i.e., Germanic, Balto-Slavic, Indo-Iranian, Sino-Tibetan) and 4 different writing systems are involved (i.e., Latin alphabet, Cyrillic alphabet, Devanagari abugida, and logograms). Therefore, we proposed a unified method that could be applied to account for the similarities and differences exhibited in the datasets of these 6 languages; this method includes regression features of the target word and of its previous word, and the surprisal for the target word within the context. Our codes are shared on Github at: https://github.com/laviniasalicchi/HkAmsters_CMCL2022.

2 Related work

Eye movement data provide valuable evidence regarding the cognitive processes underlying reading, and thus revealing how language is elaborated in our brain in every aspect, from morphology (Clifton Jr et al., 2007) to syntax (Van Schijndel and Schuler, 2015) to semantics (Ehrlich and Rayner, 1981). Since the early studies published in the last century, several studies have revealed that some features of the words themselves may influence language processing and, consequently, reading behavior; these features include word position, word length, word frequency, and the number of syllables within the word (Just and Carpenter, 1980). In addition, the *spillover effect* (Rayner et al., 1989) infers that the cognitive load of a word due to its frequency and length (Pollatsek et al., 2008) may influence the processing of its following word. Considering the multilingual nature of this task, in addition to the aforementioned features, we also included whether the word is all in uppercase, and whether it begins with a capital letter.

One additional factor that influences language comprehension is the sentence-level predictability of a word given the previous context (Kliegl et al., 2004), and in recent years, with the growth of computational linguistics, some attempts to model this kind of dynamic have been successfully achieved

Proceedings of the Workshop on Cognitive Modeling and Computational Linguistics, pages 114 - 120
May 26, 2022

using the surprisal (i.e., the negative logarithm of the probability of encountering a word given the context) computed by language models (Hale, 2001; Levy, 2008; Fossum and Levy, 2012).

In the last year's shared task, a regression model was proposed using the following features: two-word features (i.e., word length and word frequency), the cosine similarity between the vector representing the target word and the vector representing the sentence context, and the surprisal computed word-by-word (Salicchi and Lenci, 2021). However, Frank (2017) showed that given the overlaps in the information conveyed by cosine similarity and the surprisal, the latter alone is sufficient for the effective modeling of eye movements. Furthermore, in Frank's model the frequency and length of the word preceding the target one are included in the regression for modeling the spillover effect.

For these reasons, we modified the previously proposed method, increasing the number of word-specific features, and excluding the cosine similarity in our system.

3 Datasets

The shared task is formulated as a regression task to predict 2 eye-tracking features and their corresponding standard deviation across readers: (1) FFD; (2) the standard deviation of FFD across readers; (3) TRT; and (4) the standard deviation of TRT across readers. Subtask 1 (multilingual prediction) requires systems to predict these four eye-tracking features of words in 6 provided languages. The dataset includes materials from 8 openly available eye movement corpora:

- **Chinese**: Beijing Sentence Corpus (Pan et al., 2021).
- **Dutch**: GECO Corpus (Cop et al., 2017) .
- **English**: Provo Corpus (Luke and Christianson, 2018), ZuCo 1.0 Corpus (Hollenstein et al., 2018), and ZuCo 2.0 Corpus (Hollenstein et al., 2019).
- **German**: Potsdam Textbook Corpus (Jäger et al., 2021).
- **Hindi**: Postdam-Allahabad Hindi Eyetracking Corpus (Husain et al., 2015).
- **Russian**: Russian Sentence Corpus (Laurinavichyute et al., 2019).

Data statistics are given in Table 1.

Data Source	Train	Dev	Test
Chinese	1,355	82	248
Dutch	7,462	403	1,475
English(ZuCo1)	5,325	269	994
English(ZuCo2)	5,398	303	1,127
English(Provo)	5,314	152	440
German	1,463	139	293
Hindi	2,021	142	433
Russian	1,140	59	218

Table 1: Dataset statistics. The instance numbers for each portion are given.

4 Methodology

In this section, we introduce the selected features, inspired by psycholinguistic studies relying on eye-tracking data, and the investigated regression algorithms. The same set of features was used for each regression model.

4.1 Features

Given the multilingual nature of Subtask 1, we adopted several lexical features as hand-crafted features. The **Word position index** was used to provide the sequential information of a word . The **word length** of the current word and previous one was also included. Furthermore, we added two Boolean features: **Capitalization** and **Upper**. The first feature was set to 1 if the first letter of the target word was uppercase, and it was set to 0 otherwise; the second feature was set to 1 if all the letters of the target word were uppercase, and it was set to 0 otherwise. We also used language-specific tools for the following features: **Word frequencies** for all the 6 languages were computed using `wordfreq`[1]. These frequencies were collected for both the current and previous word. **Syllables counts** for Hindi words were computed using the `syllable package`[2] of `Indic NLP Library`, whereas the other languages were available in `textstat`[3]. Finally, to compute **Surprisal**, 6 different GPT versions were used: Russian GPT by Grankin et al.[4], Hindi GPT[5] by Parmar, Chinese GPT[6] by Du (2019), Dutch GPT[7] by

[1] pypi.org/project/wordfreq/
[2] github.com/anoopkunchukuttan/indic_nlp_library/find/master
[3] pypi.org/project/textstat/
[4] github.com/mgrankin/ru_transformers
[5] huggingface.co/surajp/gpt2-hindi
[6] github.com/Morizeyao/GPT2-Chinese
[7] github.com/wietsedv/gpt2-recycle

de Vries and Nissim (2021), and German GPT[8]. More specifically, for each word (w) we computed the surprisal as the negative logarithm of its probability given the previous context, from the beginning of the sentence to the word immediately preceding the target one:

$$Surprisal(w_n) = -\log(P(w_n|w_0, w_1, ..., w_{n-1})) \quad (1)$$

with P being the probability computed by GPT.

A total of 9 features were extracted. We decided to generate polynomial features from our set in order to exploit potential interactions. We used the `PolynomialFeatures` functionality of the `scikit-learn` Python package to generate interaction features of order 2, and we used only interaction features, so that the final number of features that were fed to the regressors was 46.

4.2 Regressors

Once we had computed all the regression features, we ran several experiments to find the best regression model for each language and each feature, using the mean absolute error (MAE) for all the words within the same language as our main index. We tested several regression algorithms using the implementations in the `scikit-learn` Python package. The adopted scikit-learn API and the main hyper-parameters are listed below:

- **RR** (`Ridge`): Ridge regression solves a regression model in which the loss function is the linear least-squares function, and regularization is given by the l2 norm. `alpha`=1.0, `normalize`=True.
- **MLP** (`MLPRegressor`): The multi-layer perceptron regressor optimizes the squared-loss using L-BFGS algorithm or stochastic gradient descent. `hidden layer size`=5, `activation`=identity, `solver`=adam.
- **PLSR** (`PLSRegression`): PLS regression implements the PLS2, which blocks regression in the case of a one-dimensional response. `components`=5.
- **BRR** (`BayesianRidge`): A Bayesian Ridge model implements the optimization of the regularization parameters lambda and alpha. `alpha_1, alpha_2`==1.0e-6, `lambda_1, lambda_2`=1.0e-6.
- **LR** (`LinearRegression`): Linear regression is trained based on an ordinary least-squares function. `normalize`=True.
- **RF** (`RandomForestRegressor`): A random forest is a meta estimator that fits a number of classifying decision trees on various sub-samples of the dataset and uses averaging to improve the predictive accuracy and control over-fitting. `min_samples_split`=2, `min_samples_leaf`=1.
- **SVR** (`SupportVectorRegressor`): SVR is short for epsilon-support vector regression. It uses the kernel trick to map data to map the original data space to a high-dimensional space. `kernel`='rbf', `epsilon`=0.1, `degree`=3.
- **Elast** (`ElastRegressor`): Elast regressor uses linear regression with combined L1 and L2 priors as the regularizer. `alpha`=1.0, `l1_ratio`=0.5, `selection`='cyclic'.
- **LGB** (`LGBMRegressor`): LightGBM is a gradient boosting framework that uses tree-based learning algorithms. It is designed to be distributed and is efficient with faster training speed and higher efficiency. `objective` ='regression',`learning_rate`=0.05, `mum_leaves`=31.

4.3 Metrics

The performance of the participating systems was evaluated in terms of the mean absolute error (MAE), mean squared error (MSE), R-Square ($R2$), Pearson correlation ($Pears.$), and Spearman correlation ($Spear.$) between the outputs and the annotated values. In the **Results and Discussion** section, MAE is adopted as the main comparison index.

5 Results and Discussion

To use a single model that could be applied to multilingual data, we selected the model with generally better performance. Table 2 shows the performances of different regressors over the FFD for one of the target languages. *LGB*, which is the gradient boosting regressor with the regression feature interacting, provided the best predictions. *LGB* not only had the lowest MAE, but also achieved the best results in terms of MSE, R2, Pearson correlation, and Spearman correlation.

[8]huggingface.co/dbmdz/german-gpt2

Regressor	MAE	MSE	$R2$	$Pears.$	$Spear.$
LGB	2.31	10.35	0.20	0.48	0.45
BRR	2.44	10.77	0.17	0.42	0.37
RR	2.46	10.75	0.17	0.43	0.39
PLSR	2.47	11.17	0.14	0.38	0.33
Elast	2.51	11.52	0.11	0.34	0.32
LR	2.51	11.01	0.15	0.41	0.37
SVR	2.51	11.39	0.12	0.39	0.35
RF	2.56	15.03	-0.16	0.25	0.36
MLP	2.63	13.49	-0.04	0.19	0.22

Table 2: Performance of different regressors over FFD for Hindi. Evaluation metrics including MAE, MSE, $R2$, $Pears.$, $Spear.$ are provided. LGB is the best performed model for Hindi. BRR and RR are the second and third best models, but the performance gap is rather marginal.

Considering how regressors accounted for each language dataset, we present the lowest MAE values for each feature and each language in Table 3. Despite the generally good performances of LGB1, this model was not always the best. A future direction may be to identify regression features and regression models that are more suitable for a specific language and the relevant eye-tracking features.

This conclusion is reinforced by a further analysis of the performance of our system (Table 6, Appendix); it revealed that TRTAvg was the hardest feature to predict with a mean error across languages of 5.1. Regarding the mean error, the languages that performed better in our model regarding TRTAvg were Dutch (mean error 3.37, standard deviation (std) 3.34) and English (mean error 4.76, std 4.7), but their coefficients of variation were higher, compared with other languages (English: 0.993, Dutch: 0.993), such as Hindi, for which our model registered a high mean error of 8.81 (std 7.045) but the lowest coefficient of variation (0.799). For both Russian and Chinese, LGB1 had high mean errors (approximately 10) and high coefficients of variation (0.867 and 0.931, respectively).

Given the differences in the amount of data among language datasets, our comparison mainly follows the coefficient of variation, which reveals that for FFDAvg, English, German, and Hindi were the languages for which our system performed better, followed by Dutch, Russian and Chinese. For TRTStd, the better performances were on the datasets of Hindi, Chinese, and Russian, whereas the most difficult portions of the dataset for this feature were those in English, Dutch, and German. Finally, regarding the errors for FFDStd, English was undoubtedly the language for which our system performed the best, and it showed the worst results for Chinese and Hindi datasets.

Feature	Language	Model	MAE
FFD	Chinese	ELAST1	3.18
	Dutch	LGB0	1.72
	English	LGB0	5.37
	German	SVR0	0.451
	Hindi	LGB1	2.31
	Russian	SVR1	2.45
FFD sd	Chinese	LGB1	3.61
	Dutch	ELAST0	1.47
	English	LGB1	2.21
	German	SVR1	0.45
	Hindi	LGB1	2.64
	Russian	SVR1	2.43
TRT	Chinese	LR1	6.52
	Dutch	LGB0	3.34
	English	LGB1	8.28
	German	RF0	3.052
	Hindi	LGB1	5.32
	Russian	SVR0	9.71
TRT sd	Chinese	LR1	6.84
	Dutch	LGB0	2.78
	English	LGB1	5.42
	German	RF0	2.57
	Hindi	BRR1	5.23
	Russian	LGB0	6.34

Table 3: Best models for each language and feature to be predicted. Models in this table with '0' do not have interaction between regression features while models in this table with '1' take advantage of interaction between regression features.

Finally, we performed an ablation study for the German dataset, in order to examine the contribu-

	MAE		MSE		R2		Pearson		Spearman	
	w/o	w	w/o	w	w/o	w	w/o	w	w/o	w
FFD	0.467-	0.457	0.363-	0.362	0.140-	0.142	0.406-	0.407	0.325-	0.399
FFD sd	0.464-	0.456	0.432-	0.425	0.036-	0.051	0.245-	0.274	0.272-	0.327
TRT	3.517+	3.520	29.337+	30.181	0.628+	0.618	0.865-	0.875	0.793-	0.803
TRT sd	2.892-	2.872	20.397-	20.090	0.510-	0.517	0.780-	0.788	0.717+	0.716

Table 4: Feature analyses for whether using Capital letters in processing the German dataset. '+' indicates a better performance compared with all features training, while vice verses for '-'.

	FFD	FFD sd	TRT	TRT sd
Word position index	0.451+	0.463-	3.520	2.981-
Word length	0.452+	0.463-	3.612-	2.879-
Previous word length	0.456+	0.456	3.543-	2.869+
Word log frequency	0.468-	0.475-	3.677-	3.055-
Previous word log frequency	0.459-	0.470-	3.470+	2.853+
Uppercase	0.457	0.456	3.520	2.872
Capitalization	0.467-	0.464-	3.517+	2.892-
Syllable count	0.459-	0.457-	3.527-	2.933-
Surprisal score	0.456+	0.452+	3.573-	2.889-
all	0.457	0.456	3.520	2.872

Table 5: An ablation study for the German dataset (no **Uppercase**). The MAE results are presented using leave-one comparison. '+' indicates a better performance compared with all features training, while vice verses for '-'.

tion of the different features. Table 4 shows the results of whether using the feature **Capitalization**. Despite some minor performance drop (especially for TRT), using **Capitalization** generally improves the evaluation metrics. Table 5 summarizes the MAE results of feature ablation study for the German dataset. In general, every feature incorporated in the proposed system contributes to the best practice. These preliminary results suggest that the features we adopted are tenable. We leave a more comprehensive cross-lingual comparison along this line for the future study.

In summary, in our system, TRTAvg was the most difficult one to predict, but TRTAvg and TRTStd showed better performance in Hindi, and FFDAvg and FFDStd were better in English. Our proposed system outperformed the Shared Task baseline with an average MAE of 3.0112, resulting in the best system of the competition.

6 Conclusions

In this paper, we described the system we proposed for the CMCL2022 Shared Task - Subtask 1 on multilingual data. Using a gradient boosting regressor with features of the target words as well as their previous word, and the surprisal between the target word and the previous context as regression features, we predicted two eye-tracking features and two standard deviations: first fixation duration, total reading time, and their standard deviations across readers.

Despite the multilingual nature of this task, we were able to reach our goal of creating a unified system capable of modeling the human reading behavior in 6 substantially different languages. Our results showed a tendency of better performances with FFD related features than with TRT related ones. This may partly reflect the fact that in our system, more word-level hand-crafted features were included, which could favor this token-level prediction task, given that FFD is often assumed to reflect lexical information processing, whereas TRT may be related to a later stage of language processing related to information-structural integration.

Acknowledgments

We would like to thank the reviewers for their insightful feedback. This research was made possible by the start-up research fund (BD8S) at the Hong Kong Polytechnic University.

References

Charles Clifton Jr, Adrian Staub, and Keith Rayner. 2007. Eye movements in reading words and sentences. *Eye movements*, pages 341–371.

Uschi Cop, Nicolas Dirix, Denis Drieghe, and Wouter Duyck. 2017. Presenting GECO: An Eye-Tracking Corpus of Monolingual and Bilingual Sentence Reading. *Behavior Reseach Methods*, 49(2):602–615.

Wietse de Vries and Malvina Nissim. 2021. As good as new. how to successfully recycle English GPT-2 to make models for other languages. In *Findings of the Association for Computational Linguistics: ACL-IJCNLP 2021*, pages 836–846, Online. Association for Computational Linguistics.

Zeyao Du. 2019. Gpt2-chinese: Tools for training gpt2 model in chinese language. `https://github.com/Morizeyao/GPT2-Chinese`.

Susan E. Ehrlich and Keith Rayner. 1981. Contextual Effects on Word Perception and Eye Movements During Reading. *Journal of Verbal Learning and Verbal Behavior*, 20:641–65.

Victoria Fossum and Roger Levy. 2012. Sequential vs. hierarchical syntactic models of human incremental sentence processing. In *Proceedings of the 3rd Workshop on Cognitive Modeling and Computational Linguistics (CMCL 2012)*, pages 61–69, Montréal, Canada. Association for Computational Linguistics.

Stefan L Frank. 2017. Word Embedding Distance Does not Predict Word Reading Time. In *Proceedings of CogSci*, pages 385–390.

John Hale. 2001. A Probabilistic Earley Parser as a Psycholinguistic Model. In *Proceedings of NAACL*.

Nora Hollenstein, Emmanuele Chersoni, Cassandra Jacobs, Yohei Oseki, Laurent Prévot, and Enrico Santus. 2021. Cmcl 2021 shared task on eye-tracking prediction. In *Proceedings of the Workshop on Cognitive Modeling and Computational Linguistics*.

Nora Hollenstein, Emmanuele Chersoni, Cassandra Jacobs, Yohei Oseki, Laurent Prévot, and Enrico Santus. 2022. Cmcl 2021 shared task on eye-tracking prediction. In *CMCL 2022 Shared Task on Multilingual and Crosslingual Prediction of Human Reading Behavior.*

Nora Hollenstein, Jonathan Rotsztejn, Marius Troendle, Andreas Pedroni, Ce Zhang, and Nicolas Langer. 2018. Zuco, a simultaneous eeg and eye-tracking resource for natural sentence reading. *Scientific Data*, 5.

Nora Hollenstein, Marius Troendle, Ce Zhang, and Nicolas Langer. 2019. Zuco 2.0: A dataset of physiological recordings during natural reading and annotation. *arXiv preprint arXiv:1912.00903*.

Samar Husain, Shravan Vasishth, and Narayanan Srinivasan. 2015. Integration and prediction difficulty in hindi sentence comprehension: Evidence from an eye-tracking corpus. *Journal of Eye Movement Research*, 8(2).

Lena A Jäger, Thomas Kern, and Patrick Haller. 2021. Potsdam textbook corpus (potec).

Marcel Adam Just and Patricia A. Carpenter. 1980. A theory of reading: From eye fixations to comprehension. *Psychological Review*, 87(4):329–354.

Reinhold Kliegl, Ellen Grabner, Martin Rolfs, and Ralf Engbert. 2004. Length, frequency, and predictability effects of words on eye movements in reading. *European Journal of Cognitive Psychology - EUR J COGN PSYCHOL*, 16:262–284.

Anna K Laurinavichyute, Irina A Sekerina, Svetlana Alexeeva, Kristine Bagdasaryan, and Reinhold Kliegl. 2019. Russian sentence corpus: Benchmark measures of eye movements in reading in russian. *Behavior research methods*, 51(3):1161–1178.

Roger Levy. 2008. Expectation-based Syntactic Comprehension. *Cognition*, 106(3):1126–1177.

Steven G Luke and Kiel Christianson. 2018. The Provo Corpus: A Large Eye-tracking Corpus with Predictability Norms. *Behavior Research Methods*, 50(2):826–833.

Jinger Pan, Ming Yan, Eike M Richter, Hua Shu, and Reinhold Kliegl. 2021. The beijing sentence corpus: A chinese sentence corpus with eye movement data and predictability norms. *Behavior Research Methods*, pages 1–12.

Alexander Pollatsek, Barbara J Juhasz, Erik D Reichle, Debra Machacek, and Keith Rayner. 2008. Immediate and delayed effects of word frequency and word length on eye movements in reading: a reversed delayed effect of word length. *Journal of experimental psychology: human perception and performance*, 34(3):726.

Keith Rayner, Sara C. Sereno, Robin K. Morris, A. Réne Schmauder, and Charles Clifton Jr. 1989. Eye movements and on-line language comprehension processes. *Language and Cognitive Processes*, 4(3-4):SI21–SI49.

Lavinia Salicchi and Alessandro Lenci. 2021. PIHKers at CMCL 2021 shared task: Cosine similarity and surprisal to predict human reading patterns. In *Proceedings of the Workshop on Cognitive Modeling and Computational Linguistics*, pages 102–107, Online. Association for Computational Linguistics.

Marten Van Schijndel and William Schuler. 2015. Hierarchic syntax improves reading time prediction. In *Proceedings of the 2015 conference of the North American chapter of the association for computational linguistics: Human language technologies*, pages 1597–1605.

Appendix

	FFDAvg	FFDStd	TRTAvg	TRTStd
Chinese				
$Mean$	5.884	7.152	10.096	7.804
$Stddev$	7.688	11.216	9.396	6.396
CV	1.307	1.568	0.931	0.820
Dutch				
$Mean$	1.754	1.484	3.367	2.798
$Stddev$	1.741	1.385	3.343	2.714
CV	0.993	0.933	0.993	0.970
English(Zuco1)				
$Mean$	0.960	1.010	4.180	4.102
$Stddev$	0.819	0.865	4.335	4.649
CV	0.853	0.856	1.037	1.133
English(Zuco2)				
$Mean$	1.682	1.841	4.672	4.169
$Stddev$	1.383	1.459	4.805	4.169
CV	0.822	0.793	1.028	1.000
English(Provo)				
$Mean$	2.061	2.014	5.434	5.167
$Stddev$	1.682	1.857	4.969	4.872
CV	0.816	0.922	0.915	0.943
German				
$Mean$	0.457	0.456	3.520	2.872
$Stddev$	0.392	0.468	4.233	3.453
CV	0.857	1.025	1.203	1.202
Hindi				
$Mean$	6.615	9.716	8.814	9.904
$Stddev$	6.034	11.296	7.045	7.265
CV	0.912	1.163	0.799	0.734
Russian				
$Mean$	2.669	2.703	10.152	6.649
$Stddev$	2.934	1.942	8.805	6.140
CV	1.099	0.719	0.867	0.923

Table 6: Error analysis on the performance of our proposed system on every portion of the dev dataset. $Mean$ refers to the average of the absolute error of all words in a portion. $Stddev$ refers to the standard deviation of the absolute error of all words in a portion. CV refers to the coefficient of variation (representing a relative standard deviation), which is a statistical measure of the dispersion of the absolute error of all words in a portion.

CMCL 2022 Shared Task on Multilingual and Crosslingual Prediction of Human Reading Behavior

Nora Hollenstein
University of Copenhagen
nora.hollenstein@hum.ku.dk

Emmanuele Chersoni
The Hong Kong Polytechnic University
emmanuelechersoni@gmail.com

Cassandra Jacobs
University of Buffalo
jacobs.cassandra.1@gmail.com

Yohei Oseki
University of Tokyo
oseki@g.ecc.u-tokyo.ac.jp

Laurent Prévot
Aix-Marseille Université & CNRS, LPL
laurent.prevot@univ-amu.fr

Enrico Santus
Bayer Pharmaceuticals
esantus@gmail.com

Abstract

We present the second shared task on eye-tracking data prediction of the Cognitive Modeling and Computational Linguistics Workshop (CMCL). Differently from the previous edition, participating teams are asked to predict eye-tracking features from multiple languages, including a surprise language for which there were no available training data. Moreover, the task also included the prediction of standard deviations of feature values in order to account for individual differences between readers.

A total of six teams registered to the task. For the first subtask on multilingual prediction, the winning team proposed a regression model based on lexical features, while for the second subtask on cross-lingual prediction, the winning team used a hybrid model based on a multilingual transformer embeddings as well as statistical features.

1 Introduction

The benefits of eye movement data for machine learning have been assessed in various domains, including NLP (Barrett et al., 2016, 2018; McGuire and Tomuro, 2021) and computer vision (Shanmuga Vadivel et al., 2015; Kruthiventi et al., 2017; Bautista and Naval, 2020; Tseng et al., 2020). Eye-tracking provides millisecond-accurate records on where humans look when they are reading and are useful in explanatory research of language processing. Eye movements depend on the stimulus and are therefore language-specific, but there are also universal tendencies that have been observed across languages (Liversedge et al., 2016).

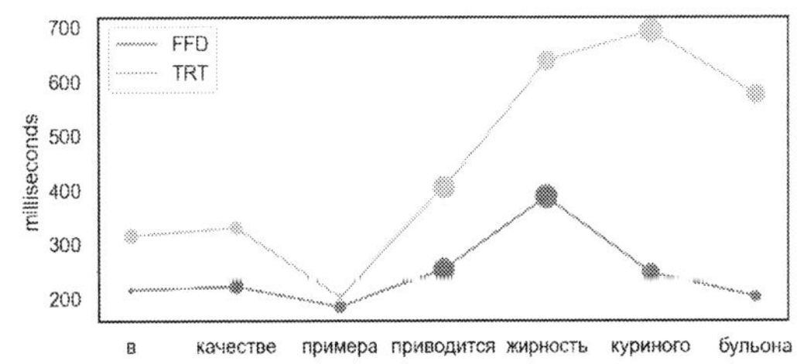

Figure 1: An example sentence from the Russian Sentence Corpus (Laurinavichyute et al., 2019) averaged across all readers. A wider diameter of the markers represents a higher standard deviation.

Modelling human reading has been researched extensively in psycholinguistics (Reichle et al., 1998; Matthies and Søgaard, 2013; Hahn and Keller, 2016). In NLP, eye-tracking prediction has been used to determine linguistic complexity (Singh et al., 2016; Sarti et al., 2021) or to analyze language models' ability to account for measures of human reading effort (Merkx and Frank). Being able to accurately predict eye-tracking features across languages will advance this field and will facilitate comparisons between models and the analysis of their varying capabilities.

In this shared task, we address the challenge of predicting eye-tracking features recorded during sentence processing of multiple languages. We are interested in both cognitive modelling approaches as well as linguistically motivated approaches (i.e., language models). This shared task is hosted on CodaLab, where the instructions and pre-processed

Proceedings of the Workshop on Cognitive Modeling and Computational Linguistics, pages 121 - 129
May 26, 2022 ©2022 Association for Computational Linguistics

eye-tracking datasets are available.[1]

Compared to the CMCL 2021 Shared Task on eye-tracking prediction (Hollenstein et al., 2021a), we introduce two major changes:

- Multilingual data: We provide an eye movement dataset with sentences from six different languages (Chinese, Dutch, English, German, Hindi, Russian) for Subtask 1 and a new Danish test set for Subtask 2.
- Eye-tracking features: To take into account the individual differences between readers, the task is not limited to predict the mean eye tracking features across readers, but also the standard deviation of the feature values.

2 Related Work

2.1 Eye-Tracking and Language Models

It is widely acknowledged by researchers on naturalistic reading that fixation patterns are influenced by the words' contextual predictability (Ehrlich and Rayner, 1981), although there is some substantial disagreement about the nature of this link (Brothers and Kuperberg, 2021). In Natural Language Processing, the most influential account of this phenomenon comes from *surprisal theory* (Hale, 2001; Levy, 2008). This theory claims that the processing difficulty of a word is proportional to its *surprisal*, i.e., the negative logarithm of the probability of the word given the context, and it served as a reference framework for several studies on language models and eye-tracking data prediction (Demberg and Keller, 2008; Frank and Bod, 2011; Fossum and Levy, 2012). Surprisal is not necessarily the only factor involved: for example, word length, word frequency, and other local statistics (e.g., bigram and trigram probabilities) also affect reading times (Rayner and Raney, 1996; Williams and Morris, 2004; Goodkind and Bicknell, 2021). Embedding-based semantic similarity was also found to be correlated with eye-tracking metrics (Mitchell et al., 2010; Salicchi et al., 2021; Yu et al., 2021), although it is not clear whether its effect is independent of surprisal (Frank, 2017).

Later research work brought evidence that language models with a lower perplexity are better at fitting to human reading times (Goodkind and Bicknell, 2018; Aurnhammer and Frank, 2019; Wilcox et al., 2020; Merkx and Frank). However, other studies suggested that perplexity may not tell the whole story. For example, Hao et al. (2020) pointed out that such a metric cannot be used for comparing models with different vocabularies and proposed, as a more reliable predictor, the correlation between surprisal values computed by a language model and the surprisal values obtained from humans by means of a Cloze test. Moreover, while most work on eye-tracking and language modeling focused on English, recent experiments on typologically distant languages like Japanese showed that lower-perplexity models may not be necessarily better at predicting eye-movement data (Kuribayashi et al., 2021). Therefore, multilingual evaluation is an important step for building cognitively plausible models of human reading processes.

2.2 Multilingual Eye-Tracking Corpora

Comparing monolingual and multilingual Transformer models, Hollenstein et al. (2021b) found that the latter are surprisingly accurate in predicting eye-tracking features across languages. In particular, multilingual BERT (Devlin et al., 2019) shows the best crosslinguistic transfer ability, even without being explicitly trained on the target language, while the XLM models (Lample and Conneau, 2019) achieve better in-language performance after fine-tuning.

Psycholinguistic research in the last two decades has led to the introduction of corpora with eye-tracking recordings in several languages, including English (Cop et al., 2017; Luke and Christianson, 2017; Hollenstein et al., 2018, 2020), German (Kliegl et al., 2006; Jäger et al., 2021), Hindi (Husain et al., 2015), Japanese (Asahara et al., 2016), Dutch (Cop et al., 2017), Russian (Laurinavichyute et al., 2019), Mandarin Chinese (Pan et al., 2021), and Danish (Hollenstein et al., 2022). However, it is not optimal to combine datasets recorded in different settings. The most recent release is the Multilingual Eye-Movement Corpus (MECO; Siegelman et al. 2022), a new resource including parallel data from 580 readers of 13 different languages following the same experiment protocol. The notable differences between these corpora and other psycholinguistic studies is the naturally occurring stimuli, the presentation of full sentences or longer text spans, and that the participants were able to read in their own speed.

[1] `https://competitions.codalab.org/competitions/36415`

Corpus	Lang.	Sents.	Tokens	Subjects	Reference
BSC	ZH	150	1685	60	Pan et al. (2021)
PAHEC	HI	153	2596	30	Husain et al. (2015)
RSC	RU	144	1417	102	Laurinavichyute et al. (2019)
Provo	EN	189	2659	84	Luke and Christianson (2017)
ZuCo 1.0	EN	300	6588	12	Hollenstein et al. (2018)
ZuCo 2.0	EN	349	6828	18	Hollenstein et al. (2020)
GECO-NL	NL	800	9218	18	Cop et al. (2017)
PoTeC	DE	101	1895	75	Jäger et al. (2021)
CopCo (*Subtask 2 only*)	DK	402	6768	5	Hollenstein et al. (2022)

Table 1: Datasets used in the shared task. Note that the number of sentences and tokens refers to the text materials we have selected and not necessarily to the complete original datasets.

Feature	min	max	mean (std)
FFDAVG	0.0	56.74	13.02 (7.34)
FFDSTD	0.0	58.54	4.47 (3.55)
TRTAVG	0.0	100.0	18.87 (11.57)
TRTSTD	0.0	100.0	9.86 (8.01)

Table 2: Minimum, maximum, mean and standard deviation of the *scaled* feature values in both training and test data of Subtask 1, after averaging across readers.

3 Task Description

The shared task is formulated as a regression task to predict 2 eye-tracking features and the corresponding standard deviation across readers for each word:

1. FFDAVG: first fixation duration (FFD), the duration of the first fixation on the prevailing word;
2. FFDSTD: standard deviation of FFD across readers;
3. TRTAVG: total reading time (TRT), the sum of all fixation durations on the current word, including regressions;
4. TRTSTD: standard deviation of TRT across readers.

3.1 Subtask 1

The goal of the first subtask is multilingual eye tracking prediction, i.e., to predict the eye-tracking features for sentences of the 6 provided languages in the training data on held-out sentences of the same languages in the test data. The dataset contains sentences from a range of openly available eye-tracking corpora.

3.2 Subtask 2

The second subtask test the models' performances in a cross-lingual prediction scenario. The training and development data are identical to Subtask 1, but the test data contains eye-tracking data from a new language. The participants were only informed about which language would be included in this subtask at the beginning of the evaluation phase.

4 Data

4.1 Subtask 1

The dataset contains sentences from the following openly available eye-tracking corpora: the Beijing Sentence Corpus (BSC; Pan et al. 2021), the Postdam-Allahabad Hindi Eye Tracking Corpus (PAHEC; Husain et al. 2015), the Russian Sentence Corpus (RSC; Laurinavichyute et al. 2019), the Provo Corpus (Luke and Christianson, 2017), the Zurich Cognitive Language Processing Corpus (ZuCo; Hollenstein et al. 2018, 2020), The Dutch part of the Ghent Eye-Tracking Corpus (GECO-NL; Cop et al. 2017), and the Potsdam Textbook Corpus (PoTeC; Jäger et al. 2021). These datasets cover a diverse range of text domains, including news articles, novels, Wikipedia sentences, scientific textbook passages, etc. The details are presented in Table 1.

The training data contains 1703 sentences, the development set contains 104 sentences, and the test set 324 sentences.

4.2 Subtask 2

As described, the training and development data are identical to Subtask 1, but the test data contains eye-tracking data from a new language, namely Danish. The Danish eye-tracking data contains 402

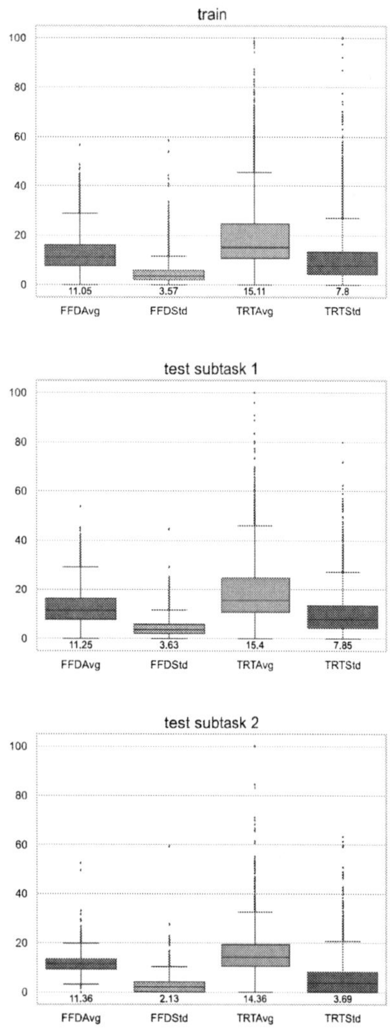

Figure 2: Boxplots showing the feature value distributions of the training data and the test sets of both subtasks. Below each box is the median value of each feature.

sentences read by 5 readers, extracted from the CopCo corpus (Hollenstein et al., 2022).

4.3 Preprocessing

Tokenization The tokens in the sentences are split in the same manner as they were presented to the participants during the reading experiments. Hence, this does not necessarily follow a linguistically correct tokenization. For example, the sequences "(except," and "don't" were presented as such to the reader and not split into "(", "except", "," and "do", "n't" as a tokenizer would do. It is the participants' decision how to deal with these tokens.

Feature Extraction The data contains scaled features in the range between 0 and 100 to facilitate evaluation via the mean absolute average (MAE). The eye-tracking feature values (FFDAVG and TRTAVG) are averaged over all available readers of a corpus. This preprocessing step is done separately for each corpus before combining them. Table 2 shows the scaled features values across the full dataset of Subtask 1. In Figure 2, we present the distributions of the feature values for the training set and the test set of Subtasks 1 and 2. Finally, Figure 3 in the Appendix shows the individual plots for each language.

5 Evaluation

In this section, we describe the evaluation procedure used to assess the submitted predictions of the participating teams.

Any additional data source was allowed to train the models, as long as it is freely available to the research community. For example, additional eye-tracking corpora, additional features such as brain activity signals, pre-trained language models, etc.

5.1 Scoring Metric

The submitted predictions are evaluated against the real eye-tracking feature values using the mean absolute error (MAE) metric, a measure of errors between paired observations including comparisons of predicted (y) versus observed (x) values for each word in the test set:

$$MAE = \frac{\sum_{i=1}^{n} |y_i - x_i|}{n} \quad (1)$$

The winning system is defined as the one with the lowest average MAE across all 4 features. We reported additional metrics for analysis, namely R^2 for all features individually and aggregated, but only MAE was used for the ranking.

5.2 Mean Baseline

We use the mean central tendency as a baseline for this regression problem, i.e., we calculate the mean value for each feature from the training data and use it as a prediction for all words in the test data. Table 3 shows the MAE scores achieved by this mean baseline for each eye-tracking feature.

For Subtask 1, we add an additional stronger mean baseline calculated over the training set of each language individually. This baseline assumes that the language of each sentence is known to the

Rank	Team Name	MAE	FFDAVG	FFDSTD	TRTAVG	TRTSTD	R^2	Reference
1	HkAmsters	3.01	4.40	4.15	1.76	1.73	0.61	Salicchi et al. (2022)
2	DMG	3.65	5.65	4.43	2.61	1.92	0.49	Takmaz (2022)
-	Lang. baseline	4.27	3.55	2.03	6.56	4.94	0.34	-
3	NU HLT	5.49	6.67	8.38	3.93	2.99	-0.18	Imperial (2022)
4	Poirot	5.50	8.37	5.68	5.47	2.50	-0.03	Srivastava (2022)
5	UFAL	5.72	8.81	5.73	5.77	2.58	0.00	Bhattacharya et al. (2022)
-	Mean baseline	5.73	8.82	5.89	5.69	2.54	0.00	-
6	TorontoCL	11.09	18.84	8.89	13.06	3.57	-2.04	

Table 3: Overall results of **Subtask 1** showing the best submission per team and the mean baselines, including the overall MAE and R^2 scores, as well as the individual MAE scores for each feature. The teams are ranked by the MAE averaged across all five eye-tracking features (third column).

Rank	Team Name	MAE	FFDAVG	FFDSTD	TRTAVG	TRTSTD	R^2	Reference
1	Poirot	4.23	5.60	5.65	2.95	2.73	-0.26	Srivastava (2022)
2	DMG	4.97	6.90	5.77	5.45	1.73	-0.57	Takmaz (2022)
-	Mean baseline	5.73	8.82	5.89	5.69	2.54	0.00	-
3	NU HLT	7.09	14.65	4.04	7.53	2.12	-1.83	Imperial (2022)

Table 4: Overall results of **Subtask 2** showing the best submission per team and the mean baseline, including the overall MAE and R^2 scores, as well as the individual MAE scores for each feature. The teams are ranked by the MAE averaged across all five eye-tracking features (third column).

system. This second baseline was not reported in the rankings, but serves for further analysis.

6 Participating Teams & Systems

Six teams and a total of 37 participants registered on the competition website. All six teams submitted their predictions during the evaluation phase for Subtask 1. Four of the teams also submitted predictions for Subtask 2. Each team was allowed three submissions for each subtask during the evaluation phases. Finally, 5 teams published system description papers outlining their approaches (see Table 3 for all references).

6.1 Methods

The participating teams submitted predictions generated from various approaches, from regression algorithms such as random forests (NU HLT) and linear regression models (HkAmsters) with a wide range of lexical, cognitively and phonetically-motivated features (NU HLT), to neural approaches that fine-tune large pre-trained transformer models with additional regression heads, and integrate adapters into pre-trained transformer language models (DMG) (Pfeiffer et al., 2020; Han et al., 2021).

Some teams chose to build language-specific models (e.g., HkAmsters, DMG), while others merged the words from all languages into a common vocabulary space in which all words are converted to their IPA forms (NU HLT). Moreover, representations from both monolingual models such as GPT-2 (Radford et al., 2019) as well as multilingual transformer models such as mBERT (Devlin et al., 2019) and XLM (Lample and Conneau, 2019) were also included (Poirot). For the second subtask, dealing with a new unseen language was handled again through a common phonetic vocabulary space (NU HLT), through translation (i.e., translating the Danish text to German and then using a German model for prediction) (DMG), or zero-shot learning (Poirot).

7 Results

In this section, we describe the prediction performance achieved by the participating teams. The official results of this shared task are presented in Tables 3 and 4 for Subtask 1 and 2, respectively. The best results for the first subtask on multilingual prediction were achieved by Team HkAmsters with language-specific regression models based on word-level features such as word length, word frequency, and surprisal scores estimated with GPT-2 (Radford et al., 2019). For the second subtask on cross-lingual prediction, the winning team (Poirot) used a zero-shot hybrid model based on a multilingual transformer embeddings as well as statistical features.

8 Outlook & Conclusion

We presented the results of the second shared task on predicting token-level eye-tracking features recorded during natural reading of sentences or longer text spans. In this second edition, we focused on multilingual and crosslingual prediction. We hope the CMCL Shared Task makes a lasting contribution to the field of linguistic cognitive modelling by providing researchers with a standard evaluation framework and a high quality dataset. Despite the limited size of the training and test sets as well as the diversity of text domains within the eye-tracking corpora, many previously reached conclusions can now be tested more thoroughly and future models can be compared on a shared multilingual benchmark.

Acknowledgements

Emmanuele Chersoni acknowledges the Start-up Fund for RAPs under the Strategic Hiring Scheme from the Hong Kong Polytechnic University (PolyU UGC, BD8S).

References

Masayuki Asahara, Hajime Ono, and Edson T Miyamoto. 2016. Reading-Time Annotations for "Balanced Corpus of Contemporary Written Japanese". In *Proceedings of COLING: Technical Papers*.

Christoph Aurnhammer and Stefan L Frank. 2019. Evaluating Information-theoretic Measures of Word Prediction in Naturalistic Sentence Reading. *Neuropsychologia*, 134:107198.

Maria Barrett, Joachim Bingel, Nora Hollenstein, Marek Rei, and Anders Søgaard. 2018. Sequence Classification with Human Attention. In *Proceedings of the 22nd Conference on Computational Natural Language Learning*, pages 302–312.

Maria Barrett, Joachim Bingel, Frank Keller, and Anders Søgaard. 2016. Weakly Supervised Part-of-speech Tagging Using Eye-tracking Data. In *Proceedings of ACL*.

Louise Gillian Bautista and Prospero Naval. 2020. Towards Learning to Read Like Humans. In *International Conference on Computational Collective Intelligence*, pages 779–791. Springer.

Sunit Bhattacharya, Rishu Kumar, and Ondrej Bojar. 2022. Team ÚFAL at CMCL 2022 Shared Task: Figuring Out the Correct Recipe for Predicting Eye-Tracking Features Using Pretrained Language Models. In *Proceedings of the ACL Workshop on Cognitive Modeling and Computational Linguistics*.

Trevor Brothers and Gina R Kuperberg. 2021. Word Predictability Effects Are Linear, Not Logarithmic: Implications for Probabilistic Models of Sentence Comprehension. *Journal of Memory and Language*, 116:104174.

Uschi Cop, Nicolas Dirix, Denis Drieghe, and Wouter Duyck. 2017. Presenting GECO: An Eyetracking Corpus of Monolingual and Bilingual Sentence Reading. *Behavior Research Methods*, 49(2):602–615.

Vera Demberg and Frank Keller. 2008. Data from Eye-tracking Corpora as Evidence for Theories of Syntactic Processing Complexity. *Cognition*, 109(2):193–210.

Jacob Devlin, Ming-Wei Chang, Kenton Lee, and Kristina Toutanova. 2019. BERT: Pre-training of Deep Bidirectional Transformers for Language Understanding. In *Proceedings of NAACL*.

Susan E. Ehrlich and Keith Rayner. 1981. Contextual Effects on Word Perception and Eye Movements During Reading. *Journal of Verbal Learning and Verbal Behavior*, 20:641–65.

Victoria Fossum and Roger Levy. 2012. Sequential vs. Hierarchical Syntactic Models of Human Incremental Sentence Processing. In *Proceedings of the NAACL Workshop on Cognitive Modeling and Computational Linguistics*.

Stefan L Frank. 2017. Word Embedding Distance Does Not Predict Word Reading Time. In *Proceedings of CogSci*.

Stefan L Frank and Rens Bod. 2011. Insensitivity of the Human Sentence-processing System to Hierarchical Structure. *Psychological Science*, 22(6):829–834.

Adam Goodkind and Klinton Bicknell. 2018. Predictive Power of Word Surprisal for Reading Times Is a Linear Function of Language Model Quality. In *Proceedings of the LSA Workshop on Cognitive Modeling and Computational Linguistics*.

Adam Goodkind and Klinton Bicknell. 2021. Local Word Statistics Affect Reading Times Independently of Surprisal. *arXiv preprint arXiv:2103.04469*.

Michael Hahn and Frank Keller. 2016. Modeling Human Reading with Neural Attention. In *Proceedings of EMNLP*.

John Hale. 2001. A Probabilistic Earley Parser as a Psycholinguistic Model. In *Proceedings of NAACL*.

Wenjuan Han, Bo Pang, and Yingnian Wu. 2021. Robust Transfer Learning with Pretrained Language Models through Adapters. In *Proceedings of ACL*.

Yiding Hao, Simon Mendelsohn, Rachel Sterneck, Randi Martinez, and Robert Frank. 2020. Probabilistic Predictions of People Perusing: Evaluating Metrics of Language Model Performance for Psycholinguistic Modeling. In *Proceedings of the EMNLP Workshop on Cognitive Modeling and Computational Linguistics*.

Nora Hollenstein, Maria Barrett, and Marina Björnsdóttir. 2022. The Copenhagen Corpus of Eye-Tracking Recordings from Natural Reading of Danish Texts. In *Proceedings of the 13th Conference on Language Resources and Evaluation (LREC 2022)*.

Nora Hollenstein, Emmanuele Chersoni, Cassandra L Jacobs, Yohei Oseki, Laurent Prévot, and Enrico Santus. 2021a. CMCL 2021 Shared Task on Eye-tracking Prediction. In *Proceedings of the Workshop on Cognitive Modeling and Computational Linguistics*.

Nora Hollenstein, Federico Pirovano, Ce Zhang, Lena Jäger, and Lisa Beinborn. 2021b. Multilingual Language Models Predict Human Reading Behavior. In *Proceedings of NAACL*.

Nora Hollenstein, Jonathan Rotsztejn, Marius Troendle, Andreas Pedroni, Ce Zhang, and Nicolas Langer. 2018. ZuCo, a Simultaneous EEG and Eye-tracking Resource for Natural Sentence Reading. *Scientific Data*.

Nora Hollenstein, Marius Troendle, Ce Zhang, and Nicolas Langer. 2020. ZuCo 2.0: A Dataset of Physiological Recordings During Natural Reading and Annotation. In *Proceedings of LREC*.

Samar Husain, Shravan Vasishth, and Narayanan Srinivasan. 2015. Integration and Prediction Difficulty in Hindi Sentence Comprehension: Evidence from an Eye-Tracking Corpus. *Journal of Eye Movement Research*, 8(2).

Joseph Marvin Imperial. 2022. NU HLT at CMCL 2022 Shared Task: Multilingual and Crosslingual Prediction of Human Reading Behavior in Universal Language Space. In *Proceedings of the Workshop on Cognitive Modeling and Computational Linguistics*.

Lena Jäger, Thomas Kern, and Patrick Haller. 2021. Potsdam Textbook Corpus (PoTeC): Eye Tracking Data from Experts and Non-experts Reading Scientific Texts. Available on OSF, DOI 10.17605/OSF.IO/DN5HP.

Reinhold Kliegl, Antje Nuthmann, and Ralf Engbert. 2006. Tracking the Mind During Reading: The Influence of Past, Present, and Future Words on Fixation Durations. *Journal of Experimental Psychology*, 135(1):12.

Srinivas SS Kruthiventi, Kumar Ayush, and R Venkatesh Babu. 2017. Deepfix: A Fully Convolutional Neural Network for Predicting Human Eye Fixations. *IEEE Transactions on Image Processing*, 26(9):4446–4456.

Tatsuki Kuribayashi, Yohei Oseki, Takumi Ito, Ryo Yoshida, Masayuki Asahara, and Kentaro Inui. 2021. Lower Perplexity Is Not Always Human-like. In *Proceedings of ACL*.

Guillaume Lample and Alexis Conneau. 2019. Cross-lingual language model pretraining. In *Advances in Neural Information Processing Systems*.

AK Laurinavichyute, Irina A Sekerina, SV Alexeeva, and KA Bagdasaryan. 2019. Russian Sentence Corpus: Benchmark Measures of Eye Movements in Reading in Cyrillic. *Behavior Research Methods*, 51(3):1161–1178.

Roger Levy. 2008. Expectation-based Syntactic Comprehension. *Cognition*, 106(3):1126–1177.

Simon P Liversedge, Denis Drieghe, Xin Li, Guoli Yan, Xuejun Bai, and Jukka Hyönä. 2016. Universality in Eye Movements and Reading: A Trilingual Investigation. *Cognition*, 147:1–20.

Steven G Luke and Kiel Christianson. 2017. The Provo Corpus: A Large Eye-tracking Corpus with Predictability Norms. *Behavior Research Methods*, pages 1–8.

Franz Matthies and Anders Søgaard. 2013. With Blinkers On: Robust Prediction of Eye Movements across Readers. *Proceedings of EMNLP*, pages 803–807.

Erik McGuire and Noriko Tomuro. 2021. Relation Classification with Cognitive Attention Supervision. In *Proceedings of the NAACL Workshop on Cognitive Modeling and Computational Linguistics*.

Danny Merkx and Stefan L Frank. Human Sentence Processing: Recurrence or Attention? In *Proceedings of the NAACL Workshop on Cognitive Modeling and Computational Linguistics*.

Jeff Mitchell, Mirella Lapata, Vera Demberg, and Frank Keller. 2010. Syntactic and Semantic Factors in Processing Difficulty: An Integrated Measure. In *Proceedings of ACL*.

Jinger Pan, Ming Yan, Eike M Richter, Hua Shu, and Reinhold Kliegl. 2021. The Beijing Sentence Corpus: A Chinese Sentence Corpus with Eye Movement Data and Predictability Norms. *Behavior Research Methods*, pages 1–12.

Jonas Pfeiffer, Andreas Rücklé, Clifton Poth, Aishwarya Kamath, Ivan Vulić, Sebastian Ruder, Kyunghyun Cho, and Iryna Gurevych. 2020. AdapterHub: A Framework for Adapting Transformers. In *Proceedings of EMNLP: System Demonstrations*.

Alec Radford, Jeffrey Wu, Rewon Child, David Luan, Dario Amodei, Ilya Sutskever, et al. 2019. Language models Are Unsupervised Multitask Learners. *OpenAI blog*, 1(8):9.

Keith Rayner and Gary E Raney. 1996. Eye Movement Control in Reading and Visual Search: Effects of Word Frequency. *Psychonomic Bulletin & Review*, 3(2):245–248.

Erik D Reichle, Alexander Pollatsek, Donald L Fisher, and Keith Rayner. 1998. Toward a Model of Eye Movement Control in Reading. *Psychological Review*, 105(1):125.

L. Salicchi, R. Xiang, and Y. Hsu. 2022. HkAmsters at CMCL 2022 Shared Task: Predicting Eye-Tracking Data from a Gradient Boosting Framework with Linguistic Features. In *Proceedings of the Workshop on Cognitive Modeling and Computational Linguistics*.

Lavinia Salicchi, Alessandro Lenci, and Emmanuele Chersoni. 2021. Looking for a Role for Word Embeddings in Eye-Tracking Features Prediction: Does Semantic Similarity Help? In *Proceedings of IWCS*.

Gabriele Sarti, Dominique Brunato, and Felice Dell'Orletta. 2021. That Looks Hard: Characterizing Linguistic Complexity in Humans and Language Models. In *Proceedings of the NAACL Workshop on Cognitive Modeling and Computational Linguistics*, pages 48–60.

Karthikeyan Shanmuga Vadivel, Thuyen Ngo, Miguel Eckstein, and BS Manjunath. 2015. Eye Tracking Assisted Extraction of Attentionally Important Objects from Videos. In *Proceedings of the IEEE Conference on Computer Vision and Pattern Recognition*, pages 3241–3250.

Noam Siegelman, Sascha Schroeder, and V Kuperman. 2022. Expanding Horizons of Cross-linguistic Research on Reading: The Multilingual Eye-Movement Corpus (MECO). *Behavior Research Methods*.

Abhinav Deep Singh, Poojan Mehta, Samar Husain, and Rajkumar Rajakrishnan. 2016. Quantifying Sentence Complexity Based on Eye-tracking Measures. In *Proceedings of the COLING Workshop on Computational Linguistics for Linguistic Complexity*, pages 202–212.

Harshvardhan Srivastava. 2022. Poirot at CMCL 2022 Shared Task: Zero Shot Crosslingual Eye-Tracking Data Prediction using Multilingual Transformer Models. In *Proceedings of the Workshop on Cognitive Modeling and Computational Linguistics*.

Ece Takmaz. 2022. Team DMG at CMCL 2022 Shared Task: Transformer Adapters for the Multi- and Cross-Lingual Prediction of Human Reading Behavior. In *Proceedings of the ACL Workshop on Cognitive Modeling and Computational Linguistics*.

Ching-Hsi Tseng, Yen Hsu, and Shyan-Ming Yuan. 2020. Eye-tracking Data for Weakly Supervised Object Detection. In *2020 IEEE Eurasia Conference on IOT, Communication and Engineering (ECICE)*, pages 223–225.

Ethan Gotlieb Wilcox, Jon Gauthier, Jennifer Hu, Peng Qian, and Roger Levy. 2020. On the Predictive Power of Neural Language Models for Human Real-Time Comprehension Behavior. *arXiv preprint arXiv:2006.01912*.

Rihana Williams and Robin Morris. 2004. Eye Movements, Word Familiarity, and Vocabulary Acquisition. *European Journal of Cognitive Psychology*, 16(1-2):312–339.

Qi Yu, Aikaterini-Lida Kalouli, and Diego Frassinelli. 2021. KonTra at CMCL 2021 Shared Task: Predicting Eye Movements by Combining BERT with Surface, Linguistic and Behavioral Information. In *Proceedings of the NAACL Workshop on Cognitive Modeling and Computational Linguistics*.

A Appendix

Figure 3 shows the distributions of the feature values for the data of all six languages.

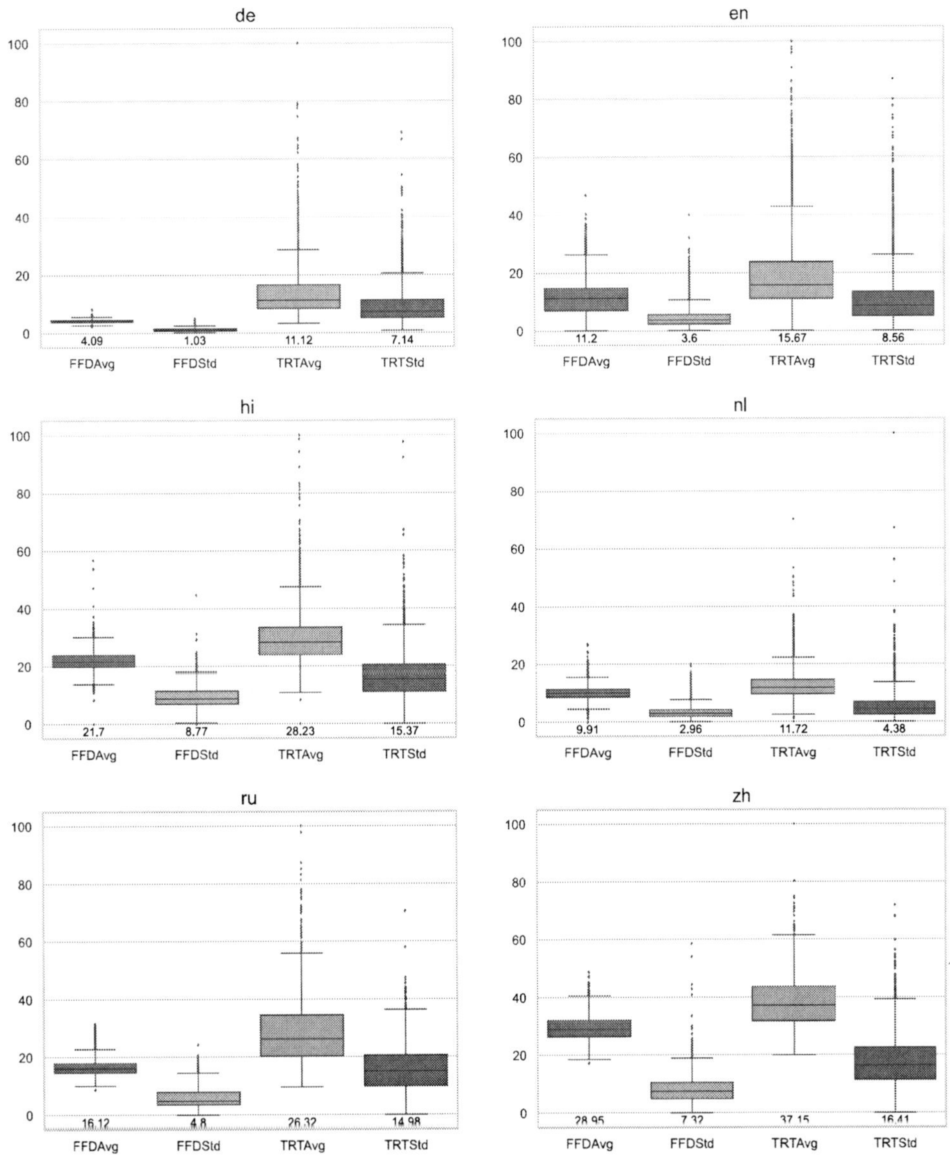

Figure 3: Boxplots showing the feature value distributions of the eye-tracking data of all languages of Subtask 1. Below each box is the median value of each feature.

Team ÚFAL at CMCL 2022 Shared Task: Figuring out the correct recipe for predicting Eye-Tracking features using Pretrained Language Models

Sunit Bhattacharya, Rishu Kumar and **Ondřej Bojar**
Charles University
Faculty Of Mathematics and Physics
Insititute of Formal and Applied Linguistics
bhattacharya,kumar,bojar@ufal.mff.cuni.cz

Abstract

Eye-Tracking data is a very useful source of information to study cognition and especially language comprehension in humans. In this paper, we describe our systems for the CMCL 2022 shared task on predicting eye-tracking information. We describe our experiments with pretrained models like BERT and XLM and the different ways in which we used those representations to predict four eye-tracking features. Along with analysing the effect of using two different kinds of pretrained multilingual language models and different ways of pooling the token-level representations, we also explore how contextual information affects the performance of the systems. Finally, we also explore if factors like augmenting linguistic information affect the predictions. Our submissions achieved an average MAE of 5.72 and ranked 5th in the shared task. The average MAE showed further reduction to 5.25 in post task evaluation.

1 Introduction and Motivation

In the last decade that has seen rapid developments in AI research, the emergence of the Transformer architecture (Vaswani et al., 2017) marked a pivotal point in Natural Language Processing (NLP). Fine-tuning pretrained language models to work on various downstream tasks has become a dominant method of obtaining state-of-the-art performance in different areas. Their capability to capture linguistic knowledge and learn powerful contextual word embeddings (Liu et al., 2019) have made the transformer based models the work-horses in many NLP tasks. Pretrained models like the multilingual BERT (Devlin et al., 2019) and XLM (Conneau et al., 2020) have also shown state-of-the-art performance on cross-lingual understanding tasks (Wu and Dredze, 2019; Artetxe et al., 2019). In some cases like machine translation, there are even claims that deep learning systems reach translation qualities that are comparable to professional translators (Popel et al., 2020).

Language processing and its links with cognition is a very old research problem which has revealed how cognitive data (eg. gaze, fMRI) can be used to investigate human cognition. Attempts at using computational methods for such studies (Mitchell et al., 2008; Dehghani et al., 2017) have also shown encouraging results. However recently, there have been a number of works that have tried to incorporate human cognitive data collected during reading for improving the performance of NLP systems (Hollenstein et al., 2019). The CMCL 2022 Shared Task of multilingual and cross-lingual prediction of human reading behavior (Hollenstein et al., 2022) explores how eye-gaze attributes can be algorithmically predicted given reading data in multilingual settings.

Informed by the previous attempts at using pretrained multilingual language models to predict human reading behavior (Hollenstein et al., 2021) we experiment with multilingual BERT and XLM based models to test which fares better in this task. For the experiments with the pretrained models, we use the trained weights from Huggingface (Wolf et al., 2020) and perform the rest of our experiments using PyTorch[1]. Inspired by the psycholinguistic research on investigating context length during processing (Wochna and Juhasz, 2013), we experiment how different contexts affect model performance. Finally, we merged the principles of the "classical" approach of feature-based prediction with the pretrained-language model based prediction for further analysis. In the following sections, we present our results from a total of 48 different models.

2 Task Description

The CMCL 2022 Shared Task of Multilingual and Cross-lingual prediction of human reading behavior frames the task of predicting eye-gaze attributes associated with reading sentences as a regression

[1]https://pytorch.org/

Proceedings of the Workshop on Cognitive Modeling and Computational Linguistics, pages 130 - 135
May 26, 2022

task. The data for the task was comprised of eye movements corresponding to reading sentences in six languages (Chinese, Dutch, English, German, Hindi, Russian). The training data for the task contained 1703 sentences while the development set and test set contained 104 and 324 sentences respectively. The data was presented in a way such that for each word in a sentence there were four associated eye-tracking features in the form of the mean and standard deviation scores of the Total Reading Time (TRT) and First Fixation Duration (FFD). The features in the data were scaled in the range between 0 and 100 to facilitate evaluation via the mean absolute average (MAE).

3 Experiments

A total of 48 models of different configurations were trained with the data provided for the shared task. The different configurations used to construct the models are based on intuition and literature survey.

Thee models were primarily categorized as System-1 (sys1) and System-2 (sys2) models. For some word corresponding to a sentence in the dataset, System-1 models provided no additional context information. System-2 models on the other hand, contained the information of all the words in the sentence that preceded the current word, providing additional context. This setting was inspired by works (Khandelwal et al., 2018; Clark et al., 2019) on how context is used by language models.

All systems under the System-1/2 labels were further trained as a BERT (bert) based system or a XLM (xlm) based system. BERT embeddings were previously used by Choudhary et al. (2021) for the eye-tracking feature prediction task in CMCL 2021.

Corresponding to each such language models (bert and xlm), the impact of different fine-tuning strategies(Sun et al., 2019) on system performance was studied. Hence, for one setting, only the contextualized word representation (CWR) was utilized by freezing the model weights and putting a learnable regression layer on top of the model output layer (classifier). Alternatively, the models were fine-tuned with the regression layer on top of them (whole). This setting is similar to the one used by Li and Rudzicz (2021). However in our case, we experiment with a BERT and XLM pretrained model.

Additionally, we also performed experiments with pooling strategies for the layer representations by either using the final hidden representation of the first sub-word encoding of the input (first) or aggregating the representations of all sub-words using mean-pooling (mean) or sum-pooling (sum). The rationale behind using different pooling strategies was to have a sentence-level representation of the input tokens. The impact of different pooling strategies has previously been studied (Shao et al., 2019; Lee et al., 2019) for different problems. In this paper, we analyze the effect of pooling feature-space embeddings in the context of eye-tracking feature prediction.

Finally, for the experiments where we augmented additional lexical features (augmented) to the neural features for regression, we used word length and word-frequency as the additional information following Vickers et al. (2021).

Constructing the experiments in this manner provided us with models with a diverse set of properties and in turn provided insights into how well the model behaves when all other things stay the same, and only one aspect of learning is changed.

4 Results

The results corresponding to the top 10 systems based on the experiments described above are shown in Table 1.

Model	MAE
bert_sys2_augmented_sum_classifier	5.251
bert_sys2_unaugmented_first_classifier	5.267
bert_sys2_augmented_mean_classifier	5.272
bert_sys1_augmented_mean_classifier	5.279
bert_sys2_augmented_first_classifier	5.295
xlm_sys1_augmented_first_classifier	5.341
xlm_sys2_augmented_first_whole	5.346
bert_sys1_augmented_sum_classifier	5.353
bert_sys2_augmented_sum_whole	5.367
xlm_sys2_augmented_first_classifier	5.373

Table 1: Top 10 best performing systems

It was observed that the maximum MAE scores (and the maximum variance of scores) for all the models was obtained for the attribute "TRT_Avg". The attribute wise variances corresponding to the test-data for all the models are shown in Table 2. Similarly, the mean values of the attributes for all models are shown in Table 3.

An analysis of the models based on the different experimental configurations are described in the

FFD_Avg	FFD_Std	TRT_Avg	TRT_Std
0.194	0.403	0.637	0.489

Table 2: Attribute wise variance of scores for all models

FFD_Avg	FFD_Std	TRT_Avg	TRT_Std
5.691	2.646	8.633	5.806

Table 3: Attribute wise mean of scores for all models

following sections.

4.1 System-1 vs System-2

Table 4 shows the average model performance across System-1 and System-2 configurations for both BERT and XLM based models (based on the average MAE values of the configurations). We see that for the BERT based models, the average MAE for System-1 is lower than that of System-2. But for XLM-based models, the difference is almost non-existent.

Model	Average MAE across models
Sys1_BERT	5.66
Sys1_XLM	5.70
Sys2_BERT	5.72
Sys2_XLM	5.69

Table 4: System-1 vs System-2 performance across models

However, it should be noted that 12 out of the first 20 best performing models were System-2 models. Hence we posit that although the availability of the full sentence context is a factor for having more efficient systems, independently the factor does not seem to boost the overall performance much.

4.2 BERT vs XLM

Table 5 shows that there is only a tiny difference in average MAE for all four attributes (FFD_μ, FFD_σ, TRT_μ, TRT_σ) for all BERT vs XLM models . However, a brief look at Table 6 and Table 7 reveal that it was the XLM models that were responsible for slightly decreased MAE scores for 3 of the 4 attributes that were being predicted.

We also see that the amount of variance for XLM based models was also smaller for 3 of the 4 attributes.

Model	Average MAE across models
BERT	5.6920
XLM	5.6960

Table 5: BERT vs XLM performance across models

Model	FFD_μ	FFD_σ	TRT_μ	TRT_σ
BERT	0.141	0.776	0.952	0.792
XLM	0.236	0.045	0.349	0.204

Table 6: Attribute wise variance of scores for all BERT and XLM based models

Model	FFD_μ	FFD_σ	TRT_μ	TRT_σ
BERT	5.592	2.679	8.645	5.852
XLM	5.789	2.612	8.622	5.760

Table 7: Attribute wise mean of scores for all BERT and XLM based models

4.3 Augmented vs Un-Augmented models

Fig. 1 shows that augmented models. i.e. models that were fed information like word-frequency and word-length along with the neural representation information before being fed to the regression layer performed better than models that used only contextual word embeddings resulting from pretrained language models. Table 8 and Table 9 show the 5 best performing models of this category sorted by their MAE.

Model	MAE
bert_sys2_unaugmented_first_classifier	5.267
bert_sys2_unaugmented_mean_classifier	5.405
xlm_sys1_unaugmented_mean_classifier	5.5
xlm_sys2_unaugmented_mean_classifier	5.55
xlm_sys1_unaugmented_mean_classifier	5.557

Table 8: Performance of 5 best Un-Augmented models.

Model	MAE
bert_sys2_augmented_sum_classifier	5.251
bert_sys2_augmented_mean_classifier	5.272
bert_sys1_augmented_mean_classifier	5.279
bert_sys2_augmented_first_classifier	5.295
xlm_sys1_augmented_first_classifier	5.341

Table 9: Performance of 5 best Augmented models

The mean and variance of attributes across models of these families presented in Table 10 & 11 show that augmented models show way less vari-

Model	FFD_μ	FFD_σ	TRT_μ	TRT_σ
Aug	5.502	2.511	8.181	5.436
Uaug	5.88	2.78	9.086	6.176

Table 10: Attribute wise mean of scores for all Augmented and Un-augmented models

Model	FFD_μ	FFD_σ	TRT_μ	TRT_σ
Aug	0.017	0.004	0.015	0.007
Uaug	0.292	0.749	0.823	0.678

Table 11: Attribute wise variance of scores for all Augmented and Un-augmented models

ance in their predictions in comparison with neural-representation only model families.

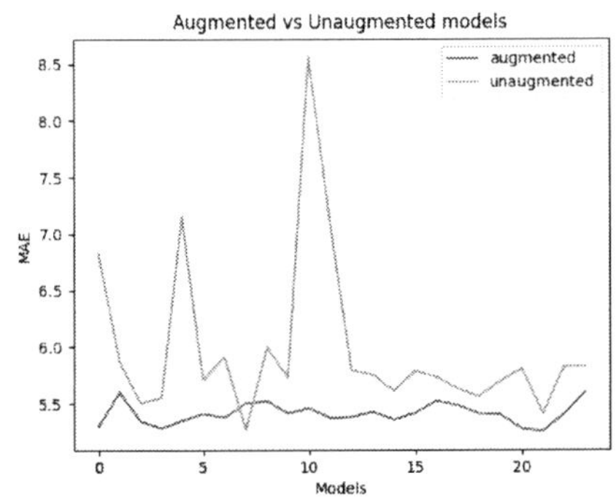

Figure 1: Augmented vs Un-augmented model performance. The x-axis represents the 24 different models of each category. The y-axis shows the MAE corresponding to each model.

4.4 Nature of representation of input tokens (Pooling strategies)

Fig. 2 shows that using the first sub-word token or the mean-pooled representation of the entire input gives lesser MAE scores than the sum-pooled representations. It was also observed that for System-2 family of models, the mean-pooled representations were associated with lesser MAE scores in comparison to the first sub-word representation. The attribute wise mean in Table 15 and attribute wise variance of model MAEs shown in Table 16 illustrates this point. Table 12,Table 13 and Table 14 show the 5 best performing models of this category sorted by their MAE.

4.5 Fine-tuning

Fine-tuning on large pretrained language models has become the standard way to conduct NLP research after the widespread adoption of the transformer architecture. And unsurprisingly, our experiments reveal (Fig. 3) that fine-tuning of models give smaller MAE scores than training only the regression layers. The stark difference in the variance for the predicted attributes between fine-tuned models and regression only models (as illustrated in Table 17-18) further demonstrates the advantage of fine-tuning.

Model	MAE
bert_sys2_unaugmented_first_classifier	5.267
bert_sys2_augmented_first_classifier	5.295
xlm_sys1_augmented_first_classifier	5.341
xlm_sys2_augmented_first_whole	5.346
xlm_sys2_augmented_first_classifier	5.373

Table 12: Performance of 5 best first models

Model	MAE
bert_sys2_augmented_mean_classifier	5.272
bert_sys1_augmented_mean_classifier	5.279
bert_sys2_augmented_mean_whole	5.375
bert_sys2_unaugmented_mean_classifier	5.405
xlm_sys1_augmented_mean_whole	5.413

Table 13: Performance of 5 best Mean models

Model	MAE
bert_sys2_augmented_sum_classifier	5.251
bert_sys1_augmented_sum_classifier	5.353
bert_sys2_augmented_sum_whole	5.367
bert_sys1_augmented_sum_whole	5.402
xlm_sys2_augmented_sum_classifier	5.456

Table 14: Performance of 5 best Sum models

Model	FFD_μ	FFD_σ	TRT_μ	TRT_σ
first	5.549	2.505	8.434	5.615
Mean	5.57	2.538	8.416	5.636
Sum	5.954	2.894	9.05	6.167

Table 15: Attribute wise mean of scores for models with different input token representations

Model	FFD_μ	FFD_σ	TRT_μ	TRT_σ
first	0.036	0.004	0.118	0.054
Mean	0.047	0.005	0.118	0.048
Sum	0.383	1.082	1.374	1.139

Table 16: Attribute wise variance of scores for models with different input token representations

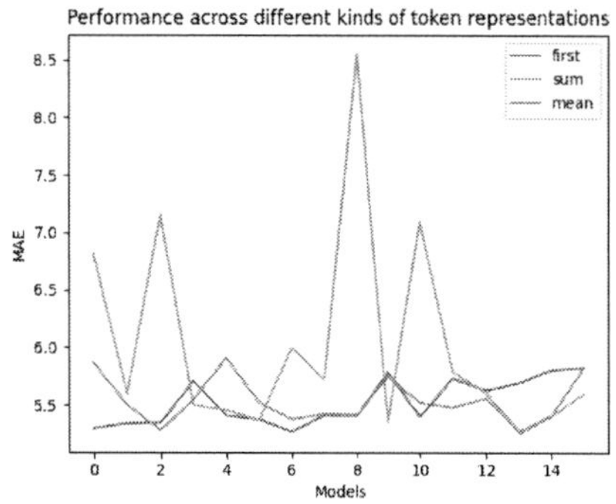

Figure 2: Model performance based on the nature of representation of input tokens.The x-axis represents the 16 different models of each category. The y-axis shows the MAE corresponding to each model.

Model	FFD_μ	FFD_σ	TRT_μ	TRT_σ
Aug	5.502	2.511	8.181	5.436
Uaug	5.88	2.78	9.086	6.176

Table 17: Attribute wise variance of scores for fine-tuned models vs regression-layer only models

Model	FFD_μ	FFD_σ	TRT_μ	TRT_σ
Aug	0.017	0.004	0.015	0.007
Uaug	0.292	0.749	0.823	0.678

Table 18: Attribute wise mean of scores for fine-tuned models vs regression-layer only models

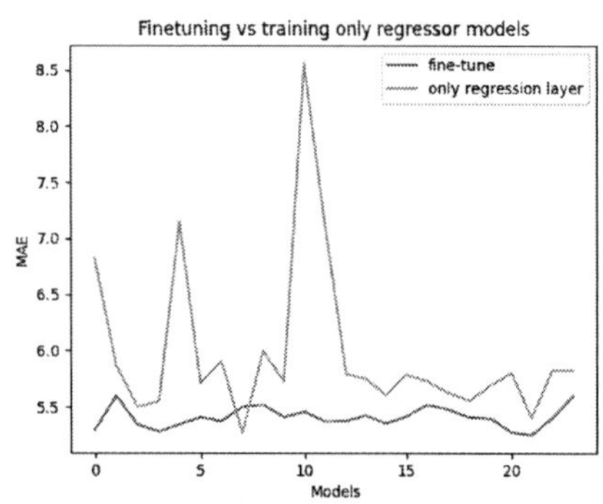

Figure 3: Fine-tuning vs training only regression layer in the models. The x-axis represents the 24 different models of each category. The y-axis shows the MAE corresponding to each model.

5 Conclusion

In this paper, we have described our experiments with different kinds of models that were trained on the data provided for this shared-task. We have identified five ways in which we can make better systems to predict eye-tracking features based on eye-tracking data from a multilingual corpus. First, the experiments demonstrate that the inclusion of context (previous words occurring in the sentence) helps the models to predict eye-tracking attributes better. This reaffirms previous observations made with language models that more context is always helpful. Second, we find that XLM based models perform relatively better than the BERT based models. Third, our experiments show the advantages of augmenting additional linguistic features (word length and word frequency information in this case) to the contextual word representations to make better systems. This is in agreement with the findings from eye-tracking prediction tasks from last iterations of CMCL. Fourth, we see how different pooling methods applied on the input token representations affect the final performance of the systems. Finally, the experiments re-validate the approach of fine-tuning pretrained language models for specific tasks. Hence we conclude that contextualized word representations from language models pretrained with many different languages, if carefully augmented, engineered, and fine-tuned, can predict eye-tracking features quite successfully.

6 Acknowledgement

This work has been funded from the grant 19-26934X (NEUREM3) of the Czech Science Foundation.

References

Mikel Artetxe, Sebastian Ruder, and Dani Yogatama. 2019. On the cross-lingual transferability of monolingual representations. *arXiv preprint arXiv:1910.11856.*

Shivani Choudhary, Kushagri Tandon, Raksha Agarwal, and Niladri Chatterjee. 2021. Mtl782_iitd at cmcl 2021 shared task: Prediction of eye-tracking features using bert embeddings and linguistic features. In *Proceedings of the Workshop on Cognitive Modeling and Computational Linguistics*, pages 114–119.

Kevin Clark, Urvashi Khandelwal, Omer Levy, and Christopher D Manning. 2019. What does bert look at? an analysis of bert's attention. *arXiv preprint arXiv:1906.04341.*

Alexis Conneau, Kartikay Khandelwal, Naman Goyal, Vishrav Chaudhary, Guillaume Wenzek, Francisco Guzmán, Édouard Grave, Myle Ott, Luke Zettlemoyer, and Veselin Stoyanov. 2020. Unsupervised cross-lingual representation learning at scale. In *Proceedings of the 58th Annual Meeting of the Asso-*

ciation for Computational Linguistics, pages 8440–8451.

Morteza Dehghani, Reihane Boghrati, Kingson Man, Joe Hoover, Sarah I Gimbel, Ashish Vaswani, Jason D Zevin, Mary Helen Immordino-Yang, Andrew S Gordon, Antonio Damasio, et al. 2017. Decoding the neural representation of story meanings across languages. *Human brain mapping*, 38(12):6096–6106.

Jacob Devlin, Ming-Wei Chang, Kenton Lee, and Kristina Toutanova. 2019. Bert: Pre-training of deep bidirectional transformers for language understanding. In *Proceedings of the 2019 Conference of the North American Chapter of the Association for Computational Linguistics: Human Language Technologies, Volume 1 (Long and Short Papers)*, pages 4171–4186.

Nora Hollenstein, Maria Barrett, Marius Troendle, Francesco Bigiolli, Nicolas Langer, and Ce Zhang. 2019. Advancing nlp with cognitive language processing signals. *arXiv e-prints*, pages arXiv–1904.

Nora Hollenstein, Emmanuele Chersoni, Cassandra Jacobs, Yohei Oseki, Laurent Prévott, and Enrico Santus. 2022. Cmcl 2022 shared task on multilingual and crosslingual prediction of human reading behavior.

Nora Hollenstein, Federico Pirovano, Ce Zhang, Lena Jäger, and Lisa Beinborn. 2021. Multilingual language models predict human reading behavior. In *Proceedings of the 2021 Conference of the North American Chapter of the Association for Computational Linguistics: Human Language Technologies*, pages 106–123, Online. Association for Computational Linguistics.

Urvashi Khandelwal, He He, Peng Qi, and Dan Jurafsky. 2018. Sharp nearby, fuzzy far away: How neural language models use context. *arXiv preprint arXiv:1805.04623*.

Juho Lee, Yoonho Lee, Jungtaek Kim, Adam Kosiorek, Seungjin Choi, and Yee Whye Teh. 2019. Set transformer: A framework for attention-based permutation-invariant neural networks. In *International Conference on Machine Learning*, pages 3744–3753. PMLR.

Bai Li and Frank Rudzicz. 2021. Torontocl at cmcl 2021 shared task: Roberta with multi-stage finetuning for eye-tracking prediction. *arXiv preprint arXiv:2104.07244*.

Nelson F Liu, Matt Gardner, Yonatan Belinkov, Matthew E Peters, and Noah A Smith. 2019. Linguistic knowledge and transferability of contextual representations. In *Proceedings of the 2019 Conference of the North American Chapter of the Association for Computational Linguistics: Human Language Technologies, Volume 1 (Long and Short Papers)*, pages 1073–1094.

Tom M Mitchell, Svetlana V Shinkareva, Andrew Carlson, Kai-Min Chang, Vicente L Malave, Robert A Mason, and Marcel Adam Just. 2008. Predicting human brain activity associated with the meanings of nouns. *science*, 320(5880):1191–1195.

Martin Popel, Marketa Tomkova, Jakub Tomek, Łukasz Kaiser, Jakob Uszkoreit, Ondřej Bojar, and Zdeněk Žabokrtský. 2020. Transforming machine translation: a deep learning system reaches news translation quality comparable to human professionals. *Nature communications*, 11(1):1–15.

Taihua Shao, Yupu Guo, Honghui Chen, and Zepeng Hao. 2019. Transformer-based neural network for answer selection in question answering. *IEEE Access*, 7:26146–26156.

Chi Sun, Xipeng Qiu, Yige Xu, and Xuanjing Huang. 2019. How to fine-tune bert for text classification? In *China national conference on Chinese computational linguistics*, pages 194–206. Springer.

Ashish Vaswani, Noam Shazeer, Niki Parmar, Jakob Uszkoreit, Llion Jones, Aidan N Gomez, Łukasz Kaiser, and Illia Polosukhin. 2017. Attention is all you need. In *Advances in neural information processing systems*, pages 5998–6008.

Peter Vickers, Rosa Wainwright, Harish Tayyar Madabushi, and Aline Villavicencio. 2021. CogNLP-Sheffield at CMCL 2021 shared task: Blending cognitively inspired features with transformer-based language models for predicting eye tracking patterns. In *Proceedings of the Workshop on Cognitive Modeling and Computational Linguistics*, pages 125–133, Online. Association for Computational Linguistics.

Kacey L Wochna and Barbara J Juhasz. 2013. Context length and reading novel words: An eye-movement investigation. *British Journal of Psychology*, 104(3):347–363.

Thomas Wolf, Lysandre Debut, Victor Sanh, Julien Chaumond, Clement Delangue, Anthony Moi, Pierric Cistac, Tim Rault, Remi Louf, Morgan Funtowicz, Joe Davison, Sam Shleifer, Patrick von Platen, Clara Ma, Yacine Jernite, Julien Plu, Canwen Xu, Teven Le Scao, Sylvain Gugger, Mariama Drame, Quentin Lhoest, and Alexander Rush. 2020. Transformers: State-of-the-art natural language processing. In *Proceedings of the 2020 Conference on Empirical Methods in Natural Language Processing: System Demonstrations*, pages 38–45, Online. Association for Computational Linguistics.

Shijie Wu and Mark Dredze. 2019. Beto, bentz, becas: The surprising cross-lingual effectiveness of BERT. In *Proceedings of the 2019 Conference on Empirical Methods in Natural Language Processing and the 9th International Joint Conference on Natural Language Processing (EMNLP-IJCNLP)*, pages 833–844, Hong Kong, China. Association for Computational Linguistics.

Team DMG at CMCL 2022 Shared Task: Transformer Adapters for the Multi- and Cross-Lingual Prediction of Human Reading Behavior

Ece Takmaz
Institute for Logic, Language and Computation
University of Amsterdam
ece.takmaz@uva.nl

Abstract

In this paper, we present the details of our approaches that attained the second place in the shared task of the ACL 2022 Cognitive Modeling and Computational Linguistics Workshop. The shared task is focused on multi- and cross-lingual prediction of eye movement features in human reading behavior, which could provide valuable information regarding language processing. To this end, we train 'adapters' inserted into the layers of frozen transformer-based pretrained language models. We find that multilingual models equipped with adapters perform well in predicting eye-tracking features. Our results suggest that utilizing language- and task-specific adapters is beneficial and translating test sets into similar languages that exist in the training set could help with zero-shot transferability in the prediction of human reading behavior.

1 Introduction

Eye movements provide valuable information about the contents of underlying cognitive processes and where our attention falls (Rayner, 1977). Predicting human reading behavior as reflected in eye movements is an important task that requires capturing universal aspects of language processing as well as its language-specific properties (Liversedge et al., 2016; Hollenstein et al., 2021b). This task could help us gain insight into language-related eye movements and the predictive capabilities of the models of human reading behavior.

Various approaches have been proposed for the modeling of human reading behavior (Rayner, 1998; Reichle et al., 1998; Hahn and Keller, 2016). The CMCL 2021 shared task focused on the prediction of 'monolingual' reading behavior and the participants applied various methodologies to predict eye-tracking features, e.g. gradient boosting, ensembling, using handcrafted features, deep learning (Hollenstein et al., 2021a; Bestgen, 2021; Li and Rudzicz, 2021; Oh, 2021; Vickers et al., 2021).

With regard to deep learning-based approaches, there exist findings suggesting that, as compared to transformer-based models (Vaswani et al., 2017), recurrent neural networks exhibit attention patterns closer to human attention (Sood et al., 2020). However, more recently, transformer-based models have been shown to better account for human reading behavior than recurrent neural networks (Merkx and Frank, 2021). Moreover, pretrained language models (PLM) such as BERT (Devlin et al., 2019) and XLM (Conneau and Lample, 2019) can predict multilingual human reading behavior well (Hollenstein et al., 2021b), in addition to having advanced the state-of-the-art in many downstream NLP tasks.

The focus of the CMCL 2022 shared task (Hollenstein et al., 2022) is to predict four eye-tracking features for data containing sentences in 6 different languages as well as transferring to a new language. For this purpose, we train 'adapters' inserted into transformer layers of frozen PLMs (Houlsby et al., 2019). We find that training adapters for each language separately within multilingual transformers leads to good performance, attaining the second place in the leaderboard. In addition, we show that such models can transfer to new languages via simply translating the new test sets into closely-related languages (e.g. lexically or grammatically) that the model was exposed to during training.[1]

2 Background

2.1 Data and Subtasks

The CMCL 2022 shared task consists of 2 subtasks. The data for Subtask 1 includes publicly-available eye-tracking corpora for 6 languages (English, Chinese, Russian, Hindi, German, Dutch). These corpora differ in size as well as the nature of the sentences they contain (i.e. news articles, scientific texts, Wikipedia entries). The data is already par-

[1]Our repository: https://github.com/ecekt/cmcl2022_dmg

Proceedings of the Workshop on Cognitive Modeling and Computational Linguistics, pages 136 - 144
May 26, 2022

titioned into train, validation and test splits. For Subtask 2, we are only supplied with a test set comprised of Danish sentences. We only use the data provided in the shared task and preprocess the textual input utilizing the tokenizers of PLMs. For more details, see Appendix A.

The eye-tracking features provided in the data correspond to 'first fixation duration' (FFD, duration of the first fixation on the current word) and 'total reading time' (TRT, total duration of all fixations on the current word including regressions). The values of these features were provided per token entry, averaged across all the readers: **FFDAvg** and **TRTAvg**. In addition, to account for the individual differences between readers, the data also includes the standard deviations of these features across readers: **FFDStd** and **TRTStd**.

The aim of the subtasks is to predict these 4 features for each token. The submissions are ranked with respect to test-set Mean Absolute Error (MAE): the average of the absolute differences between the ground-truth values and the values output by the model (see Appendix B). The shared task system also reports coefficients of determination (R^2), which we provide in Appendix F.

2.2 Adapters

The common method for using PLMs in downstream tasks is to fine-tune them for each task. If there are multiple tasks the model should handle at the same time, this could lead to some issues (Pfeiffer et al., 2021). For instance, learning tasks in parallel could cause interference and the model might learn a certain task better than the others. In the case of sequential training, we might observe catastrophic forgetting, where the model forgets the previously learned tasks. In addition, usually the whole model is fine-tuned; hence, we might need to save a new model per task, which increases compute and memory requirements.

To overcome these issues, 'adapters' have been proposed (Houlsby et al., 2019; Bapna and Firat, 2019). Adapters are bottleneck layers consisting of new weights integrated into each layer of a transformer model. They first project down ($W_D \in \mathbb{R}^{h \times d}$) the dimensions of the transformer hidden state h_l at layer l, apply a non-linearity, and then project the activations back up ($W_U \in \mathbb{R}^{d \times h}$) to the original dimensions. The outcome is then summed up with the residual r_l via a skip-connection to obtain the output of the adapter A_l:

$$A_l = W_U(ReLU(W_D h_l)) + r_l \quad (1)$$

Keeping the pretrained model frozen and only training adapters have been shown to yield performances close to those of fully-fine-tuned models while also maintaining efficiency (Houlsby et al., 2019; Bapna and Firat, 2019; Rücklé et al., 2021). Various types of adapters, insertion and training schemes have been proposed for machine translation, multi-task settings and cross-lingual transfer (Ansell et al., 2021; Pfeiffer et al., 2020b, 2021; Philip et al., 2020; Üstün et al., 2020, 2021; Poth et al., 2021).

Given their relevant advantages, we use Adapters from AdapterHub framework (Pfeiffer et al., 2020a)[2] built on HuggingFace Transformers (Wolf et al., 2020), to insert trainable adapters into frozen PLMs for the prediction of eye-tracking features. Then, we train language- and task-specific adapters and store their trained weights along with a single model. The details of the models and adapters used in Subtasks 1 and 2 are provided in Sections 3 and 4, respectively. For reproducibility, the hyperparameters for the best models selected with respect to their MAE scores on the validation set and the details of the development environment are provided in Appendices C and D.

3 Subtask 1: Multi-lingual

In this subtask, the aim is to predict eye-tracking features for data from 6 languages, for which we have training, validation and test sets. We focus on comparing a single setup for all languages vs. separate setups for different languages.

3.1 Methodology

Single adapter for all languages We first train a single task-specific adapter integrated into a frozen PLM on all the languages per eye-tracking feature. We utilize the XLM-RoBERTa-base (XLM-R) model (Conneau et al., 2020), which is a multilingual version of RoBERTa (Liu et al., 2019), trained with the masked language modeling objective on 100 languages covering all of the shared task languages.[3]

We place a token-level regression head on top of XLM-R. We then train this head and the adapters

[2] https://adapterhub.ml

[3] https://huggingface.co/xlm-roberta-base

to predict eye-tracking features for each contextualized token in a given sentence. Since we keep the underlying model frozen, this method only learns a small set of parameters for the eye-tracking features, which we expect would capture universal patterns in human reading behavior.

Language-specific adapters When a single model is trained on multiple languages, its capacity for certain languages might decrease, which is called 'the curse of multilinguality' (Conneau et al., 2020; Pfeiffer et al., 2020b). To avoid this issue, we increase the language-specific capacity by training adapters separately for each language.

In this approach, we train a single adapter that is specific to a language-task pair (yielding $6*4 = 24$ adapters) integrated into frozen XLM-R. In addition, we also implement another setup where we *stack* language- and task-specific adapters on top each other (Pfeiffer et al., 2020b). In the latter setup, per language, we utilize a frozen language-specific adapter that was trained on Wikipedia articles with the masked language modeling objective, as provided on AdapterHub (Pfeiffer et al., 2020b, 2021).[4] We train the new task-specific adapter and the token regression head to predict eye-tracking features specific to each language. For Dutch, AdapterHub did not have a language adapter trained on Wikipedia; therefore, we only use a single new adapter.[5]

PLM tokenizers produce multiple wordpieces for some tokens. For such tokens, the models output predictions for each wordpiece. We calculate their average value and assign it as the prediction for the whole token entry. To explore whether the way the wordpieces are treated has an effect on accuracy, we also train and test the stacked setup only keeping the first wordpiece to represent the full token entry.

3.2 Results

In the top half of Table 1, we present the results for Subtask 1. Overall, our models outperform the mean baseline and seem to predict FFD features better than TRT features. XLM-R with new adapters trained from scratch on all languages together performs the worst. XLM-R with new language-specific adapters further improves the results, in particular decreasing the MAE of features corresponding to averages.

The XLM-R setup that stacks adapters per language yields our best results for Subtask 1 achieving second place in the leaderboard of the shared task (MAE $= 3.6533$, our second submission). The breakdown of results per language is provided in Table 2 in Appendix E. It can be observed from this table that the model performs well for languages such as German and Dutch, yet struggles with languages such as Chinese and Russian, which could be due to the differences in their typologies, the nature of the corpora, vocabulary size and the issues that might have been caused by the multilinguality of the underlying PLM.

Finally, utilizing only the first wordpieces seems to degrade the performance across the features (MAE $= 3.7261$, our third submission). This finding indicates that retaining all wordpieces provides a better picture of the value to be predicted, as each wordpiece might contribute to the processing of the full token, affecting fixation duration times.

4 Subtask 2: Cross-lingual

For this subtask, we conduct various experiments to obtain results for the Danish test set in the absence of training and validation data in this language.

4.1 Methodology

Zero-shot We first feed the Danish test set directly into the XLM-R all-languages model. Since the adapters in this case are expected to have learned universal eye movement features and XLM-R includes Danish in its training, we expect to see this model to transfer well to Danish without being exposed to eye-tracking data in this language.

Translate train In this approach, we translate the training and validation set from their source language into the target language to be used in the training of a new model (Conneau et al., 2018). We have chosen English as the source language, as it constitutes almost half of the whole shared task data and XLM-R performs well in English (Conneau et al., 2020). We translate the English training and validation data word-by-word[6] into Danish

[4]`https://adapterhub.ml/explore/text_lang/` The names of the language-specific adapters are '{x}/wiki@ukp', where {x} is to be replaced by the abbreviation corresponding to the language, e.g. 'en/wiki@ukp'.

[5]We also experiment with training two new adapters stacked together for Dutch to make the setups more comparable. See Appendix E for the outcomes of additional models including the use of RoBERTa and XLM-RoBERTa-large.

[6]Sentence-by-sentence translation could yield more reliable outcomes; however, it may cause issues in word order and count: source and translated text would need to be aligned.

Model setup	FFDAvg	FFDStd	TRTAvg	TRTStd	MAE
All languages together	3.1449	1.9697	6.4339	4.6253	4.0434
Language-specific	2.8563	1.9741	5.5682	4.6956	3.7736
Language-specific-stack	2.6086	1.9219	5.6542	4.4284	**3.6533**
First wordpiece-only	2.6876	1.9609	5.7059	4.5501	3.7261
Zero-shot	3.4955	2.7370	7.1336	7.1502	5.1291
Translate train	14.6278	4.4001	19.8624	14.2824	13.2932
Translate test - EN	13.7903	5.1338	20.9214	13.5084	13.3385
Translate test - EN (without Provo)	4.5843	3.9382	9.3022	6.8426	6.1668
Translate test - DE	5.4512	1.7349	6.9036	5.7730	**4.9657**
Mean baseline	5.6858	2.5395	8.8200	5.8877	5.7332

Table 1: Test set results for Subtask 1 and Subtask 2. The best models per subtask are indicated in bold.

using the MarianMT en-da model.[7] Since AdapterHub currently does not host a language-specific adapter for Danish, we do not implement stacking and only train task-specific adapters for Danish.

Translate test In this setup, we translate the test set into a language for which we have training and validation data (Conneau et al., 2018) using MarianMT models. We first translate the Danish test set into English word-by-word. Using the best English model we obtained in Subtask 1, we generate predictions for the translated test set. In addition, we notice that the Provo corpus (Luke and Christianson, 2018) in the English subset has rather higher values for the features as compared to the other English corpora existing in the data. As a result, we retrain the best English setup using the same hyperparameters and skipping the Provo data.

In our final setup for Subtask 2, we translate Danish into German and utilize the best German model from Subtask 1 to obtain predictions. The main reason for opting for German was to better account for the effects of word order, e.g. inversions in main and subordinate clauses, exploiting the syntactic similarities between Danish and German.

4.2 Results

The bottom half of Table 1 provides the results for Subtask 2. First of all, the translate train approach does not seem to be a viable option, as its accuracy is much lower than the mean baseline (MAE = 13.2932, our first submission). Using the translate test approach in English yields very similar results. However, as we hypothesized, removing the Provo corpus from the training improves the translate test performance substantially (MAE = 6.1668, our second submission), albeit still underperforming. The zero-shot setup, on the other hand, yields a MAE score better than the mean baseline, suggesting that our adapters learn universal eye-tracking feature across languages combined with the multilingual pretraining of XLM-R.

Finally, the translate test setup in German yields our best results for this subtask achieving second place in the leaderboard (MAE = 4.9657, our third submission). These results indicate that the selection of source language and data has an effect on the results. Furthermore, it can be claimed that translate test is a viable option for adapters integrated into PLMs for achieving good transfer to a test set in a new language, without being exposed to actual eye-tracking data in this language.

5 Conclusion

We have trained language- and task-specific adapters for the prediction of eye-tracking features reflecting human reading behavior in multi- and cross-lingual settings. Our best models performed well, attaining the second place in the CMCL 2022 leaderboard. This suggests that pretrained language models enhanced with small adapter layers possess the capability to predict eye-tracking features.

In addition to our setups, other methods such as dropping adapters or adapter fusion could be implemented (Rücklé et al., 2021; Pfeiffer et al., 2021). It would also be informative to consider autoregressive models and the possibility of making use of various lexical and syntactic features and additional cognitive signals. The prediction of

[7] https://huggingface.co/docs/transformers/model_doc/marian

each eye-tracking feature could also be informed by other eye-tracking features, as each of them represents different aspects of human reading behavior. Similar approaches could also be of help in the modeling of other human cognitive signals, opening up novel ways of predicting and inspecting cognitive processes in humans.

Acknowledgments

We would like to thank Raquel Fernández, Sandro Pezzelle and Ahmet Üstün for their valuable feedback regarding the project and the paper. This project has received funding from the European Research Council (ERC) under the European Union's Horizon 2020 research and innovation program (grant agreement No. 819455).

References

Alan Ansell, Edoardo Maria Ponti, Jonas Pfeiffer, Sebastian Ruder, Goran Glavaš, Ivan Vulić, and Anna Korhonen. 2021. MAD-G: Multilingual adapter generation for efficient cross-lingual transfer. In *Findings of the Association for Computational Linguistics: EMNLP 2021*, pages 4762–4781, Punta Cana, Dominican Republic. Association for Computational Linguistics.

Ankur Bapna and Orhan Firat. 2019. Simple, scalable adaptation for neural machine translation. In *Proceedings of the 2019 Conference on Empirical Methods in Natural Language Processing and the 9th International Joint Conference on Natural Language Processing (EMNLP-IJCNLP)*, pages 1538–1548, Hong Kong, China. Association for Computational Linguistics.

Yves Bestgen. 2021. LAST at CMCL 2021 shared task: Predicting gaze data during reading with a gradient boosting decision tree approach. In *Proceedings of the Workshop on Cognitive Modeling and Computational Linguistics*, pages 90–96, Online. Association for Computational Linguistics.

Alexis Conneau, Kartikay Khandelwal, Naman Goyal, Vishrav Chaudhary, Guillaume Wenzek, Francisco Guzmán, Edouard Grave, Myle Ott, Luke Zettlemoyer, and Veselin Stoyanov. 2020. Unsupervised cross-lingual representation learning at scale. In *Proceedings of the 58th Annual Meeting of the Association for Computational Linguistics*, pages 8440–8451, Online. Association for Computational Linguistics.

Alexis Conneau and Guillaume Lample. 2019. Cross-lingual language model pretraining. In *Advances in Neural Information Processing Systems*, volume 32. Curran Associates, Inc.

Alexis Conneau, Ruty Rinott, Guillaume Lample, Adina Williams, Samuel Bowman, Holger Schwenk, and Veselin Stoyanov. 2018. XNLI: Evaluating cross-lingual sentence representations. In *Proceedings of the 2018 Conference on Empirical Methods in Natural Language Processing*, pages 2475–2485, Brussels, Belgium. Association for Computational Linguistics.

Jacob Devlin, Ming-Wei Chang, Kenton Lee, and Kristina Toutanova. 2019. BERT: Pre-training of deep bidirectional transformers for language understanding. In *Proceedings of the 2019 Conference of the North American Chapter of the Association for Computational Linguistics: Human Language Technologies, Volume 1 (Long and Short Papers)*, pages 4171–4186, Minneapolis, Minnesota. Association for Computational Linguistics.

Michael Hahn and Frank Keller. 2016. Modeling human reading with neural attention. In *Proceedings of the 2016 Conference on Empirical Methods in Natural Language Processing*, pages 85–95, Austin, Texas. Association for Computational Linguistics.

Nora Hollenstein, Emmanuele Chersoni, Cassandra L. Jacobs, Yohei Oseki, Laurent Prévot, and Enrico Santus. 2021a. CMCL 2021 shared task on eye-tracking prediction. In *Proceedings of the Workshop on Cognitive Modeling and Computational Linguistics*, pages 72–78, Online. Association for Computational Linguistics.

Nora Hollenstein, Emmanuele Chersoni, Cassandra L. Jacobs, Yohei Oseki, Laurent Prévot, and Enrico Santus. 2022. CMCL 2022 shared task on multilingual and crosslingual prediction of human reading behavior. In *Proceedings of the Workshop on Cognitive Modeling and Computational Linguistics*. Association for Computational Linguistics.

Nora Hollenstein, Federico Pirovano, Ce Zhang, Lena Jäger, and Lisa Beinborn. 2021b. Multilingual language models predict human reading behavior. In *Proceedings of the 2021 Conference of the North American Chapter of the Association for Computational Linguistics: Human Language Technologies*, pages 106–123, Online. Association for Computational Linguistics.

Neil Houlsby, Andrei Giurgiu, Stanislaw Jastrzebski, Bruna Morrone, Quentin De Laroussilhe, Andrea Gesmundo, Mona Attariyan, and Sylvain Gelly. 2019. Parameter-efficient transfer learning for NLP. In *Proceedings of the 36th International Conference on Machine Learning*, volume 97 of *Proceedings of Machine Learning Research*, pages 2790–2799. PMLR.

Bai Li and Frank Rudzicz. 2021. TorontoCL at CMCL 2021 shared task: RoBERTa with multi-stage fine-tuning for eye-tracking prediction. In *Proceedings of the Workshop on Cognitive Modeling and Computational Linguistics*, pages 85–89, Online. Association for Computational Linguistics.

Yinhan Liu, Myle Ott, Naman Goyal, Jingfei Du, Mandar Joshi, Danqi Chen, Omer Levy, Mike Lewis, Luke Zettlemoyer, and Veselin Stoyanov. 2019. Roberta: A robustly optimized bert pretraining approach. *arXiv preprint arXiv:1907.11692*.

Simon P. Liversedge, Denis Drieghe, Xin Li, Guoli Yan, Xuejun Bai, and Jukka Hyönä. 2016. Universality in eye movements and reading: A trilingual investigation. *Cognition*, 147:1–20.

Ilya Loshchilov and Frank Hutter. 2019. Decoupled weight decay regularization. In *International Conference on Learning Representations*.

Steven G. Luke and Kiel Christianson. 2018. The Provo corpus: A large eye-tracking corpus with predictability norms. *Behavior research methods*, 50(2):826–833.

Danny Merkx and Stefan L. Frank. 2021. Human sentence processing: Recurrence or attention? In *Proceedings of the Workshop on Cognitive Modeling and Computational Linguistics*, pages 12–22, Online. Association for Computational Linguistics.

Byung-Doh Oh. 2021. Team Ohio State at CMCL 2021 shared task: Fine-tuned RoBERTa for eye-tracking data prediction. In *Proceedings of the Workshop on Cognitive Modeling and Computational Linguistics*, pages 97–101, Online. Association for Computational Linguistics.

Jonas Pfeiffer, Aishwarya Kamath, Andreas Rücklé, Kyunghyun Cho, and Iryna Gurevych. 2021. AdapterFusion: Non-destructive task composition for transfer learning. In *Proceedings of the 16th Conference of the European Chapter of the Association for Computational Linguistics: Main Volume*, pages 487–503, Online. Association for Computational Linguistics.

Jonas Pfeiffer, Andreas Rücklé, Clifton Poth, Aishwarya Kamath, Ivan Vulić, Sebastian Ruder, Kyunghyun Cho, and Iryna Gurevych. 2020a. AdapterHub: A framework for adapting transformers. In *Proceedings of the 2020 Conference on Empirical Methods in Natural Language Processing: System Demonstrations*, pages 46–54, Online. Association for Computational Linguistics.

Jonas Pfeiffer, Ivan Vulić, Iryna Gurevych, and Sebastian Ruder. 2020b. MAD-X: An Adapter-Based Framework for Multi-Task Cross-Lingual Transfer. In *Proceedings of the 2020 Conference on Empirical Methods in Natural Language Processing (EMNLP)*, pages 7654–7673, Online. Association for Computational Linguistics.

Jerin Philip, Alexandre Berard, Matthias Gallé, and Laurent Besacier. 2020. Monolingual adapters for zero-shot neural machine translation. In *Proceedings of the 2020 Conference on Empirical Methods in Natural Language Processing (EMNLP)*, pages 4465–4470, Online. Association for Computational Linguistics.

Clifton Poth, Jonas Pfeiffer, Andreas Rücklé, and Iryna Gurevych. 2021. What to pre-train on? Efficient intermediate task selection. In *Proceedings of the 2021 Conference on Empirical Methods in Natural Language Processing*, pages 10585–10605, Online and Punta Cana, Dominican Republic. Association for Computational Linguistics.

Keith Rayner. 1977. Visual attention in reading: Eye movements reflect cognitive processes. *Memory & Cognition*, 5:443–448.

Keith Rayner. 1998. Eye movements in reading and information processing: 20 years of research. *Psychological bulletin*, 124 3:372–422.

Erik D. Reichle, Alexander Pollatsek, Donald L. Fisher, and Keith Rayner. 1998. Toward a model of eye movement control in reading. *Psychological review*, 105 1:125–57.

Andreas Rücklé, Gregor Geigle, Max Glockner, Tilman Beck, Jonas Pfeiffer, Nils Reimers, and Iryna Gurevych. 2021. AdapterDrop: On the efficiency of adapters in transformers. In *Proceedings of the 2021 Conference on Empirical Methods in Natural Language Processing*, pages 7930–7946, Online and Punta Cana, Dominican Republic. Association for Computational Linguistics.

Ekta Sood, Simon Tannert, Diego Frassinelli, Andreas Bulling, and Ngoc Thang Vu. 2020. Interpreting attention models with human visual attention in machine reading comprehension. In *Proceedings of the 24th Conference on Computational Natural Language Learning*, pages 12–25, Online. Association for Computational Linguistics.

Erik F. Tjong Kim Sang and Fien De Meulder. 2003. Introduction to the CoNLL-2003 shared task: Language-independent named entity recognition. In *Proceedings of the Seventh Conference on Natural Language Learning at HLT-NAACL 2003*, pages 142–147.

Ahmet Üstün, Alexandre Berard, Laurent Besacier, and Matthias Gallé. 2021. Multilingual unsupervised neural machine translation with denoising adapters. In *Proceedings of the 2021 Conference on Empirical Methods in Natural Language Processing*, pages 6650–6662, Online and Punta Cana, Dominican Republic. Association for Computational Linguistics.

Ahmet Üstün, Arianna Bisazza, Gosse Bouma, and Gertjan van Noord. 2020. UDapter: Language adaptation for truly Universal Dependency parsing. In *Proceedings of the 2020 Conference on Empirical Methods in Natural Language Processing (EMNLP)*, pages 2302–2315, Online. Association for Computational Linguistics.

Ashish Vaswani, Noam Shazeer, Niki Parmar, Jakob Uszkoreit, Llion Jones, Aidan N Gomez, Ł ukasz Kaiser, and Illia Polosukhin. 2017. Attention is all you need. In *Advances in Neural Information Processing Systems*, volume 30. Curran Associates, Inc.

Peter Vickers, Rosa Wainwright, Harish Tayyar Madabushi, and Aline Villavicencio. 2021. CogNLP-Sheffield at CMCL 2021 shared task: Blending cognitively inspired features with transformer-based language models for predicting eye tracking patterns. In *Proceedings of the Workshop on Cognitive Modeling and Computational Linguistics*, pages 125–133, Online. Association for Computational Linguistics.

Thomas Wolf, Lysandre Debut, Victor Sanh, Julien Chaumond, Clement Delangue, Anthony Moi, Pierric Cistac, Tim Rault, Remi Louf, Morgan Funtowicz, Joe Davison, Sam Shleifer, Patrick von Platen, Clara Ma, Yacine Jernite, Julien Plu, Canwen Xu, Teven Le Scao, Sylvain Gugger, Mariama Drame, Quentin Lhoest, and Alexander Rush. 2020. Transformers: State-of-the-art natural language processing. In *Proceedings of the 2020 Conference on Empirical Methods in Natural Language Processing: System Demonstrations*, pages 38–45, Online. Association for Computational Linguistics.

Appendix

A Data preprocessing

We use the XLM-RoBERTa tokenizer containing 250002 tokens. When converting the words into IDs, the tokenizer maintains the cases of the words, which could provide crucial information regarding human reading behavior. However, the way the tokens were presented to the readers differ from how the tokenizer would partition a given sentence. For instance, in the data, we see full stop appended to the last word or '(1917-1919)' as a single entry. For such cases, the tokenizer yields multiple wordpieces per token. We assign the eye-tracking feature values of the full entry to each of its wordpieces and during training and validation, we include them in the loss separately. For the test set predictions, we calculate the average of the predictions for the wordpieces and assign it as a single prediction for the whole entry.

We combine the token entries having the same sentence ID into a single sentence. Since the sentences do not include start- and end-of-sentence tokens, we also add such special tokens where necessary. In addition, we pad or truncate the input to maintain a total wordpiece length of 200. For all special tokens, we assign '-1' as the dummy eye-tracking feature value.

B Metric

We implement MAE as below:

$$\frac{\sum_{i=1}^{N} |o_i - t_i|}{N} \quad (2)$$

where N is the number of tokens in the data, o_i is the value output by the model for a given token, and t_i is the ground-truth value for this token. We calculate MAE for all 4 eye-tracking features and take their average to obtain the final MAE.

C Hyperparameters

For each model, we have performed hyperparameter search for learning rate (0.001, 0.0001, 0.00001, 0.00002) and batch size (4, 8, 16, 32). All the models were trained up to 50 epochs.[8] We saved the best model based on the validation MAE per epoch and ran random initializations of the best model with 4 different seeds. The adapters were optimized using the AdamW optimizer (Loshchilov and Hutter, 2019) with respect to MSELoss following a linear learning rate schedule. In Table 3, we provide the hyperparameters of our best models for Subtask 1 and Subtask 2.

D Environment details

We use AdapterHub version 2.2.0 based on HuggingFace Transformers version 4.11.3.[9] We implement and train our models in Python version 3.7.11 and PyTorch version 1.10.1.[10] All models were run on a computer cluster running Debian Linux OS, with 4 NVIDIA GeForce GTX 1080 Ti GPUs with driver version 470.103.01 and CUDA version 11.4.

E More results

RoBERTa + NER Our first submission to Subtask 1 was built on RoBERTa-base (Liu et al., 2019),[11] with a Named Entity Recognition (NER) adapter trained on the CoNLL2003 dataset[12] (Poth et al., 2021; Tjong Kim Sang and De Meulder, 2003). We used the NER adapter as we noticed a lot of named entities in the data. In this setup, we remove the NER token classification head and create a token-level regression head. The head is trained from scratch and the NER adapter is finetuned. The results revealed that this setup already

[8]It is possible that a higher epoch cap could produce better results; however, in most cases, we observed declining performance as the number of epochs approached 50.

[9]`https://huggingface.co/docs/transformers/`

[10]`https://pytorch.org/`

[11]`https://huggingface.co/docs/transformers/model_doc/roberta`

[12]`https://adapterhub.ml/adapters/AdapterHub/roberta-base-pf-conll2003/`

Model setup	FFDAvg	FFDStd	TRTAvg	TRTStd	MAE	Baseline MAE
EN stack	3.2360	1.9582	6.8383	4.9501	4.2456	5.2736
EN large stack	3.0390	1.9921	6.1242	4.8968	4.0130	
ZH stack	3.1586	3.3608	6.8213	6.6955	5.0091	5.4616
ZH large stack	3.1571	3.4448	7.3876	6.5892	5.1447	
DE stack	0.4304	0.4346	3.7796	2.8918	1.8841	2.8679
HI stack	2.5493	2.7178	5.7471	5.5693	4.1459	4.5668
RU stack	2.6062	2.6443	8.3637	5.5609	4.7938	4.9007
NL 1 new	1.8772	1.5720	3.3467	2.9443	2.4351	2.4176
NL 2 new stack	1.8904	1.5911	3.2836	3.0673	2.4581	

Table 2: Test set results for Subtask 1 for the XLM-R language-specific models with stacking, broken down into languages. Baseline MAE is calculated with respect to the means of the language-specific data. EN: English, ZH: Chinese, DE: German, HI: Hindi, RU: Russian, NL: Dutch.

Model	LR	Batch size	Seed
EN stack	0.0001	4	42
ZH stack	0.001	4	8
DE stack	0.001	8	42
HI stack	0.001	4	42
RU stack	0.001	4	8
NL 1 new	0.001	4	42

Table 3: Hyperparameters for our best submission for Subtask 1 (Language-specific-stack). DE stack model is also used in obtaining our best results for Subtask 2. LR: Learning rate.

improves over the mean baseline across all features (MAE = 4.0317, our first submission). Although RoBERTa is monolingual (English) and its vocabulary is much smaller than XLM-R's vocabulary (50265, also its tokenizer converts non-Latin scripts into unintelligible wordpieces), this model seemed to work quite well. However, we wanted to make sure that the wordpieces work properly and that the underlying frozen PLM was exposed to multilingual data, which is why we switched to XLM-RoBERTa.

Language breakdown The details of the language-specific-stack models for Subtask 1 are provided in Table 2. The majority of these models outperform the corresponding mean baselines computed with respect to the language-specific means (except for the Dutch setup, which does not include a pretrained language-specific adapter).

Dutch-specific models For Dutch, we only employed a single adapter as we did not have a Dutch-specific adapter pretrained on Wikipedia articles. As a result, we also tried stacking 2 new adapters. This setup yielded slightly worse scores than the former setup. Therefore, we opted for keeping the single-adapter model in our submissions.

Large models We also use the large version of XLM-RoBERTa.[13] At the time of writing, only English and Chinese Wikipedia MLM adapters were available on AdapterHub (Pfeiffer et al., 2020b, 2021).[14] For English, the utility of the large model was not substantially high, and for Chinese, the large model caused a decrease in accuracy. These findings suggest that the adapters are able to capture the patterns in eye-tracking features, without the need to resort to larger language models. However, more hyperparameter tuning could be beneficial to explore the capacity of the large models.

F R^2 scores

In Table 4, we provide the R^2 (coefficient of determination) scores as reported by the shared task system. The top half lists the results for Subtask 1 and the bottom half for Subtask 2.

[13]https://huggingface.co/xlm-roberta-large

[14]EN: https://adapterhub.ml/adapters/ukp/xlm-roberta-large-en-wiki_pfeiffer/, ZH: https://adapterhub.ml/adapters/ukp/xlm-roberta-large-zh-wiki_pfeiffer/

Model	FFDAvg	FFDStd	TRTAvg	TRTStd	R^2
RoBERTa + NER	0.6963	0.3437	0.3293	0.2677	0.4093
Language-specific-stack	0.7581	0.3689	0.4868	0.3517	0.4914
First wordpiece-only	0.7506	0.3564	0.4836	0.3362	0.4817
Translate train	-13.5708	-3.1490	-6.1914	-5.4032	-7.0786
Translate test - EN (without Provo)	-1.0249	-2.3468	-0.8361	-0.7824	-1.2475
Translate test - DE	-1.2176	-0.1296	-0.4203	-0.4929	-0.5651

Table 4: R^2 scores for the submissions to Subtask 1 and 2.

Author Index

Association for Computational Linguistics
209 N. Eighth Street
Stroudsburg, Pennsylvania 18360

CURRAN ASSOCIATES INC.
proceedings.com

ISBN 978-1-7138-6729-6